Past Lives, Dreams and Inspiration

by

Jen Ward

ISBN-13: 978-0-9994954-6-9
ISBN-10: 0-9994954-6-1

CONTENTS

Jen Ward

INTRODUCTION

There is so much of the human experience that is never talked about in a practical way. Dreams are considered flights of fancy with no substance. Past lives bleed through our dreams and our memories. But we are trained to deny them. So much of what we are is a compilation of what we have experienced in past times. But we are trained to deny anything that hasn't transpired in a short section of our existence. It is insanity to exist so blindly to our own journey. It is no wonder so many people can't find inspiration in their lives. The inspiration comes from exploring their own depths.

Imagine judging a movie from coming in at midway. Would the hero be everything that they could be? That is what we do with our own lives. If someone wants someone to admire, they could piece together their own journey of many lifetimes. By the clues they are given in this life, they could marvel at their own capacity to thrive. All their fears, talents, preferences and denials etch a course through the tapestry of time to reveal a dynamic plight of adventure, sorrow, love and loss.

This book is your encouragement to open up the pages to yourself. Question all your fears and preferences in life. Question why you think, feel, believe, fear and love the way you do. I guarantee that your own story is much more fascinating than any imagination could conjure up to be on the big screen. Here is to you discovering your own story.

Jen Ward

SECTION ONE: PAST LIVES

Open to a Session

A man came to me who was dealing with grave issues that were getting in the way of his quality of life, two of which were extreme panic attacks and extreme fear of hospitals or anything of a medical nature. Also, he had an aversion to being a parent.

It took many sessions to peel away an underlying lifetime. I saw how difficult it was for him to get himself to work in this life and how it mimicked the same difficulty in a past life. But in the past lifetime, he had definite reasons for not wanting to venture out.

In a past life, he was Jewish in a German occupied country. He was in hiding with his children. They had started rounding up Jews and putting them in camps. He knew of this and was relatively safe in hiding as long as he didn't venture out.

If it were just him, he could go months without supplies, but the children needed food regularly. He knew if he ventured out, he could be arrested on the spot. But his children were hungry and watching them go without was unbearable. One day, he struggled with this very dilemma of going out and risking the consequences or staying in hiding and watching his children go hungry. This struggle played out at the front door daily in his present life.

He was arrested by the Nazis while going for supplies and he never saw his children again. He was taken to a camp where they used him for torturous medical experiments. Leaving the house, being put in a position of needing to be around medical staff, or the thought of having children all triggered that horrific lifetime.

The good news is that when the pain is great enough, one is willing to look outside their comfort zone for relief. When everything is being done from a Western medicine point of view and issues still exist, I am very happy and grateful that my validation of past trauma and releasing its stagnant effect on the body brings back a quality of life to those who are open to sessions with me.

A Mouthpiece for Wisdom

People may not realize how their past lives are so close to the surface replaying in their energy fields. When I connect to people, their past life memories go to very dark places. Because we are love and light at the core, the happy memories don't make the impression that the negative ones do because there is no contrast.

As I am connecting with someone, I am toggling being present in the moment while also experiencing them being tortured, raped, bleeding out on a battlefield, being terrorized by negative forces, feeling forsaken by God and being abandoned by all that they love. My training in many lifetimes, including this one, has strengthened my ability to assist people who are reliving devastating experiences through their present life circumstances while still maintaining my composure.

Two eras that have seemed to mark almost every person are the centuries of the Crusades and the Dark Ages that ensued. During the Dark Ages, people lost their drive to succeed because they experienced such atrocities at the hands wielding power. Many have vowed never to abuse power again and prefer to be the victim rather than tap into the horrific images of abusing power or killing innocence that they have stored in their energy field. At an energetic level, they don't understand the difference between abusing power and self-empowerment. This is one of the things I assist with.

The Dark Ages that ensued created in people the fear of speaking their mind, being judged or even showing the ways that they outshine others. In the Dark Ages, a jealous lord could pull anyone who showed any signs of intelligence out of the crowd and have them tortured on a whim. It is during those times that so many people learned to mute their truth and hide their skillset and talents. Even a person's beauty could mean the threat of being taken from their life to serve a ruthless lord in his bed.

During the Dark Ages, intelligence was revered because most lived in ignorance. Only the noble class could read. Someone could be tortured for their ability to read because it was a threat to the power system of the time. That is why we worship the intelligence. It has become synonymous with freedom. But there is a difference between being intelligent and being able to think for one's self. Differentiating between the two and empowering the latter is another thing that I do.

But just as it was a crime to read during the Dark Ages, it has become a crime in the present time to think for one's self. I am met with contempt for my writings. Speaking one's truth creates such a reaction in people that it seems like it is not worth it to many to even do. They confuse an opinion with truth. They have opinions that are threatened by truth. It is a freedom for them when I can break free and show them the limitations of the former.

A Series of Blessings

The deep dark abyss

Between reality and truth

The cynical scrutiny

Of the decrepit to youth

The mucus thin sheath

Between real and illusion

An amniotic connection between

Pain, joy, and their fusion

An ill equipped father

An adept old sage

Both play their parts handsomely

On life's Shakespearean stage

Insights can accrue from having many lifetimes

Or can be an epiphany, flash in the pan

Lightning can't strike twice or seldom even once

But most assuredly, experience can

Again and again

We meet death as our fate

Carry over our lessons

To another embryonic state

Ignorance or bliss

Can repeat verse for verse

Life can be a series of blessings

Or a perpetual curse

One key factor

That rings as clear as a bell

We make our own heaven

Or live our own hell

It all depends

On what we see or deny

Will we ground ourselves in concepts

Or let ourselves fly

The choice is the "you"

You are willing to be

Grounded in fear

Or loving and free.

A Therapeutic Exercise

Do you notice all the doomsday movies and scenarios that are created and by really talented people? They are so convincing that something bad is going to come along and destroy the planet. They are created by people who met their demise in the last days of Atlantis, Lemuria, or some other long forgotten civilization, perhaps even Pompeii.

So you see, these movies aren't depicting some fate that is looming towards us. They are telling the story of the devastation that already has transpired. These movies aren't foreshadowing the future. They are working out the trauma of those who lived and died in such circumstances. They are a therapeutic exercise in releasing deep-seated terror.

And since this culture doesn't embrace the concept of past

lives, making and viewing these movies releases the past in a way that doesn't challenge the current belief system. In fact, carrying such heavy engrams of these past experiences creates the adoption of a single life belief system because people don't want to look at these things. It is easier to stay in denial. It may be easier, but it doesn't support spiritual freedom.

This is the time to release the past. The techniques I share help people do that. People don't have to relive these memories. They just need to learn how not to stuff them down anymore. That is what the taps and visualizations I share teach people to overcome. It is a huge opportunity for personal growth and freedom. The process has to eventually happen. You may as well accept the assistance and get on with spiritual endeavors.

Releasing Aversion to Change

I facilitated a session recently with a client who was making a major move. They were selling their house and moving to another state. It wasn't the best scenario for the family, but it was becoming more devastating than it needed to be.

The move was bringing up a lot of trauma from past lives when the family was burned off the land and forced to leave. There were many other times of a similar scenario of the family losing everything due to war. There were also lifetimes that were revealed of being nomads. Those were happy lives, but the joy and freedom of those

ing displaced by war.

In the session, we released a lot of the trauma of associating moving with war. That isn't a connection that people come to on their own, but it was really effective for the client. By the end of the session, they were telling me that they remembered their gypsy lives and knew that they were happy. We were laughing together.

If this story resonates with you, you may want to do this tap:

(Say this three times while tapping on your head and say it a fourth time while tapping on your chest.)

"I release associating change with the devastation of war; in all moments."

Agenda for Control

Many people are alone and without a companion. They think that God has forsaken them or that there is something innately wrong with them. Or, they attract adversaries as partners. They wonder what it would be like to truly have someone in their life who loved and respected them.

They are not being punished. In many lifetimes, we have given ourselves completely to God. This means taking vows to him. These included vows of solitude, chastity, celibacy and being married only to God. That vow is still

lifetimes were buried under the traumatic memories of being displaced by war.

In the session, we released a lot of the trauma of associating moving with war. That isn't a connection that people come to on their own, but it was really effective for the client. By the end of the session, they were telling me that they remembered their gypsy lives and knew that they were happy. We were laughing together.

If this story resonates with you, you may want to do this tap:

(Say this three times while tapping on your head and say it a fourth time while tapping on your chest.)

"I release associating change with the devastation of war; in all moments."

Agenda for Control

Many people are alone and without a companion. They think that God has forsaken them or that there is something innately wrong with them. Or, they attract adversaries as partners. They wonder what it would be like to truly have someone in their life who loved and respected them.

They are not being punished. In many lifetimes, we have given ourselves completely to God. This means taking vows to him. These included vows of solitude, chastity, celibacy and being married only to God. That vow is still taken in the present lifetime by so many. These vows stay into play throughout our lifetimes because many of them were taken to last "forever".

In the past, the concept of many lifetimes was more prevalent. It was accepted knowledge. The concept of only one lifetime was introduced as a form of control, and it works very well in that regard. Our biggest political conflict presently is based on the premise of only one lifetime. This is a great way to control the reproduction of our species. What better control is there than that?

Akashic Records

As a teen, I discovered that if I looked intently at someone, I could see them at a different age than the present one. If it were an old man, I could see what he looked like as a child or a young adult. I could look at a baby and see the adult they were going to become.

Back then, I didn't realize that I was viewing others' Akashic records. The Akashic records hold the memories of everything that we have ever experienced. When I do sessions with people, I am allowed to see different experiences from their past to help them release old hurts that may be getting in their way in the present.

Alleviating a Bad Temper

I facilitated a session with a woman who had a very bad

temper. It was so much a part of her that she was almost proud of it. In her session, the reason for it opened up.

In a past life, she was a strong, vibrant warrior who was chained in a dungeon at the prime of his life. He was very frustrated. He was torn from his people and his family and his dignity. He became a maniacal ball of rage that went insane in that dungeon. This is the place that the woman would "go" whenever she felt slighted.

In her session, we went to "the her" from the past and calmed him down. We took off his chains and freed him. We washed his body, healed his wounds and fed, shaved and clothed him. We educated him and gave him a comfortable home where he could rest. We gave him a wife and loving children and activities that he enjoyed.

In freeing this man, we were validating a very deep aspect of herself that felt the need to bubble to the surface in the present to get its needs met. She no longer needed to do that. The frenzy inside her was dissipated when the warrior was freed.

Armed Aggression

I facilitated a session once with a man who lost most of the feeling in his right arm due to an accident. His past life images came through very quickly.

He was a very gifted soldier. He killed many people easily and without thought. But one day, something happened where he had a shift within himself. He saw one of his young victims as human instead of merely a mission or an object to conquer. He saw the vulnerability in his eyes, his life, and his desire to live. He was devastated by his last kill.

The emotional shift was unbearable. He vowed that he would rather cut off his own arm than harm another person again. He let himself be taken down and killed. He did not fight back.

In this present life, the vow that he put into motion way back in the past was playing itself out. His arm in the present was useless to wield a weapon. During his session, we released some of the angst. Some of the feeling returned into his arm with the one session.

Being Homesick

In private sessions, many people secretly admit that they don't feel like they are in their natural habitat. Some feel like they come from a different land and feel isolated from their true home. Many don't want to admit this because they are afraid of seeming strange. Some of them have imagery of being on another planet. They never share this because they are very sane and don't want to appear otherwise.

I also have had clients who have vivid recall of being in a situation where the waters were rising quickly and there was no hope for escape. The waves were very high and they were flooding the land at the highest point. They have watched their whole civilization drown. In the present, they live with that dread within themselves. Some have identified it as Atlantis. Some have felt a kinship to Lemuria. Some of them have vivid recall of dynamic civilizations that still live somewhere within their memories.

May these taps assist in releasing the inner stress for those who have nothing in this world to validate an inner turmoil that they have difficulty admitting even to themselves.

(Say each statement three times while tapping on your head and say it a fourth time while tapping on your chest.)

"I release being homesick; in all moments."

"I release hating earth; in all moments."

"I release associating life on earth with dread; in all moments."

"I release living in anticipation of a cataclysm; in all moments."

"I release the fear of remembering; in all moments."

"I release the trauma of being usurped from my homeland; in all moments."

"I release the grief and devastation of the cataclysm; in all moments."

"I release the fear of cataclysm; in all moments."

"I release the devastation of mass translation; in all moments."

"I release the fear of mass translation; in all moments."

"I remove all the pain, trauma and limitations that the cataclysm has put on me; in all moments."

"I take back all the Joy, Love, Abundance, Freedom, Peace, Life and Wholeness that the cataclysm has taken from me; in all moments."

"I shift my paradigm from cataclysm to Joy, Love, Abundance, Freedom, Peace, Life and Wholeness; in all moments."

Some things don't need to make sense to the conscious mind to be effective. In fact, sometimes dealing with things in the abstract is a way to bypass the mind's sometimes menacing control. If this exercise brings relief in any small way, then it is worth doing. Sometimes the more the conscious mind objects, the more one would benefit from them. The energy that is freed up can be better put to use in having a happy life.

Being Killed During Sleep

I have a client who refuses to fall asleep in her bed. She has to end each night by falling asleep in front of the television. She also wakes up at the same time every night. It is very unsettling.

In a past life, she was killed in her bed. It has created an unsettling pattern within her. She wakes up every night at the time she was murdered. The one place that should be a sanctuary is a place of unrest.

Once a memory is brought to the surface, it is easier to release the unconscious programming. When trauma from the past is remembered and validated, the behavior it created serves no purpose any more. There is much freedom in releasing past trauma.

Book of Life

Take a bow to things you fear

That have captured your attention

They have put a face upon

What's too hideous to mention

Past life memories buried deep

Incest, Torture, Murder, Rage

They are teachers, perhaps mentors

Dog-eared chapters in your page

Insert your page among the others

Take a bow to their strife

Love denotes your humble presence

Honoring the book of life.

Breaking Through the Facade

I recently had a private session with one of my clients who had trouble relating to others. She is smart and articulate and wants close relationships but comes across as materialistic and condescending. In her past lives, she has had to present a façade to survive.

During the session, I saw an image in the depth of an abyss. It was a chaotic scene of a time when a war was ending. It was on foreign soil. There was a four-year old blond girl walking around in a daze. She was alone and abandoned. She was in shock and numb. This was the state that, on some level, my client was stuck in. Because she had removed herself from so much of life, she made herself small in this abyss.

In this life, she equated security with love. It was very important to her. To others she may seem shallow, but in reality, she feels like a lost little girl. Material items make her feel loved.

In her session, it was revealed that she created a mini microcosm within herself. A microcosm is something that represents the universe, or humanity, in miniature. A single human being is a microcosm of the whole of humanity. In this instance, humanity is the macrocosm of the woman.

Here are some of the releases that I led her through to help the trapped little girl come out of her shell. We called the shell a mini microcosm. These may help anyone feeling small, ineffective, unworthy, materialistic or lost.

(Say each statement three times while tapping on your head and say it a fourth time while tapping on your chest.)

"I release confusing security for love; in all moments."

"I release hiding within a mini microcosm; in all moments."

"I recant all vows and agreements between myself and the mini microcosm; in all moments."

"I remove all curses between myself and the mini microcosm; in all moments."

"I dissolve all karmic ties between myself and the mini microcosm; in all moments."

"I release identifying with the mini microcosm; in all moments."

"I remove all the pain, burden, and limitations that the mini microcosm has put on me; in all moments."

"I take back all the Joy, Love, Abundance, Freedom, Life and Wholeness that the mini microcosm has kept from me; in all moments."

"I implode the mini microcosm; in all moments."

"I am centered in Joy, Love, Abundance, Freedom, Security and Wholeness; in all moments."

"I remove all unnecessary masks, walls and armor; in all moments."

"I am safe, happy, abundant, and free; in all moments."

A Better Life for All

If you have a child and wish merely that they be happy, you are setting them up to be takers. You are using your children to fulfill your need to give. This is selfish and shortsighted. We see evidence of this all over the world and are at the mercy of it.

If you have a child and instill in them the intention to be happy by sharing their gifts and giving to others, then you have done a service to humanity. To procreate merely to fulfill the desire of a petty God is shortsighted at best.

All children deserve to be gestated and raised in an environment of love and acceptance. If you are not capable, then you should not be forced, coerced or shamed into afflicting your lack onto the world in the embodiment of the next generation. Doing this is the true sin. Doing this is the true abomination. Doing this is the true crime against humanity.

I was forced into a loveless home and world by an immoral decree. It took all my resilience to absorb any breadcrumbs of love that were strewn around. I am the exception I believe. I have sidestepped fifteen pedophiles and have endured endless humiliations and abuse. It is a cold existence coming into a world where there is no warmth or acceptance of you. How dare outsiders who are ignorant of spiritual law thrust that fate on so many. If I were not here, I would be somewhere else where perhaps there was some love for me.

Yes, I hear the arguments you want to give of how special I am because of the tragedy of a loveless life. But that is not the point. The point is condemning new souls to be born into hostile homes because of the misguided belief that terminating a life is murder.

I have many vivid memories of dying and living again. So do many others. To be beholden to a law that says otherwise is not separation of church and state. It is dictatorship of the church. Their only recourse in control is crying victim. It is funny how every abuser that I have known justifies the abuse by crying victim. It is a natural ploy of abuse. This is now being done on a systemic level when it comes to forcing women to have babies. The ignorance is so ensconced that those immersed in it are not able to reason beyond their own indoctrination. The woman impregnated in poverty is not the perpetrator, she is the victim of circumstance.

Unless we make a loving place for every soul venturing into the physical realm, we are subjecting them to an apathetic life of poverty, crime and demoralization. Why is it so easy to accept young people on the brink of adulthood murdering themselves and others out of desperation to be loved and valued than it is to accept a termination of a pregnancy. The hypocrisy is mind boggling. If all the energy that was used to demonize women who aren't capable of providing for a new life was used to assist those who were already here, then progress would be made.

There are people suffering and dying on the other side of the world who simply are looking for a home. If we weren't so hell bent as a group on people having unwanted babies, then perhaps there would be more room for those who are already here in the world. They wouldn't have to be locked up in containment camps like criminals. What does a petty God say about that? As a group, are we really loving each other or using them as a number? Do we care about every soul or are we glamorizing babies for their potential? There is so much untapped potential in the world that apathy is just about bursting at the seams.

We need to wake up and start discerning for ourselves and stop mindlessly perpetuating living by the rhetoric that was fed to us. If this message makes you angry, then that is on you. That means that you are incapable of discerning truth for yourself. You should be mad at that and not at the message. It is time for society to take responsibility for the conditions that it has created and stop demonizing those who envision a better life for all.

A Bubble of Pure Love

Some people may think I am abrupt when I engage them. Let me try to explain. Holding a place of pure love in a world that gravitates to negativity is a conscious thing. It is like holding an air bubble under water. I hold a space for everyone to join me in this bubble of pure love. There is just a pressure bracing against that space. To let them in, I have to be a bouncer at the door. It is to make certain the lesser vibrations don't inundate the space and collapse it.

Most people carry with them the vibrations of a lower nature just by being around it. It is the same as someone's clothes smelling like smoke after they were with a smoker. Only so much can be allowed for the air to continue to be fresh. They don't know that. When I am abrupt, I am actually addressing that vibration. To the person, it feels like their feelings are being hurt because a sheath of vibration is being stripped off. For myself, it isn't a conscious thing and is done energetically. But I am aware it is being done.

Some of it is a protection for myself. When someone introduces discussion, they are unconsciously trying to pull me down to the mental realms. I refuse to go. Some people are stuck in the mental realms and by going there with them, it is like going into a hostile environment. That is where they feel comfortable so they will try to pull people there. I refuse. When I was a child, I learned not to ride with pedophiles. It is a similar thing to me, although sincere questions are a different vibration and are welcome.

Some people will quote someone else when I write an original quote. This is insulting to me because they are saying, "Your truth is not good enough. Now THIS person is saying something important. Everyone should listen to THEM." Don't they realize that truth is always more relevant in the now. In that way, what I am saying is more substantial. It is imbued in the now.

I get protective of other people when they have to back up their statement with a book. I prefer to listen to someone fumble around for their own truth rather than have a quote from someone else that got them closer to their truth.

When a person adds a link on my page directing someone to another person's page, it is offensive sometimes because it is like having a conversation in truth with a group of people and someone interrupts that truth and diverts everyone's attention to what someone else is saying. It is no different than speaking and having someone interrupt and telling everyone to listen to someone else. Or, it is like crashing a party and telling everyone there is a better party somewhere else.

When someone compares me to someone else, they are diminishing my specialness. I work diligently on staying in the highest truth. I live like a monk and guard my actions and thoughts continuously. Apparently, I live to serve others. There really is no other Joy. I feel alone and separate in this. I have healed so many people in ways that are not socially accepted for them to even admit. My assistance drastically changes lives and even saves them, in ways society does not allow anyone to accept. So when someone casually says that they know someone who does what I do, it is a diminishing statement. It is dismissive of all that I have endured to serve in this humbling way.

I only explain because I don't want people to think that I don't love them because I protect my truth. I would hope that others would do the same thing in their life. It takes constant awareness to be a bubble of love in this world. I hold that intention for all others to do the same. If you can be supported in that, that is wonderful. But if you can do it with little outer support, that makes it all so sweeter. I support you in this. You are Joy, Love, Abundance, Beauty, Health and Wholeness to me. To see you as any less would do you a disservice.

Aversion to Beauty Being Sacrificed

I have had a few clients who had a real aversion to being beautiful. This following scenario is more common than you might think.

A past life opened up in which a client was a girl who was just discovering her womanhood. An important man started coming around her family and giving her attention. She started being treated special. It was all so wonderful and overwhelming. She was receiving gifts and respect from even the elders. She accepted it as it came.

They started preparing her for a huge celebration. She was going to be the guest of honor. The nice man that she met spent time with her, and in her naivete, she thought they were going to be mated. The night of the ceremony they adorned her from head to foot. She was cleansed and tended to.

When she was finally presented, the nice man was there. Everyone was there and then her joy turned to terror when she saw her fate. She was going to be sacrificed. There was a procession up to the volcano that she would be thrown into. The man no longer talked to her but led the procession. No one would meet her eyes. No one helped as she screamed out. She was in a hellish situation that sealed her fate in that lifetime.

By releasing the trauma of this memory, the client could now be comfortable in her own skin and not associate such dread with being attractive.

Being Beautiful

I recently facilitated a session with an attractive woman who believed she wasn't beautiful. This is a very common belief. For some, being beautiful translates to happiness.

This issue ran very deep. The surface belief is that she wasn't attracting happiness in the form of a loving relationship because she wasn't beautiful enough. Her past lives showed me how she was so mistreated in past lives that she correlated relationships with abuse. Physical features were not a factor.

She lived in times when most women were abused, treated poorly, called horrible names and degraded. In a past life, she saw a beautiful woman who seemed respected and sought after. From that vantage point, that woman seemed to have happiness. So she correlated beauty with happiness. It meant not being abused and being appreciated.

I have facilitated other sessions where women who were beautiful had an aversion to it because they had been sacrificed to the Gods for being beautiful. One woman correlated beauty and adulation with fear and distrust. She happily creates a "plain Jane" persona. To her, that is peace and contentment.

In the session with the first woman, her mother, who had crossed, came through and stroked her face and gave her a pep talk. Her little grandmother came through as well to remind her how special she is. Sometimes, loved ones on the other side seem to help their living loved one (even loving pets) make a connection with me as a means to either give them a message or just to help them. This seemed to be one of those instances.

Many people waste so much energy in thinking and believing badly about themselves. If they only could accept that who they are and how they react is all formulated by their experiences and their unconscious fears and aversions. Then people would accept that they are doing the best they can to take care of their own needs and stop making themselves suffer more for survival tactics.

Here are some SFT taps to help:

(Say each statement three times while tapping on the head and say it a fourth time while tapping on the chest.)

"I release the aversion to being beautiful; in all moments."

"I release correlating beauty with happiness; in all moments."

"I release the trauma of being sacrificed; in all moments."

"I release being invisible; in all moments."

"I release feeling unworthy; in all moments."

"I release the belief that I am undesirable; in all moments."

"I release burying my gifts; in all moments."

May these releases help women who choose to mute their own beauty through a lack of self-care or by putting on layers of weight as a means to hide.

Cannibalism

I facilitated a session with a client who had a past life memory of being washed ashore from a shipwreck. He was terrified to get there because someone was waiting on the beach to eat him. I was going to focus on releasing her issues with cannibalism, but then her past lifetimes of being ingested as an animal were revealed.

Her energy was still attached to the flesh and when she was ingested, she was broken up into pieces and allotted to each person who ate her. It left her feeling discombobulated and lost. This happens all over the world daily in the plant and animal kingdom and even with man on an energetic level.

These are the taps that I led her through. You are welcome to do them too.

(Say each statement three times while tapping on your head, and say it a fourth time while tapping on your chest.)

"I release the trauma of being cut up and quartered; in all moments."

(Sometimes the soul is still connected to the body after death and witnesses the terror.)

"I release the trauma of being ingested; in all moments."

"I recant all vows and agreements between myself and all those who have eaten me; in all moments."

"I remove all curses between myself and all those who have eaten me; in all moments."

"I dissolve all karmic ties between myself and all those who have eaten me; in all moments."

"I take back all the essence that those who have eaten me

have taken from me; in all moments."

As she did these taps, I realized that she had eaten and taken from others too. So we completed the circle and freed them up from her. For the most part, maybe they are one and the same but these taps felt satisfying to do:

"I release the guilt and trauma of eating others; in all moments."

"I recant all vows and agreements between myself and those I have eaten; in all moments."

"I remove all curses between myself and those I have eaten; in all moments."

"I dissolve all karmic ties between myself and those I have eaten; in all moments."

"I give back all the essence that I have taken from those I have eaten; in all moments."

Maybe this is the most important reason for saying grace. Maybe when we say grace, we are releasing any residual essence of the life force that shortly before operated in our food. Maybe saying grace isn't about uplifting the food for us at all. Maybe it is just the humane thing to do for the soul that is sacrificed for our meal.

Cyclical Depression

Sometimes people get depressed during certain parts of the year. They have no explanation for it. It feels like there is some ominous kind of trigger, like the changing of the seasons. But knowing it is looming doesn't help deal with it. It could be triggered by the holidays approaching or getting less light in the day which is called Seasonal Affective Disorder.

May I suggest a deeper solution?

Some of us may be mourning a past life where we were having a pleasant day-to-day existence and were killed or pulled into slavery or imprisonment at a certain time of year. The change in the seasons could trigger an unconscious memory of a past state of mourning. It just feels like this is a time in the cycle of the year when being conquered, in general, happened more than at other times.

If this is an issue that you deal with, you may want to try these taps:

(Say each statement three times while tapping on your head and say it a fourth time while tapping on your chest.)

"I release mourning the loss of my freedom; in all moments."

"I release mourning my life; in all moments."

"I release the belief that I am missing out; in all moments."

"I release lamenting the future; in all moments."

"I release being enslaved to loss; in all moments."

"I release the belief that life is imprisonment; in all

moments."

"I release defining this season with sadness; in all moments."

"I shift my paradigm to Joy, Love, Abundance and Freedom; in all moments."

"I am centered and satisfied in Divine Love; in all moments."

Dawn's Fate

I had a client that would wake up before dawn and not be able to get back to sleep. He was fitful and anxious and thought it was merely a fear of not getting enough rest. But it was a past life memory of a particular day when he was going to be hanged at dawn.

Sometimes, just knowing that the angst one is feeling runs way deeper than realized helps to alleviate it. The client could forgive himself now for being anxious at this time. It didn't seem ridiculous any more.

Dealing with Jealousy

There are two reasons to be jealous. The first reason is because on some level, one realizes that their present mate isn't their soul mate, and they realize they will be leaving them at some point and they aren't ready to do that. They are taking themselves out of the moment and living in a perpetual state of break up.

The other reason one is jealous is because they are reliving a past experience of losing a dear love. They are playing it over and over in their subliminal energy field. The love that they are enjoying shares close quarters with a painful memory of loss. Jealousy is a private excruciating hell of various degrees. Here are some taps to alleviate the angst:

(Say each statement three times while tapping on your head and say it a fourth time while tapping on your chest.)

"I release the anguish of being separated from my Love; in all moments."

"I release the fear and trauma of my Love leaving me; in all moments."

"I release being frozen in abandonment; in all moments."

"I release confusing Love with competition; in all moments."

"I release competing for Love; in all moments."

"I release seeing other women/men as the enemy; in all moments."

"I release feeling lonely and desperate in relationships; in all moments."

"I release pulling my Love into a lonely and desperate place; in all moments."

"I release defining Love as emptiness and need; in all moments."

"I release having relationships pull me into a void; in all moments."

"I redefine relationships as fullness and completion; in all moments."

"I shift the paradigm of my relationship from taking to giving; in all moments."

"I release being jealous; in all moments."

"I shift my paradigm from jealousy to peace; in all moments."

"My relationship is centered in Joy, Love, Abundance, Freedom, Peace, Contentment and Wholeness; in all moments."

"I am totally centered in the moment; in all moments."

I have a dear friend whose soul mate crossed over. Every day, a hawk flew over her house and called to her. She felt it was her husband reminding her of their love. It was very comforting to her and she had many dream experiences with them together.

One day, she called me very upset. There were two hawks together. In her grief, she thought that her husband had moved on and she was in excruciating pain. Because of jealousy, she failed to realize that she was the second hawk. She was being shown that she was still with her husband in the higher realms. It was only in the physical that she was experiencing separation. But on all other levels, they were still together.

Death Is the New Birth

Many people have such an aversion to death. But it can be a beautiful and humbling experience. To help someone cross over in comfort and peace is the most natural and spiritual thing to do. People get confused between fighting to live and the resistance to death. They are not the same.

When the fight is over and the crossing is inevitable, choose to spend the remaining time left to honor that person and prepare them for their passing. Usually, the person crossing is concerned with leaving loved ones behind. So reassure them that you will be okay without them but will just miss them terribly.

People have so many misunderstandings about what happens when one dies that it creates fear. Here is what happens. The person you love slips out of their physical body and continues their existence on the astral plane. The astral plane is a lot like the physical world except the vibratory rate is different so the two of you can't physically connect in the same way. But they are alive, well and happy in the astral plane. When they are on the astral plane, it is as real to them as the physical plane once was.

When they slip out of the body, they are usually greeted

by loved ones who have already crossed and their spirit guides or angels. It is a wonderful experience to be welcomed to the other side. Immediately, the person is caught up in the happiness of their new life on the astral plane and the only thing that really distracts them from that is the anguish of people they have left on earth.

Earth is such a coarse vibratory rate compared to the astral plane that people who are hurting emotionally on earth gain much stamina by pulling themselves out of it. That is the experience of the physical life. People on the astral plane can now see that and have great compassion for their loved ones left behind. They want to use any means to comfort you by sending you a sign somehow that you are misguided because they are fine and you are still connected by the love. Someone may say something that was their catch phrase or you may hear a song on the radio that depicts their connection with you. And the more that you look for these signs, the more they will be there.

When someone is crossing over, know that this is a wonderful time for them. Reminisce about all that you have experienced together and be grateful for the love. Let them pass on in peace and the understanding that you will not pull on them when they are on the other side. The love is the commonality in your vibratory rates so that you can connect through subtle means regardless of where one is residing. Connect through the love; it is the only viable means anyway.

A technique when one has crossed over is to imagine that

they are merely off on an errand or in another room. Because they are.

Decapitation and Choking

I facilitated a session with a woman who was having terrible neck pains. It was really easy to tune into her for some reason.

She seemed really benevolent and gracious, but she also came across as very proper. The image I saw of her past was ominous. It was a long, graceful walk to the guillotine. She was proud and dignified and dearly loved the people she had served. It manifested in this life as not showing people how she really felt. She had to always put up a good front.

There was another life where she was choked from behind. Usually, when there is one form of injury to the body, there will be layers of a similar injury to the same area. It manifested as her not liking anyone standing behind her. She acknowledged this fact about people standing behind her as true. Also, obviously she didn't care to wear choker necklaces.

There were many other "coincidences" that were revealed from me telling her these lifetimes. Part of the acknowledgement of the past trauma is a validation to the individual. The pain is the body crying out to be comforted after trauma of such a deep and devastating level. It tries to reenact the injury as an attempt to be heard. In a private session, I validate the trauma with the client, and I also release the traumatic energy around the events and the body so the client can be in ease.

She mused at one silly hobby she had that validated her life as a queen. She loved to collect tiaras.

See the Totality of You: Who We Are Is an Incredible Mystery to Unravel

Technique: Take inventory of the things that you are afraid of, things that you naturally excel at, time periods that you gravitate to in the movies, and places you want to travel to or avoid. All are keys to who you have been and what you have experienced in past lives.

Some people avoid the concept of past lives because the trauma that they have endured is too close to the surface and they prefer to keep it buried. But if people can look at who they have been, they can make some adjustments to who they are now and save themselves a lot of unnecessary dis-ease.

For example, someone who has nightmares or is depressed may be able to uncover the underlying cause of such things and face the intensity of them in the light of the present existence.

Embedded Souls

I facilitated a session with a woman who was going to her

hometown. The initial sense was to release all her connections with it and all the karmic pulls it had on her, which we did. But the session took on a more profound aspect.

In the session, I saw the earth. Just as blood seeps into the ground, I saw people dying in layers upon layers into the ground and being embedded there. There wasn't always the convenience of honoring each body as it fell. And souls didn't always conveniently walk into the light. In the history of earth, due to war, indifference or inability, the dead lay where they fell and sometimes their energy just dripped into the ground. That is what I saw.

It seemed that some of my client's energies were still entangled with the ground where she had fallen in past lives. It was time to collect herself. And to make the most of the session, we used her as a surrogate to collect the energies of all others who have fallen and assist them as well. Why do this? Because I was directed to and given the insight to release them.

In a vision that was happening simultaneously as I facilitated her session, I saw the client and myself on the side of a dark hill seeped and layered with energies. Behind us stood our spirit guides. This woman is very attuned to her purpose and was open to assist in this. What I saw was her and me with our arms outstretched pulling up energies from the ground. They were in the form of people. We pulled them up from the ground and sent them back to where they originated.

At first, we did this for her hometown. Then I envisioned the earth and we did the same thing globally. After her session, she was to get on her flight and fly home. She reported that she never has experienced such a peaceful and restful flight.

Emergency Session

I finished facilitating an emergency remote session. My client has had a very swollen abdomen for the last three days. Her husband was going to take her to emergency care, but they are scheduled to go on vacation and really didn't want to put their plans on hold.

In her session, we released a lot of issues around babies. She was carrying a lot of guilt around babies and children. This person is very kind all the time. The thought of not being kind was not even in her wheelhouse. She was in total denial that she could ever be unkind. Because of her condition, I forced the issue. I had to make her understand that she has had the same experiences of harming others that every other human has had.

A past life of hers revealed itself to me. She was in the army out in the West. The railroad was moving in and the army was rounding up Native American children to send them to orphanages. The commander was short tempered and lacked compassion. The train that was going to take them away was delayed. As a solution, he ordered all the children killed. My client was forced to follow orders of the commander. She also then had to keep it a secret.

There was something about this experience that was being triggered now in my client. When I asked about her vacation, the only uneasy thing about it was that she was going to visit her father's grave for the first time in years. Her father was selectively cantankerous. She was not excited about this part of the vacation. He was the reason she was having the physical reaction that she was having. He was the commander who ordered the children killed.

We combed out all her dynamics with her father and released the stagnant energy in regards to him. Her deep loathing of keeping secrets was also revealed and we released the stagnant energy around that issue as well. By the end of the hour, some of the swelling in her abdomen already went down.

Here are some taps I used around secrets:

(Say each statement three times while tapping on your head and say it a fourth time while tapping on your chest.)

"I release keeping secrets; in all moments."

"I release the trauma of carrying secrets; in all moments."

"I release storing secrets in my body; in all moments."

"I shift my paradigm from secrets to Joy, Love, Abundance, Freedom, Health, Life and Wholeness; in all moments."

"I am centered in truth; in all moments."

Empowering Female Energy

As I facilitate sessions with many people, I see some recurring themes show up in their past lives. There are many lifetimes when women were diminished and defiled. It is not only a female issue. I see it show up in most people's Akashic records.

Through history, woman have been defiled and seen as inferior. This still plays out around the world in women not being allowed the same freedoms as men. It is mind boggling for those in a more free culture that women are being denied simple human rights. Yet it still plays out in America in more subtle forms of discrimination.

This imbalance between male energy and female energy in the world affects us all. It shows up as incredible abuse of power, lack of compassion and inequality between men and woman on subtle levels. The good news is that more people are becoming savvy to the direct connection between the individual and the whole. The more that individuals release their lifetimes of programming that men are superior, the more the whole can indeed come into balance.

We have all been men. We have all diminished women. We have all added our energies to the condition the world is in today. Here is a way energetically to undo what we have all contributed to. These taps are for all men and women to do to assist in helping the dynamics in the world balancing out. We can help the world by doing these taps as surrogates for those who have abused and those who have been abused. By doing these taps, we will be assisting the world in drawing more upon the strengths of the female energy in the world.

(Say each statement three times while tapping on your head and say it a fourth time while tapping on your chest.)

"I release the belief that women are evil; in all moments."

"I release the belief that woman are whores; in all moments."

"I release the belief that women are weak; in all moments."

"I release hating women; in all moments."

"I release diminishing women; in all moments."

"I release raping women; in all moments."

"I release the trauma of being raped; in all moments."

"I release beating women; in all moments."

"I release killing women; in all moments."

"I release the trauma of childbirth; in all moments."

"I release robbing the womb; in all moments."

"I release the trauma of having my baby ripped from my womb; in all moments."

"I release the belief that women are inferior to men; in all moments."

"I release the belief that men are superior to women; in all moments."

"I release stealing women's gifts; in all moments."

"I release enslaving women; in all moments."

"I recant all vows and agreements between myself and female energy; in all moments."

"I remove all curses between myself and female energy; in all moments."

"I dissolve all diminishing views about women; in all moments."

"I remove all negative programming in regards to women; in all moments."

"I dissolve all karmic ties between myself and female energy; in all moments."

"I remove all the pain, burden and limitations that being female has put on me; in all moments."

"I remove all the pain, burden and limitations that I have put on all women; in all moments."

"I take back all the Joy, Love, Abundance, Freedom, Health, Success, Security, Companionship, Creativity, Peace, Life, Wholeness and Balance that being female has taken from me; in all moments."

"I give back all the Joy, Love, Abundance, Freedom, Health, Success, Security, Companionship, Creativity,

Peace, Life, Wholeness and Balance that I have taken from all women; in all moments."

"I release defining being female as inferior; in all moments."

"I empower female energy; in all moments."

"I release the power struggle between women and men; in all moments."

"I balance out the Yin and Yang; in all moments."

"I am centered in equality between women and men; in all moments."

"I define women as Joy, Love, Abundance, Freedom, Health, Success, Security, Companionship, Creativity, Peace, Life, Wholeness and Balance; in all moments."

"I make space in this world for empowered, valued female energy equal to male energy; in all moments."

"I remove all blockages to having empowered, valued female energy equal to male in the world; in all moments."

"I stretch the world's capacity to accept empowered, valued female energy equal to male in the world; in all moments."

Enlightening the Masses

Recently, I facilitated a session with a woman who felt it

was her passion to educate everyone against the ills of the controlling factions. She would do anything she could to lead others to the truth. What she did not realize was, in past lives, she was the one that had controlled others. Her gifts and talents were used to suppress the lives of others. This was a point of contention that she was trying to undo in the present life. It was less about her trying to uplift humanity than to undo the times when she suppressed the freedom of others.

A past life of hers opened up to reveal when this issue played out in real time. She was a very intelligent young officer in a cavalry outpost. Their mission was to clear away Indians so that settlers could move in. She was able to use her skills to help her company make better ground with their mission. This directly resulted in the death and displacement of many Indians.

When I revealed this lifetime to my client, it resonated as truth to her. One of her special projects in this lifetime was highlighting the plight of the Native Americans. Now she understood why. In that past lifetime, she died disillusioned defending the fort. She was disheartened by her part in the genocide and died because she couldn't defend her position wholeheartedly anymore.

Here are the taps that we used to release the angst of this connection within her:

"I release using my gifts and talents to advance mass control; in all moments."

"I release taking part in genocide; in all moments."

"I release the guilt and trauma of controlling the masses; in all moments."

"I recant all vows and agreements between myself and mass control; in all moments."

"I remove all curses between myself and mass control; in all moments."

"I release being enslaved to mass control; in all moments."

"I dissolve all karmic ties between myself and mass control; in all moments."

"I remove all the pain, burden and limitations that partaking in mass control has put on me; in all moments."

"I remove all the pain, burden and limitations that I have put on all others by partaking in mass control; in all moments."

"I withdraw all my energy, talents and gifts from mass control in all moments."

"I take back all the Joy, Love, Abundance, Freedom, Life and Wholeness that mass control has taken from me; in all moments."

"I give back to all others all the Joy, Love, Abundance, Freedom, Life and Wholeness that I have taken from them via mass control; in all moments.

"I release resonating with mass control; in all moments."

"I release emanating with mass control; in all moments."

"I remove all mass control from my sound frequency; in all moments."

"I remove all mass control from my light body; in all moments."

"I shift my paradigm from mass control to Joy, Love, Abundance, Freedom, Life and wholeness; in all moments."

Many of those who are adamant at exposing those who reign power over the masses are trying to release their own history of abusing power at the mercy of the vulnerable. By doing this series of taps, one can release themselves of the angst that is involved in enlightening the masses.

Escaping Jack the Ripper

I facilitated a private, remote session with a client with a prestigious position and who travels a lot for her job. She has done many sessions with me. Every time she gets a new job offer in an exciting city, she wants to do a session to see if it is a good energetic move for her. Of course, I never tell her what is best for her, but the sessions seem to help her figure it out. The last session was revealing.

She was offered a job in London. It was really thrilling for her. She wanted to know if it was a good move for her. I led her through a lot of taps on power and using male energy in a female body. As we unpeeled these layers, one of her past lives revealed itself. I told her that I saw her as a prostitute in the same era as Jack the Ripper. She responded by saying she was terrified by the thought of him.

It was revealed that she was targeted by Jack the Ripper, but she was one who got away from being a victim of his. Somehow that gave her prestige. She gained a little bit of attention that was huge for her in that era. In this life, she was trying to relive that rush of energy by being offered jobs she didn't really want but was excited to have them offered to her. She got a rush in turning down exciting jobs that she didn't really want. It was like escaping a dreadful fate all over again.

The thrill was like a famous celebrity coming back in their next incarnation as someone ordinary. What would that feel like? What experiences could possibly satiate the attention that they were accustomed to receiving? That is a fraction of what my client is experiencing in this life. Her job offers in exciting cities are more about feeding a need for thrill than for figuring out where she would be happy.

This awareness will help her change her dynamics with jobs in the future. This awareness is her escaping a fate of having to go through many habitual experiences to uncover it on her own. Her sessions with me are her escaping a fate in itself. She had strong reactions in releasing these issues and that lifetime.

Also, there was a guy she was interested in who was in London and that was factoring into her decision. She asked me about him hoping for a love interest. Everyone who piques our interest in life is not meant to be in our life. I asked her if she knew that it was not a john from that incarnation or Jack himself. This put the attraction into perspective. It helped her to finally realize that such big decisions can't be decided by personal attractions. It was a good session for her.

Experience of Reincarnation

Calico Cat Named Poodie:

The saddest news was getting the call from the vet telling me our little Poodie had FIPS. There is no cure. It was a death sentence. We did everything we could to keep Poodie as comfortable as possible. We put the fish bowl next to her bed on the end table so she would get lots of water. We gave her all the shrimp she wanted.

At the end, I told her emphatically to come back to us. Before she crossed, I envisioned a white cat with a black spot on it as a clue to what she would look like in her next life. We grieved deeply.

Months later, I needed to find an apartment. I had a nudge to go into a suburb that wasn't where I wanted to live at all. But I had to go to this one place. The apartment was wrong for me and I was curious why I was led there until I saw a white cat with a black spot in the apartment. She was a stray they had recently rescued.

I arranged to adopt one of the kittens. I figured I would know which one Poodie was because it would be white with a black spot, and I sensed it would be a boy. When the litter was born, there were four kittens all with white fur and black spots. I ended up adopting three of the kittens to make certain I had the one that was Poodie.

Shortly after arriving home with the new kittens, one of them displayed a personality similar to Poodie. He was a take charge kind of kitten, mature beyond his years. His new dad looked at me and said, "Wow! It really is Poodie, isn't it?" At that, the little kitten responded as if to say yes by walking between the both of us rubbing us both with the side of his face.

"Yes, I am Poodie! Here I am."

I think it is good that most Americans don't believe in reincarnation. We, in general, are incredible control freaks. To realize that our loved ones are out there is a terrible stress for those who want to reclaim the relationship. The search for Poodie was a stressful time. Thank goodness the owners of the mama were so loving and agreeable. But I am sure the Universe arranged that, too. Poodie is now called Smudge and we have a strong love bond. It was an incredible gift to find him and to experience the miracle of the quest.

Fear of Commitment

I tuned in to someone who had an aversion to getting married. After this experience, it is quite obvious to me why so many people meet it with dread.

In a past life, she was marrying a prince. She was chosen because she was beautiful. It was less about love than about responsibility. The pressure was overwhelming. Until then, in that lifetime, she had less status and so lived with more freedom.

There were now all kinds of bodyguards tending the betrothed. In that culture, the bodyguards were more like spies and a death squad. The pressure to learn the ways of the royal family, and the threat of death if she did not perform, were beyond stressful. She lived as a prisoner.

Four years later, it was discovered that she had taken a lover. She and her lover were executed.

After being privy to this experience, it occurred to me why so many people are afraid to get married. Ceremonies for the commoner are a relatively new cultural phenomenon. People want to have a big wedding because in the past only the most influential people had such celebrations. And some have such an aversion to being married because they unconsciously recall a trauma surrounding such responsibility from a past life.

This may be why two people who agree on so much may be at cross purposes about marriage because we all bring our own experiences to the table.

Fear of Speaking

In many of my sessions, the client has suffered an incredible trauma simply because they spoke truth. I have seen people tortured in ways that are unfathomable because they showed leadership qualities and stood apart in the crowd. This threatened the ruling lord of the land. There have been endless corrupt governing parties in the past.

How that shows up in this lifetime is that people are afraid to speak up. They had not pulled back the conscious memory of being tortured, but the reaction is so strong in them that it may make sense.

Here are some SFT taps to alleviate the reaction:

(Say each statement three times while tapping the top of your head and say it a fourth time while tapping on your chest.)

"I release the trauma of being martyred; in all moments."

"I release the trauma of being tortured; in all moments."

"I recant my vow of silence; in all moments."

"I recant my vow of martyrdom; in all moments."

"I release the fear of speaking; in all moments."

"I release the fear of sharing my Truth; in all moments."

"I release the fear of being tortured; in all moments."

"I release the fear of being martyred; in all moments."

If someone is being affected by debilitating inability to express themselves, these may help.

Forgetting

Many people wonder if there is such a thing as past lives, connecting to the other side and perceiving more subtle realities, why don't they have any unique abilities. There are many reasons.

There is a mechanism within us that acts as a curtain to keep out all the experiences of a more subtle nature. Its purpose is to keep us focused on the lessons of this particular lifetime without overwhelming us. If an individual knew of all they had experienced, it would be distracting from their life's lessons at hand and could be overwhelming.

In the human experience, we have all abused power in the past and learned from our own actions how horrific it is to cause another pain. If we were to remember our gifts, it may allow some of these instances in as well. I am not sure that those who have the greatest compassion and do the greatest good in the world are not undoing their own blemishes from the past.

If someone knew they were royalty in a past life, that knowledge alone could lighten the impact of the lesson of living in humility in this life. The truth of the opposite would see them through. They would just live this life in quiet resolve waiting for the throw of the dice to give them better circumstances. They would not be as motivated to absorb their spiritual lessons.

This life is indeed a classroom. If one accepts this, they can accept their own potential and take spiritual responsibility for every thought, feeling and action. In that self-responsibility lies the key to true empowerment.

Freeing Those You Have Caused to Be Killed

What is worse, killing someone with little remorse, or being in a position to stop someone who is killing others and doing nothing about it? How about being forced to kill someone and feeling bad, or choosing to kill someone with absolute indifference? Is it less of a moral issue to kill someone that is inferior, or is that just a form of not taking responsibility? Are humans a more important life form than an animal? Are they more important than nature? Is it okay to kill as long as there is a reason, like food or safety? What if one does not understand the vantage point of those they have killed or are indifferent?

This is the dilemma that has been played out in all eras through history. The moral issue of taking life is so subjective that one wonders if the karmic consequences are subjective as well. Sometimes, someone who was not directly responsible for the death of others carries more of a guilty burden than those who carried out the kill. How does that register in guilt and heaviness? How does each get rectified?

Here are some taps that I led a client through. They weren't privy to the images that I had to endure in releasing the following imbalances from her energy field. She knew it was a devastating shift from my horrific wailing after she performed taps. I was crying her anguish.

In doing this technique, it is like energetically going back to the incidents that caused so much anguish and guilt and releasing the imbalance. It is also an energetic way to give back what was taken from others unjustly. We cannot fully heal until we rectify our actions and these taps are the way to do just that. If there is a lot of sadness released in doing these, there is also a lot of relief in releasing the sadness that we have caused. Knowing that one is giving back what they have taken from the innocent helps in pushing past the resistance. The client had a hard time doing these taps, but when I explained that it would free those she has wronged, she got through them.

Here are the taps:

(Say each statement three times out loud while tapping your head and say it a fourth time while tapping your chest.)

"I recant all vows and agreements between myself and all those I have caused to be killed; in all moments."

"I remove all curses between myself and all those I have caused to be killed; in all moments."

"I remove all the guilt and anguish that I have been carrying for all those I have caused to be killed; in all moments."

"I dissolve all karmic ties between myself and all those I have caused to be killed; in all moments."

"I remove all the pain, burden, limitations and engrams that I have put on all those I have caused to be killed; in all moments."

"I remove all the pain burden, limitations and engrams from myself due to all those I have caused to be killed; in all moments."

"I give back all that I have taken or caused to be taken from all those I have caused to be killed; in all moments."

"I take back all the Joy, Love, Abundance, Freedom, Health, Success, Security, Companionship, Creativity, Peace, Life, Wholeness, Beauty, Enthusiasm and Contentment that was taken from me due to all those I have caused to be killed; in all moments."

"I remove all those I have caused to be killed from my sound frequency; in all moments."

"I remove all those I have caused to be killed from my light body; in all moments."

"I release resonating with the guilt of all those I have caused to be killed; in all moments."

"I release emanating with the guilt of all those I have caused to be killed; in all moments."

"I transcend all transgressions between myself and all those I have caused to be killed; in all moments."

"I shift my paradigm from all those I have caused to be killed to Joy, Love, Abundance, Freedom, Health, Success, Security, Companionship, Creativity, Peace, Life,

Wholeness, Beauty, Enthusiasm and Contentment; in all moments."

"I am centered, empowered and interconnected with all life in Divine Love; in all moments."

Freezing to Death

A friend of mine has purple hands and feet. She can never get them warm. The condition has a nice name so she knows how to refer to it. It is called Raynaud's Disease. There is no known cause, but when I look at her, I see flashes of her past life.

She is in very cold water clinging on for dear life. The image looks like one of the scenes nearing the end of the movie *Titanic*. She froze to death in a past lifetime. That was the pain and trauma she is trying to validate in this life. It is as if her hands and feet are saying, "Look what you have been through. Look at the trauma so you can let it go."

Recognizing the true cause of anything is the way of dissipating its effects. At least this is what I have found regarding the emotional and physical pain of the body.

Frozen in Indifference

A dear friend of mine has been working with me for a couple of years now. Every time an issue comes up for her, we will work through it to release any pain or angst it causes her. She has become so open and even more loving and kind than she had been in her life. She exudes contentment, humility and a sweet loving resolve. She even credits not needing high blood pressure medicine after 25 years of taking it to her work with me.

Lately, she has been having a pain in her right leg. It is a deep issue and when we connect, I will assist her in discovering an underlying cause of it. It is not easy to look at our own issues. It is similar to cleaning house. Sometimes it is easier to clean a friend's house instead of our own. Many times, it is easier to love and validate others and stifle our own cry for help. Physical pain on some level is a cry for validation and love.

She has a habit of diminishing the importance of events and situations for herself. It is a deep-seated way to prevent her from being hurt. For example, if she is going to a special event, she will say something like, "I don't really care what I wear. I will just throw on the outfit I wore the last time." Or, she will say, "It doesn't really matter. I will just have a few people over and just throw some food out. It will be good enough."

For the last couple of months, her leg has been hurting and she has been asking for my help. I have been assisting, but the pain has not been totally released. As we visited last night, a past life of hers opened up. I saw her as an animal in a metal trap. Her leg was half-frozen off. She was retrieving food for her family and anxious to get back to them when she got caught in one of those claw metal traps. As excruciating as it was, the emotional pain of not getting home to her family and feeling her life body freeze and the life force slipping farther away from them left an emotional numbness in her. She showed this in the present life by diminishing the importance of special occasions to her.

This was the moment to address it. I shared with her the connection between her physical pain and this past life. She deflected and would not look at it. She was numb to it. She moved all too quickly to another subject about something unrelated and she used those words again, "I don't care." It was time to pin the emotional issue to its manifestation.

"You do too care. You do!" I took her by surprise. "Imagine your babies are waiting for you. They are hungry and your teats are full of milk. Your husband is alone at home with them and they are all waiting for you to be cozy and safe. But you are trapped in the cold metal jaw and freezing to death not able to get to them. You know they will most likely starve without you and think you have abandoned them. You care!"

She was taken aback and cried a deep soulful cry. If there were no connection to the scenario I had just painted, the sobs would not have continued like they did.

Here are some taps that helped as well:

(Say each statement three times while tapping on your head and say it a fourth time while tapping on your chest.)

"I release being frozen in indifference; in all moments."

"I release the trauma of freezing to death; in all moments."

"I release the guilt and trauma of abandoning my family; in all moments."

"I forgive myself; in all moments."

Her husband had trapped animals in his youth. She was able to compartmentalize this as being "okay." After the sobbing, we visualized the scenario that I saw and freed her in the trapped body. We poured incredible Love into its little body. We changed the story of it to undo the emotional scar it left. We also visualized freeing all the animals that were ever trapped and killed in such a ruthless way. We poured love and healing into them all and the whole scenario.

Frozen Shoulder

Recently, I facilitated a private, remote session with someone who came to me for help with a frozen shoulder. Immediately, I got an impression of the issue. I saw her in a past life with a huge shield in her left hand, pulled clenched to the body and in a very defensive stance. When we connected by phone for her session, she validated that it was indeed her left shoulder. She also validated that people in this lifetime seemed to attack her for no reason and it did make her defensive. I explained to her that the attacks were reminders or hints to the conscious mind of what she had suffered in the past without having to remember details. Her inner energy was not fluid but stuck in the position of the warrior.

I can tell that I am accurate in accessing an issue because the client will have difficulty in hearing the taps I give them, retaining them enough to say them, and repeating them back to me. It was very difficult for this client to get through any of the taps. The energy was so stagnant and locked in her body that it was difficult to connect with her enough to help her release it by saying the taps.

The imagery of different lifetimes in war were layered within her. Besides the initial image, I saw her rotting in a dank dungeon chained to a wall in many different battle scenarios and definitely spending many lifetimes living, fighting and dying in the Crusades. When someone has been in the Crusades, the *Hallelujah* song comes to me as a way to release the issues. She was so congested with these lifetimes that I sang the *Hallelujah* song to her. She cried profusely during it. This released the issues in her a bit. I then was able to lead her through some taps to free up her energy more.

Here are some taps that I was then able to lead her through:

(Say each statement three times while tapping on your head and say it a fourth time while tapping on your chest.)

"I declare myself a surrogate for humanity; in all moments." (Optional)

"I release fighting for my life; in all moments."

"I release the trauma of being attacked; in all moments."

"I release being in attack mode; in all moments."

"I release defending my life; in all moments."

"I release being defensive; in all moments."

"I release the guilt and trauma of killing others; in all moments."

"I release hating the Church; in all moments."

"I release fighting and dying for a cause I don't believe in; in all moments."

"I release the trauma of being at war; in all moments."

"I release infusing apathy into life; in all moments."

"I release the trauma of being tortured; in all moments."

"I release the trauma of being imprisoned; in all moments."

"I recant all vows and agreements between myself and all battles; in all moments."

"I remove all curses between myself and all battles; in all moments."

"I dissolve all karmic ties between myself and all battles; in all moments."

"I remove all the pain, burden and limitations that all

battles have put on me; in all moments."

"I take back all the Joy, Love, Abundance, Freedom, Health, Peace, Life and Wholeness that all battles have taken from me; in all moments."

"I withdraw all my energy from all battles; in all moments."

"I release resonating with all battles; in all moments."

"I release emanating with all battles; in all moments."

"I remove all battles from my sound frequency; in all moments."

"I remove all battles from my light body; in all moments."

"I shift my paradigm from all battles to Joy, Love, Abundance, Freedom, Health, Life and Wholeness; in all moments."

"I repair and fortify my Wei Chi; in all moments."

"I am centered am empowered in Divine Love; in all moments."

At the end of the session, the client could feel the energy in her body as more fluid. She was happy and enthused with her session. She had been to many alternative and conventional healers. None were able to assist. I understood why. I had to really pin her down energetically to help her strip these issues off. It is similar to sitting on someone and stripping layers of tight clothing off them. I went deep and was more relentless than they were able to be.

Maybe by doing the taps above, we all can shift the tide of current events. Maybe we can work as inside agents to free and uplift humanity. Maybe we can unhinge the unconscious allure for war and move humanity to peace! Who is willing to do this?

Gypsy Freedom

I facilitated a couple of back to back sessions with a woman who is in the middle of a huge move. Although there were some aspects of the move that weren't desirable, she was allowing it to devastate her. She seemed pretty wilted.

In the first session, I saw many past lives where she was pushed off the land by war. She was a refugee. This was the cause of the feelings of devastation she was feeling in this life. But digging a little deeper, I found some experiences that contradicted the fear of being displaced from her home.

She also had lifetimes of being a gypsy. They were very free and happy lifetimes. When I mentioned them, they resonated with the woman. We released a lot of the angst that was caused by being uprooted by war. We uncovered the joy she had experienced in the past so that she could feel it in this lifetime. She was much more excited about the present move after her session.

In her next session, I picked up that she was having

difficulty packing. She was way too attached to possessions. In her session, the gypsy life came up again. In that lifetime, things made her feel powerful. She had a ruby ring that was her most prized possession and she would manipulate and scheme to get more possessions. She then told me she that she had a ruby ring in this lifetime and was devastated when it lost its stone.

We released her attachment to possessions, and I helped her see that the love of material things did not bring her closer to the people that they represented but actually got in the way of the love. She had an "aha" moment. After her session, she was able to go back and lighten her load before the move.

Hallowed Ground

I facilitated a private, remote session for a dynamic healer. She has been a champion for truth, awareness and individual empowerment. When I tuned into her, I felt a deep anger buried under sadness. As her session unfolded, the cause of this sadness and anger was revealed

In her past lives, I saw a few lifetimes and scenarios where she was considered a traitor to America. In each instance, she was doing the best she could in an impossible situation. Her loyalty, service and devotion were somehow misconstrued as her being a traitor. The lifetimes went all the way back to the birth of America and her being a Native American who inadvertently betrayed her own people somehow.

These taps created an incredible shift in her energy. Doing them did not feel un-American. They were releasing past scenarios of war and false imprisonment that left her feeling betrayed or abandoned. There have been injustices in every era of history. She just happened to be on the receiving end of many regarding America. If you are from another country, you can do these taps and put the name of your country.

(Say each statement three times while tapping the top of your head over your crown chakra and say it a fourth time while tapping on the chest.)

"I release being imprisoned by America; in all moments."

"I release being enslaved by America; in all moments."

"I release being abandoned by America; in all moments."

"I release being betrayed by America; in all moments."

"I release being manipulated by America; in all moments."

"I release being duped by America; in all moments."

"I release being demonized by America; in all moments."

"I release being executed by America; in all moments."

"I release being used by America; in all moments."

"I release being ostracized by America; in all moments."

"I release being hated by America; in all moments."

"I release hating America; in all moments."

"I recant all vows and agreements between myself and America; in all moments."

"I remove all curses between myself and America; in all moments."

"I dissolve all karmic ties between myself and America; in all moments."

"I remove all the pain, burden, limitations and engrams that America has put on me; in all moments."

"I remove all the pain, burden, limitations and engrams that I have put on all others due to America; in all moments."

"I take back all the Joy, Love, Abundance, Freedom, Health, Success, Security, Companionship, Creativity, Peace, Life, Wholeness, Spirituality, Enlightenment and Confidence that America has taken from me; in all moments."

"I give back all the Joy, Love, Abundance, Freedom, Health, Success, Security, Companionship, Creativity, Peace, Life, Wholeness, Spirituality, Enlightenment and Confidence that I have taken from all others due to America; in all moments."

"I release resonating with America; in all moments."

"I release emanating with America; in all moments."

"I remove all of America from my sound frequency; in all

moments."

"I remove all of America from my light body; in all moments."

"I shift my paradigm from America to Joy, Love, Abundance, Freedom, Health, Success, Security, Companionship, Creativity, Peace, Life, Wholeness, Spirituality, Enlightenment and Confidence; in all moments."

"I shift my paradigm from America to hallowed ground; in a moments."

"I transcend America; in all moments."

"I am centered and empowered in living on hallowed ground; in all moments."

"I am hallowed ground; in all moments."

Heart Disease

I facilitated an emergency session for a man who had been diagnosed with blockages in the heart. It was very serious because his father died early of heart disease. We agreed to do the session just a few days before he went to his appointment.

In his session, it opened up to a lifetime during the French and Indian War. He was a soldier and made enemies of the Native Americans. They were angry. They ended up capturing him and eating his heart. The trauma was like a curse on his bloodline. Heart disease was now genetic in his bloodline.

We did much releasing on the relationship between him and the Native Americans and removed all curses and dissolved all karmic ties between them. (A curse can be as simple as a negative thought towards someone or very intense.) I gave him a ton of taps to do for his heart:

"I release storing sadness in my heart; in all moments."

"I remove all blockages in my arteries; in all moments."

"I release feeding sadness from my heart to my body through my arteries; in all moments."

(Say the above three times while tapping on the head and then say them a fourth time while tapping on the chest.)

I also gave him a couple of visualizations to use:

Visualize a wire scrub brush running through the inside of the arteries and breaking up the plaque. Flush divine light through the arteries then to remove all residual issues that were stored as plaque.

Visualize an energetic artery coming out of the heart and siphoning all the anger, worry, sadness, stress and disease out of the heart and pouring it into a river of light that then dissolves it into love.

My client went to his doctor's appointment and did need a valve cleared with stents. But the overall process felt to him like a simple procedure and not the fear-based trauma that it had been.

A Letter to Jen

Hi Jen! I met you a few years back through my cousin. You helped me several times including helping my pups when they needed your specific healing expertise!

I have always been a huge animal lover and when I got my first dog as an adult, I couldn't imagine my life without my girl.

I remember telling you that exact thought one day, and your response was something similar to, "Your babies (dogs) are always with you, and they will come back to you in a new and younger body one day. Watch for it." You told me about an experience that you had with one of your cats, even.

This was a totally new and different way of thinking for me at that time and honestly, I disregarded it in a way because I couldn't fully grasp that concept. When the thought of losing one of my dogs came to my mind, I was initially selfish and thought that I'd keep my babies here as long as I can because I couldn't imagine my life without them.

Then I experienced unconditional love for the first time in my life.

My girl came into my life and was everything to me! She was a handful from day one, but I never and wouldn't have ever given up on her. She lived a short life, and went through chemo treatment and fought like a very tough cookie.

I've learned so much from my Kasey, in her short time on this earth.

I know, also, that I taught her unconditional love for the first time in her life.

I know with all of my heart and soul that she came back in a new body and is still with us--my 13 month old puppy, Axel, is totally my Kasey! He does things that only she would do, and he looks so much like her too.

Knowing, seeing and believing this has helped my broken heart on so many levels.

It was because of you and your help that this was brought to my attention, and that has helped me on many levels.

Thank you from the bottom of my heart.

Hoarding

A client who stockpiled items had an epiphany during a session. In a past lifetime, he lost everything to war. It brought such devastation that it shattered his foundation. To compensate, he would scrounge the war-torn village trying to reclaim what he had lost. It was a way to process the trauma.

During our session, he was able to look at the core reason for the need to hoard. That enabled him to begin changing the behavior.

Some of the taps to assist this behavior were:

"I release the devastation of war; in all moments."

"I release defining possessions as security; in all

moments."

"I shift my paradigm from hoarding to Joy, Love, Abundance and Freedom; in all moments."

(Say each of the above statement three times while tapping the top of your head, and say it a fourth time while tapping the middle of your chest.)

Honing an Understanding of Detachment

People misinterpret the spiritual law of noninterference in a skewed way that may leave them apathetic and indifferent. People may interpret this spiritually to not help people because they need their experiences. This is not the case. It doesn't mean not to help people. It just means not to go out of your way to interrupt experiences that are going to happen anyway.

My guides demonstrated the spiritual law of noninterference through my relationship with my female cat, Gina Lola Kittendon. When I went to meet the litter of kittens that I was going to choose as family members, I was looking for a particular cat--my little Poodie who had crossed over six months prior. I held Gina and fell in love with her. I knew she was not Poodie but adopted her anyway, as well as two of the boy kittens.

She has such a determined cry and gets so bullied by the boys that I thought, as much as I love her, perhaps she needed a different home to be happy. But my guides gave me a clear understanding of why that was not the case.

Gina was Gina. She was going to have her experiences of defending herself and being a little skittish because of it. Why would I take her out of a loving environment so she could have those same experiences elsewhere? No. I was not to try and improve Gina's quality of life by removing her from the only home she knows and causing all kinds of sadness. Gina would do best to endure just where she is. She does.

This lesson gave me a clearer understanding of the law of detachment. It doesn't mean unkindness in any way. It means not allowing the limited understanding of the human consciousness to interfere with a broader implementation of love.

How Deep the Sessions Go

I recently facilitated a private remote session with a woman who felt her energy was blocked. As soon as I tuned into her, I felt that one of her wrists was weak and her energy was bowed to one side. She confirmed that the wrist does get weak and her hips experienced a lot of pain which was reflected in the bowing energy.

I also tuned into something really unique. I felt a big thumb at her crown chakra. It was actually plugging up the energy from getting into her body. It was a huge interference that was causing dark energy where it should have been most light. It lightened up into gradients of gray going down into her body. But it was definitely dark at the top. I did not know what was causing it. But it felt like it had to do with her religious affiliation.

I asked her what religion she was. I knew she had outgrown whatever one it was, but I had to ask the question. She told me that she was raised in the Roman Catholic Church. There was resentment in her words. She also volunteered that she hated being constricted in any way. She equated Catholicism with being constricted. As she was explaining this, her Akashic records opened up to me.

It went immediately to her babyhood and the process of being baptized. The priest who facilitated it seemed to have no love for her. He was not a warm person. It also showed her past lives with this man. He was a nemesis with whom she spent many lifetimes battling. It was his mission to break her. So when she came into this world as a spiritually awakened soul in a baby form, he was here to meet her and close her down. During the ritual of baptism, instead of her energy being opened up, it was plugged shut by this man's thumb and hatred for her. Of course, this is all on subliminal levels, so outwardly, it would only seem like he was indifferent to the baby.

The baptismal is supposedly meant to open the baby to spirit. It actually is the first step to indoctrinating the baby into the religion of their parent's choice. But in this case, it was devastating. It closed the woman's energy down and caused her to feel restricted all of her life. That is what we worked on releasing. The starchy little outfit that she was baptized in was just a hammer to drive in the point of how energetically restricted she was.

This man was a key player in many lifetimes when she was tied up and restricted. It was their soul contract that he shut her down. These are the things that we release in sessions. The weakness in the one wrist was relevant to the pain in the hip. It was caused by one arm being shackled to a cold, hard wall. Her energy bowed in relationship with the torture she endured in that life. When I helped her release it, she felt warmth in the side of the hip that she was sitting on in that life.

Anything that we are experiencing can be released. It is only a matter of delving deep enough and being receptive to receiving the truth. How deep are you willing to go? People who think this is a ridiculous farce are not ready to face and release the past issue. It is fine; there are enough things in the world to distract and placate them. But some people are becoming really savvy at unlocking their inner turmoil simply to release it. The posts I share and the work I do is for them.

How the World Would Be Different If Everyone Remembered Their Past Lives

There would be no more victims. Everyone would realize that the life they are living is the one that they laid the groundwork for. Everyone may even know more readily whom they have wronged in the past by those who dislike them.

Fears could be overcome more readily by realizing they are hints of past traumas to address.

Children would be treated better knowing that they may be our caregivers when we return. Also realizing that each individual is a whole person from the beginning.

Pollution, corruption, and social issues would be dealt with from the selfish motive of knowing that the world we create is the one we inherit.

Education would be revamped because people would want every opportunity amended to them when they return.

Obsession over whom people loved would dry up realizing that loving relationships span multiple lifetimes and sometimes both partners incarnate as the same sex.

There would be more motivation to live a more ethical life to gain an overall advantage in the hierarchy of enlightenment.

There would be fewer suicides because people would realize there is no way to avoid the lessons of life but to learn from them and advance.

There would be less insanity because denying such an obvious truth creates a schism in the psyche between our innate intelligence and the inaccuracies we are taught to believe.

There would be less obsessing over a woman's right to choose realizing that people don't create souls, only a passageway into this world.

The death penalty and imprisonment wouldn't be

solutions as it would be understood that we would only be damaging people more before they were unleashed onto the world in their next life.

There would be less obsessing over being young when people realize that they will have their chance to be that again.

Religious doctrine would register with more truth and would be a blueprint on how to become enlightened rather than a means to police behavior.

It would be much easier to make decisions because we wouldn't be taught from birth inaccuracies that separate us from trusting our innate ability to know truth.

The death penalty and imprisonment wouldn't be such solutions as it would be understood that we would only be damaging people more before they were released into the world in their next life.

How to Lead Others to the High Ground

We have been CONDITIONED to be the enemy of each other lifetime after lifetime. In the early days of Greece and Rome, it was sport to watch people fight to the death. When one ruling part took over a city, they would make servants of some and send some to the coliseums to partake in blood sports. It was great entertainment.

All through history, some petty lord or king was having issues with his neighbors and sent his people to defend his honor. He did not have to be right, noble or just. He just needed to be in charge. We have been so ingrained to fight for a cause we did not believe in. All we had to do was to be pointed in the right direction and told whom to kill.

This has been an habitual thing for so long that we see it play out even in social media. People are ruthlessly unkind to each other and find the tiniest little thing to take offense at. I see people who agree on general principle quibble about details. I post about peace and love, and people still have issues with what I post. It seems systemic.

The thing is that people have been pitted against each other for so long that they fight with people out of habit. The powers that be are now using that ingrained behavior to keep us from being more aware of the way we are all diminished by controlling factions. They manipulate current events and use the media to keep us in a "them versus us" mode. We have to discontinue that behavior so as to get this world in a better state of affairs.

The next time someone offends you or tries to pick a fight with you, imagine seeing them suffering at the mercy of some ruling power that forced them to fight for their life, literally. Recognize the pain and desperation behind the biting attempts to provoke you. Then you can take the higher ground and forgive them their current offense. You can then forgive yourself of all past offenses where you were made to fight for your life.

This is what awakening is about: Meeting the you that you were and upgrading the software to empowerment. You are in control now. So don't let politics, the media, current events or a desperate attempt to engage you in battle provoke you out of your center of peace.

(Say each statement three times while tapping on your head and say it a fourth time while tapping on your chest.)

"I release being a pawn of the establishment; in all moments."

"I release myself and all others of all offenses; in all moments."

"I release maintaining enemies out of habit; in all moments."

"I remove all engrams, programs and conditioning to fight; in all moments."

"I release the need to defend myself; in all moments."

"I lay down my sword and shield; in all moments."

"I release being physically, emotionally, or mentally manipulated to fight; in all moments."

"I release all agreements to fight; in all moments."

"I nullify all contracts to fight; in all moments."

"I nullify all contracts with all those deemed an enemy; in all moments."

"I dissipate all psychic forces goading me to fight; in all moments."

"I transcend the 'them versus us' mentality; in all moments."

"I remove all the curses, blessings and connection with all those deemed an enemy; in all moments."

"I remove all that I and all adversaries have put on each other; in all moments."

"I take back all that all adversaries have taken from me and return to all adversaries all that I have taken from them; in all moments."

"I encourage and support all others in transcending; in all moments."

"I release anything in myself and all others that interferes with our transcendence; in all moments."

"I am centered and empowered in seeing all others as equal, respected and loved; in all moments."

"I resonate, emanate and am interconnected with all life in mutual respect, equality and love; in all moments."

Next time someone offends you, maybe you can send them these taps and take the high ground. It is where we are all headed. You may as well be the one that leads others there.

Individuality

A grain of sand on the shore that catches the Light

That one grounded bird that learns to take flight

The unencumbered soul that stretches to be free

That voice in dissension that learns to agree

The infant who remembers what it's like to be old

A flame that never forgets what it's like to be cold

Defeating lost hope by saying, "I can"

Experience being comfortable whether woman or man

Creating a symphony one note at a time

Knowing peace during chaos, albeit sublime

The sliver of knowledge that turns into a wedge

Being pushed past all reason and jumping over the ledge

There's no separation between the foam and the sea

Illusion's the only distinction between you and what's me.

Issues Involved in Falling to One's Death

We forget that hospitals, wheelchairs and painkillers are a relatively modern invention. In the past, when we fell or broke a limb, we lay there mangled and twisting, writhing in pain until someone put us out of our misery or death came to us. These memories still surface when we are confronted with health issues. They are the hiccups of past torments making their way to the surface for validation. They need not be permanent.

If past issues are acknowledged and the body is validated, we can move through them quite quickly. See? It is not always something settling into us. Many and most times, it is something devastating trying to leave. That is the purpose of the taps, to acknowledge the pain quickly and to help it pass through.

One of my first clients was terrified of birds. It sounds silly to some. But the image that I saw was her as a young Native American man. He was climbing on the rocks of a cliff to access eggs in the nests. He lost his footing and fell to his demise. But death wasn't swift. He lay there watching the vultures circle him as he got weaker. They did not wait for him to die before they moved in and started picking at his flesh. They made their first strikes at the moist areas where the blood drained out - the intestines and the eyeballs. This was how she left that life.

Here are some of the taps that I led her through:

(Say each statement three times while tapping on your head and say it a fourth time while tapping on your chest.)

"I release the pain and trauma of falling to my death; in all moments."

"I release the fear of heights; in all moments."

"I release the horror of being eaten alive; in all moments."

"I release the fear of being eaten by birds/dogs/
cats/natives (whatever it is); in all moments."

"I untangle the limbs of my body; in all moments."

"I untangle the energy of my body; in all moments."

"I release mingling my sense of adventure with fear; in all
moments."

"I release allowing fear to override my sense of adventure;
in all moments."

"I release feeling helpless and abandoned; in all
moments."

"I release the belief that I am helpless and abandoned; in
all moments."

"I shift my paradigm from helpless and abandoned to
empowered and free; in all moments."

"I am centered in Joy, Love, Abundance, Freedom, Health,
Success, Adventure and Wholeness; in all moments."

We are only as brave as the strongest memory of our
deepest fear. When we understand that we are
empowered by taking a non-reactive stance to
unconscious triggers, we can just address them without
being blindsided by emotional reactions. We don't even
have to fully understand the emotional reaction to just
address them head on. Our own resistance to addressing
them then becomes sabotage because the taps work easily

and effectively.

Jealousy

I have a client who has been really jealous of redheaded women all through her marriage. When she was with her husband and they saw an attractive red haired woman, she would become withdrawn and melancholy. It was so not like her, and something that she never admitted to anyone until we started working together.

She freed herself of this issue by disciplining herself to write down her dreams. By doing so, she began to consciously recall many adventures, past life scenarios and lessons that she was given during the night. In a dream, she saw the most beautiful red-haired woman standing before her. She had vibrancy, beauty, sincerity and self-confidence. Suddenly she shifted vantage points of looking at this beautiful woman to being her. She was the beautiful red-haired woman. This is how she was more comfortable looking in her past lives.

What she thought was jealousy of another was actually looking at an aspect of herself that was merely dormant in the present lifetime. In that lifetime as a red haired woman, she and her present husband were also very much in love. When she was feeling jealous, it was her feeling remorseful that she didn't look the way she did in that past lifetime for him in the present life. It was a bit of nostalgia for the past.

When we fixate on something in jealousy, we are seeing an aspect of ourselves that we once manifested but is now dormant. In the classroom of life, we need to experience every scenario to glean the wisdom and compassion to transcend. Jealousy doesn't need to set up feelings of incessant want. Twinges of it can be a gauge for us to dig deeper into life and awaken an aspect of ourselves that we didn't know existed. Jealousy and other undesirable reactions are merely part of the glorious adventure of our own self-discovery.

Karmic Burden

Many people are struggling with their burdens. The problem with our burdens is that they sometimes define us. We have had them so long that many of us would feel lost without them. That fear motivates us to cling to them with our whole being. They feel as comfortable as our own breath.

If one really wants to release carrying their burden, here are some SFT taps to help:

(Say each statement three times while tapping on your head and a fourth time while tapping your chest.)

"I recant all vows and agreements between myself and karmic burden; in all moments."

 "I remove all curses between myself and karmic burden; in all moments."

"I remove all the pain, burden and limitations that karmic burden has put on me; in all moments."

"I take back all the Joy, Love, Abundance, Freedom, Peace and Wholeness that karmic burden has taken from me; in all moments."

"I remove all karmic burden from my sound frequency; in all moments."

"I remove all karmic burden from my light body; in all moments."

"I release resonating with karmic burden; in all moments."

"I release emanating with karmic burden; in all moments."

"I shift my paradigm from karmic burden to Joy, Love, Abundance, Freedom, Peace and Wholeness; in all moments."

Learning from Past Life Memories

I have had a few past life memories of dying. Each of them was under different conditions and each of them taught me more about myself in this lifetime and assisted with my current work.

In the first scenario, I was in a farmhouse washing dishes and waiting for my husband to come home. As I was doing dishes, I looked out the window waiting for him to come home. But the scenario got crazy. I was suddenly running for my life.

I was running out of the house and into the barn for safety. But as I got to the barn, I was struck down by the ax that my husband was carrying. He planted it in my back. There was the blow, then blackness and then the scenario became peaceful, and I was floating across a river. I was murdered by my husband in that lifetime.

I learned from that experience that peace follows any trauma.

The second scenario was wartime. I was a soldier in active combat. I was at the front of the attack hiding behind trees and a shed. I was very good at what I did and was way in front of my platoon. Suddenly, everything went black and I was lying in a pile of dead soldiers. I didn't understand why.

There were some soldiers walking around, but none of them were helping me. I could not move and I could not speak. I was waiting for them to come help me. I didn't understand that I was dead too.

From that lifetime I learned that sometimes the soul stays with the body. It is a very scary and helpless feeling. I was grateful to experience, though, that I do not die after the death of the body. I am still me.

The third scenario was me in the body of a preteen boy. I had some kind of influenza that I was dying from. My parents were not good at showing affection, but it was obvious that they adored me. They were heartbroken. I tried to hang on to that life because I didn't want them to suffer. It was the most excruciating thing I have ever experienced.

As my father sat helpless near my bed, I came back to consciousness long enough to say, " I love you Dad." He was so desperate to hear it that he broke down at the words. I could feel my mother in the background starving to hear the same words. I tried to hang on long enough to tell her but was unable to. The last memory was of her anguish and resentment.

What I learned from that lifetime was how humane it is to give someone permission to cross when it is their time, also, how important it is to tell loved ones how important they are before crossing.

These life experiences happen to us all. It is so beneficial to embrace them rather than deny their existence.

Looking at Truth

A client shared with me an experience she had at a museum recently. There was a mother there with a small baby. Every time the mother carried the baby near the statues from ancient Greece and Rome, the baby got visibly upset. It was obvious to me just hearing this that the baby had bad memories from that time period and they were being stirred up by the statues.

I asked the client if she pointed out to the mother that the baby was reacting to the statues. She said no. She was afraid that the mother would think she was strange. I was a bit disappointed. This baby was someone that she had known in that lifetime in their last incarnation. Educating the mother was an opportunity to repay a kindness. It was a missed opportunity. We let so many of these opportunities slip away. It could have been said with love and nurturing. It would have been a wonderful seed for the parent and the baby's awakening.

This whole society is ruled and boxed in by fear. People are so afraid that the truth that they know in their heart of hearts will bleed through and be seen by others. They sit back and allow ignorance to reign instead of taking small steps in the direction of truth.

In past lives, we were all pulled out of the crowd and tortured or killed for speaking our truth. This memory lingers as a fear of being seen as different. This fear is our chain on the elephant's leg that keeps us enslaved to conformity.

Say these taps if you want to be less inhibited to speak your truth:

(Say each statement three times while tapping on your head and say it a fourth time while tapping your chest.)

"I recant my vow of silence; in all moments."

"I release the fear of speaking my truth; in all moments."

"I release the pain and trauma of being tortured for my truth; in all moments."

"I release being enslaved to convention; in all moments."

"I release trading truth for security; in all moments."

"I release buying security with ignorance; in all moments."

"I release the fear of being different; in all moments."

"I release perpetuating ignorance; in all moments."

"I shift my paradigm from ignorance to truth; in all moments."

"I am centered and empowered in truth; in all moments."

"I resonate with truth; in all moments."

"I infuse my sound frequency with truth; in all moments."

"I emanate with truth; in all moments."

"I imbue my light body with truth; in all moments."

"I shift my paradigm from ignorance to Joy, Love, Abundance, Freedom, Health, Success, Security, Companionship, Peace, Life and Wholeness; in all moments."

Almost every person I connect to tells me they believe in energy work and past lives but they don't think their friends and family will accept it. When I meet their family and friends, they say the same thing. Truth is everyone's "dirty little secret." Isn't it time we bring truth out of the closet and let everyone look at it in the light of day?

Lung Issues

Body parts hold memory of past lives. If there is trauma, in the past, it can show up in the present as dis-ease. It is the body's attempt to come to terms with what happened. In private sessions, I help the client release the tension that past lives have carried over into the present life. The incidents that caused the dis-ease are so traumatic that the person would rather stay in denial rather than face it. So to be able to release it by me looking at it for them, showing them parts of it and helping them decipher the lesson is, to some, a Godsend. It is like being on the fast track to one's spiritual unfoldment.

In private sessions, I see the trauma of how people have died. I see it in pictures and impressions. What I see is validated by the client because I can also tell them how it affects their present life. People who have shallow breathing or are smokers are holding trauma in their lungs. It is amazing to many clients how they feel lighter and breathe deeper after a session. The shift is permanent and becomes their new normal.

Here are some taps to open up the lungs:

(Say each statement three times while tapping on your head and say it a fourth time while tapping on your chest.)

"I release storing pain and trauma in my lungs; in all moments."

"I release the trauma of drowning; in all moments."

"I release the trauma of choking on my own blood; in all moments."

"I release the trauma of having my lung punctured; in all moments."

"I release the trauma of suffocating; in all moments."

"I release the trauma of dying of pneumonia; in all moments."

"I release the trauma of pleurisy; in all moments."

"I release the trauma of dying of smoke inhalation; in all moments."

"I release the trauma of the plague; in all moments."

"I release having the black death; in all moments."

"I release the trauma of being gassed; in all moments."

The taps that are harder to do are more relevant. Many times when a client has one lifetime with trauma to a certain area of the body; there are other lifetimes with trauma to the same part of the body. I see them overlay each other. The one that is most traumatic is usually sensed first and then when that one is addressed the other ones are easier to discern. As each issue is addressed, the person's energy opens up like a flower. The client can sometimes feel their energy unfurl like the petals of a lotus. Maybe doing the taps will help you experience that sensation.

Making It About Love

In the past, marriages were business transactions. Having the most advantageous union was a status symbol or survival tool. Being married was about keeping each other and your children alive. It wasn't a perpetual romance. There may not have been any romance there at all. Many were lucky if they could stand their life partner. Loving your mate was a luxury. Standing them was an art.

In this life, we are lucky enough to be able to choose our partner. We feel this strong attraction to them or maybe a familiarity. Most likely, someone's partner today was someone they were with in a past life.

When disagreements come or the novelty of finding someone wears off, one may see their mate in a different light. When someone is annoyed with a mate they may see them as weak, undesirable, boring, crazy, their captor, and they may feel an indescribable futility that they think is unique to them.

What they are doing is reliving past dynamics with their present spouse. These are the things that they may have come into this life to overcome. So whenever a negative perception of a mate comes through, it may be a personal challenge to realize that this may be what the two of you have come together to resolve. It is now time to come together in Love.

This is a reason why some people have an aversion to marriage. They are tapping into how the relationship ended in a past life (death), and it is too painful to look at.

Also in past lives, only those with grave responsibilities like heads of state had huge ceremonies. The ceremony itself may trigger deep-seated and valid fears.

Milk Mouth

All my current furry family are old friends that have returned. I was lovingly talking to one of my little female cats who always screams at me when she is hungry. I lovingly called her milk mouth. I wondered why I had called her milk mouth because I have never given her milk.

But then an old memory opened up with me sitting on a stool milking a cow and having this one little determined kitten screaming at me for a squirt of milk. I saw how it got all over her face and it was so amusing to me. A bond was forged.

I wondered why this little kitten would scream at me so harshly like it was life and death whenever she was hungry. Now I knew why. Mealtime was life and death in a past life, and that is what is triggered in her when she gets a hunger pain and I am in the kitchen. This is how the dynamics of our past lives interplay in the present.

Monkey Joy

A client came to me disturbed by threats from her ex-husband's family. It was causing a great reaction in her.

They had threatened to take her home from her. Immediately, my inner vision opened up to a scenario in a past life where she was a Hun. Her group had conquered a village and she was in the midst of them. She was the one who was threatening their wellbeing. The mere "memory" of her as the aggressor switched her out of victim mode so she was receptive to what came next.

In that time, they surrounded her and wore her down until one of them was able to pierce him (she was male) with a penetrating spear to the spine. I felt the blow.

"Do you feel that pain on the right side of your lower spine?" I asked. She did. That was where a debilitating blow had landed in her body in that past life. It was what we were releasing. I felt the move through her hip area and an agility return that was missing. She confirmed that although she was very agile, her lower lumbar was always locked. She was amazed. She felt the shift.

The energy continued to move down into her tailbone. I felt her have a tail. Another scene opened up. It was she in a jungle in a monkey body and the village from the past image. Her former in-laws in the present life were in that scenario as well. They were a different tribe of monkeys.

In that scenario, she had lost her monkey family and was taken in by a male in the group. She wasn't totally accepted and existed on the fringe of their group. It was a lonely and isolated existence that ended in tragedy. Before encountering this group of monkeys, she was very happy. She exuded a joy of trusting exuberance. In her session, it was time for her to return to that state. She was ready to recapture her monkey joy.

In the session, we did a bunch of energy work where we balanced the transactions between her and the group. It is like energetically balancing the karmic books so that all debts are considered paid back on both sides. There is no need to continue rehashing old debts that play out as petty issues. (It is interesting to watch how the sessions play out in the client's life afterwards).

We returned the woman to her monkey joy with the added bonus of all the insights she had learned since that naïve state. It is a wonderful experience to return to joy after forgetting what it feels like to be imbued in it. It is my hope to assist as many as I can to return to their monkey joy!

Neck Issues

So many deaths occur because of trauma to the neck. When I work with clients, many times I see their death due to choking, hanging or decapitating. When I see someone rubbing their neck, many times it takes me to a past life injury that they have had.

Sometimes, I see the trauma coming from the front, or to the side or in the back. Sometimes, I get a quick sense of the trauma instead of the whole scenario, but I have seen enough.

These taps may help neck trauma:

(Say each statement three times while tapping on your head and say it a fourth time while tapping on your chest.)

"I release the trauma of being decapitated; in all moments."

"I release the trauma of being choked to death; in all moments."

"I release the trauma of being hung; in all moments."

"I release the trauma of having my neck broken; in all moments."

"I release the trauma of having my throat slit; in all moments."

"I release drowning in my own blood; in all moments."

"I release being whiplashed; in all moments."

"I remove all the chains and shackles from my neck; in all moments."

"I mend my neck bones; in all moments."

"I heal all my neck wounds; in all moments."

When I see one lifetime of neck injury, many times there are layers of trauma to the same area. Maybe by doing these taps, one can interrupt habitual injury to the neck.

Normal

It may sound strange, but sometimes client's causal (past life) memories reveal lifetimes on other planets. Many people feel like they don't belong and that they think differently from others. They spend most of their life wondering why they are so different. They may even be homesick for a place that they have forgotten.

It is very common to feel isolated. Those who do don't want to be labeled even more different, so they suffer in silence, which isolates them even more. So many people are afraid of being called crazy that sane has become a very narrow bandwidth that people try to exist in. If everyone felt safe to be themselves, more people would experience a commonality and would relax in who they are.

Whatever one can think and feel is more common than what others on the outside could possible imagine. Every human experience is valid and surfaces to teach one more about love. Truth runs much deeper than public opinion.

Overreaction?

Recently, I facilitated a session with a woman who was very distressed. Her daughter, whom she adores, was planning on taking a vacation and not including her. She was heartbroken at being left home. It was causing excruciating emotional pain.

Coinciding with this interaction was a recurring dream

she was having. She was on a craggy shoreline where the waves were violently coming to shore. She was looking for her daughter and her granddaughter. They got separated in the chaos of the storm.

I have seen this inner scene in other people who are convinced that they are experiencing their last days on the continent Lemuria or Atlantis. My client is very sensible and balanced. She is included so much in her daughter's life that this oversight may seem like an overreaction. But the outer circumstances are merely a trigger of a life and death scenario that the woman had experienced with her daughter. The vacation was merely a means of drawing the issue to the surface so the woman can release it on a very deep level.

After the woman's session, she could see how she was projecting abandonment and loss issues onto her daughter. After the issue was released in her session, she reported that she could now look at her daughter as a blank slate. Now all that is reflected back to her is incredible deep love and appreciation for having her daughter in her life.

When we overreact to situations, it isn't an overreaction but a memory of a trauma from the past. By realizing the correlation with the past, we are able to let go of its severe significance in the present. We can be more free.

Past Life Aversions

Who you are exactly serves you. If you are not beautiful, being beautiful may have brought you the wrong attention in a past life. If you are not rich, you may have strong opinions about the poor or beliefs to be molded. All our experiences are ways to give us life from every vantage point and every spectrum. If you abused power in a past, you will learn what it feels like to feel powerless. Everyone will come to compassion for all through their experiences.

Technique: When there is something to which you feel a strong aversion, know there is something in that experience that is a learning tool for you. Look at the culture and activities that you dislike and dig into them to recognize why you don't like them. It may uncover some of your past life aversions that are holding you back.

Playing Catch Up

So much of our behavior, dislikes, fears and aversions are formulated in past lives. When I am talking to someone, it is sometimes difficult to stay present with them in the moment. A myriad of engrams from past lives comes through and I see them all at once sometimes. The most prevalent ones are the ones that cause the most dis-ease.

Sometimes when someone is talking a lot, I see it as a defense mechanism where they are literally talking themselves out of being killed in the past. When someone is rubbing their neck, I see the past life in which they were forced up to the gallows and decapitated. When someone goes on about how much they have accomplished, I see them making their case for not being kicked out of the tribe in another time. When someone is loud and obnoxious, I see that as a survival tool for living in a time when brute strength made one important. People who need to be good and perfect are also doing that to maintain their security within a group. So many behaviors and dynamics are based on means used in past lives to survive.

When we are met with difficult people, it is all we can do sometimes not to be annoyed out of our skin. A great technique to acquire is looking at them from possible past life scenarios where their behavior was warranted. If we can get a sense of the desperation and vulnerability that led a person in the past to adopt a particular behavior, we can have more compassion for them when they exhibit it. And the more awareness and understanding that we have for how others became who they are, the more compassion we can demonstrate towards them and ourselves.

This is the lifetime to absorb all these lessons. This is the lifetime to become more conscious of our spiritual journey. We are so fortunate to learn from each other here. Nowhere in the history of mankind has it been so easy to glean such truth openly. It is an incredible blessing to be aware of and to take advantage of.

Postpartum and Past Life Triggers

I recently facilitated a session where the mother was having difficulty in her role as a mom. It created a lot of angst in her because she adored her children and yet worried so much about being a good mom. She felt she wasn't able to enjoy her children.

Her past lives opened up. A similar scenario repeated itself. She was brought to a strange land as a wife and was not happy. She wanted to return home but then the babies started coming. She was then stuck in a strange land because of her inability to leave her children. The past angst was bleeding through to this life. I am wondering if a lot of the postpartum depression that happens is because new motherhood triggers trauma from past lives when it was much more difficult to care for children.

The mother felt more spacious and free after her session.

Queen Bee

This weekend, I was visiting with a friend. She is a very accomplished, balanced woman who is very positive to be around. She makes everyone feel valued.

When we were talking, she explained how much she loves women. But then I recognized that she has no close women in her life. No peers. It just stuck with me as I was talking with her. Whenever I ask a question to the Universe, I get an answer. I think this is true with everyone, but they have grown unaccustomed to listening or believing the answer. The answer I got was she was a queen bee.

I understand that it is far-fetched, but I got an image of her being a queen bee and that is why she has no equals. I shared and she was polite enough not to dismiss it. But then different evidence of how that life experience influenced the present were revealed to me. I shared many items about her I could not possibly know.

Here are the things that I listed: When you work, you are very busy and have a total overview of everything. Everyone who works for you is very efficient and the work environment is very productive. You compartmentalize everything into unique, little issues (which I saw as separate honeycombs). You don't like it when others spill out of their role. You keep others at bay. And as a queen bee, you were the only one of your kind and no one measures up to your efficiency.

All of the things I told her made sense to her. When I helped her release the limitations of being a Queen Bee, she resisted. It was a wonderful life for her, but it was still holding her back somewhat. She compartmentalized her relationships and she was overtaxed by having to be the most efficient. She had to be in control. She kept other women in a distinct holding pattern as far as connectedness. I explained to her that the releases weren't going to remove any of her great qualities but were only going to enhance her life.

Doing the SFT taps with her will hopefully open her up to

new experiences, ones in which aspects of her life can spill over into each other without causing stress. These are the unconscious things that we can outgrow. Not all are uncomfortable or obvious.

Real Time Exchange

Hi Jen,

So I've taken note that you discuss a lot about past lives, etc. I just wanted to ask you are there any tools that you can use on yourself to reveal past lives?

I'm a Christian, however deeply intuitive, and as the years pass, I keep meeting people where my soul recognizes theirs and I have strong connections with cities and places I've never visited. Lots of déjà vu.

My concern is that I don't want to waste my time dealing with soul baggage. I have a fear of the ocean and I strangely believe I drowned in a Japanese submarine. I may have died for my country. It's strange because I have a strong desire to visit Japan. I hope it's not because of this and other things.

When time permits, would love to hear from you.

Jen: Yes. You are delving into your past lives. I started out in this life devoutly Christian. But Jesus talked about past lives and men took that part out of his teachings. But yes, it was the world war. You did die there, but that doesn't erase how homesick you were at the time of your death. You were very young and were called to serve out of duty. You were a sensitive soul and not meant to fight. It brought much conflict. It is similar to your conflict with Christianity. Do you serve out of your deep loyalty? Or, do you listen to your own heart? This is a huge turning point for you.

You do not have to betray anything to follow your heart. That life was life or death. But this lifetime you have the freedom to worship and serve and love and know all at once. There is no schism in you for doing so. You are not betraying anyone and you still serve God, and it doesn't mean your demise like that lifetime.

Do this tap. Say this statement three times while tapping on your head and say it a fourth time while tapping on your chest. "I release the trauma of dying so far from home; in all moments." See if that gives you a reaction. The taps will help you unpeel the layers and thinking of all the things you enjoy in this world and all the things you fear are keys to past lives.

Her: *This made me cry, it touched deep. I serve out of loyalty and more connected to my mind than my heart. Makes loads of sense. And yes, I'm going through a transformation period in my life, last 2 years.*

Thank you so much for your time, gift and kindness.

I will try the tapping shortly.

Jen: Great! That makes me happy.

Her: *When I was tapping, I saw a skinny Asian boy, utterly confused and with no meaning to what he was doing. He was* *not a patriot; he was numb and terrified.*

Jen: Yes. That was you. Do this tap: "I release the trauma of being Shanghai'd; in all moments."

Her: *Ok.*

Jen: No. Do it now. I will assist.

Her: *This is very emotional, painful.*

Jen: I know. I am helping you. You carry this around so I am helping strip it off.

Don't you want to do the tap?

Her: *I'm doing it. My chest is feeling release.*

Jen: Yes. Do this one: "I release the trauma of drowning; in all moments." They used you because you were small. They sacrificed you. You were insignificant to them.

Her: *Ok. Yes, under right deep down I knew I was born for greatness, not like this.*

Jen: Do this one: "I release being sacrificed; in all moments."

Her: *That brought up lots of hurt.*

Jen: Great!

Her: *Is it possible this is why I have felt so much unworthiness in this life?*

Jen: Yes. That is how it works. You can strip all that away with the taps I post. See that now?

Her: *I was robbed of my childhood in this life too. [Details]…it was like a sacrifice.*

Jen: Yeah, I don't need to hear the story. It is painful when you thrust it on me. I have just validated you beyond all that pain. Yes, that is a gauge of past life experiences. That is how it works.

Her: *Do I tap every day?*

Jen: Yes, as many as you can. Make it a daily practice.

Her: (Gives details of this life)

Jen: Why are you dumping on me? Do I describe my torture to you? Do you think my body can handle your pain too?

Her: No, please I would not like that. I'm sorry if I've said anything wrong, Jen.

Jen: That is what we do to each other and how others pay me back for helping them.

Her: *I'm just new to this.*

Jen: I know.

Her: *I'm sorry.*

Jen: It is okay. But I like to make people aware.

Her: *I respect you highly.*

Jen: I am hypersensitive to pain. I feel it in everyone. To hear it is unbearable.

Her: *Yes, I understand. I'm very sensitive too. It's not easy.*

Jen: Yes it is! When you do what I just did, and use it to help others, and not wallow in the pain.

Don't indulge in saying things are hard. Flip a switch and convert all you are into a blessing because it is.

Her: *I'm still amazed how quickly you saw my past life. Just the confirmation is a miracle as I thought it was just something in my dreams. So this is a relief. Thank you.*

Jen: You are so welcome. They come that easily to me because I don't doubt.

Her: *Is there anything you would like me to pray for you? I will dedicate prayer time for you today.*

Jen: No. Prayers are sending intentions to a satellite dish and bouncing them back to you. It is stronger energy to merely hold an intention of something for me.

Her: *So what intention would you like me to hold for you?*

Jen: Getting my books out to the public.

Her: *Ok. Thank you for your time. Bless you. xx*

Jen: You are so worth it. Bless everyone through me.

Release Carrying Past Life Traumas

(Say each statement three times out loud while tapping on the top of your head at the crown chakra and say it a fourth time while tapping on your chest at the heart chakra. Say each word deliberately. They are not just words, but a vibration that you are initiating to shift energy. Pause after each word. Say it in a commanding but even tone, not as a question. Forgo saying it in a sing-song tone or with bravado. Say them all.)

"I release the trauma of being bashed in the head; in all moments."

"I release the trauma of losing my tail; in all moments."

"I release mourning my tail; in all moments."

"I release mourning my home planet; in all moments."

"I release the belief that I was forsaken; in all moments."

"I release trying too hard; in all moments."

"I release the trauma of being dissected; in all moments."

"I release the belief that God has abandoned me; in all moments."

"I release waiting to be saved; in all moments."

"I release dissipating my energy; in all moments."

"I release giving my energy to a false God; in all moments."

"I release the trauma of having my wings clipped; in all moments."

"I release the trauma of having my wings cut off; in all

moments."

"I release the trauma of being stripped of my status; in all moments."

"I release the trauma of being born; in all moments."

"I release the trauma of being trapped in a human body; in all moments."

"I release the belief that I am being punished; in all moments."

"I remove all possible limitations in being in a human form; in all moments."

"I send all energy matrices into the light that trap me in the human form; in all moments."

"I send all energy matrices into the light that cause resistance to me; in all moments."

"I repair and fortify the Wei Chi on all my bodies; in all moments."

"I release being bullied; in all moments."

"I release being inundated by a crazy person; in all moments."

"I release attracting crazy energy; in all moments."

"I release the fear of transcending; in all moments."

"I release the fear of losing everything; in all moments."

"I release the fear of losing my mind; in all moments."

"I release the fear of being separated from my consciousness; in all moments."

"I release the fear of facing myself; in all moments."

"I release being stubborn; in all moments."

"I release fighting truth; in all moments."

"I release being obtuse; in all moments."

"I release mourning my soul; in all moments."

"I release the belief that I am separate from my soul; in all moments."

"I release being attached to the illusion; in all moments."

"I remove all vivaxes between myself and the illusion; in all moments."

"I remove all tentacles between myself and the illusion; in all moments."

"I remove all programming and conditioning that the illusion has put on me; in all moments."

"I remove all engrams that the illusion has put on me; in all moments."

"I send all energy matrices into the light that immerse me in illusion; in all moments."

"I send all energy matrices into the light that have me believe the illusion; in all moments."

"I am centered and empowered in Divine Love; in all

moments."

Release the Burden of Enemies

(Say each statement three times while tapping on your head and say it a fourth time while tapping on your chest.)

"I remove all labels on me; in all moments."

"I shatter all glass ceilings that have been put on me; in all moments."

"I release carrying the burden of war; in all moments."

"I remove all engrams of war; in all moments."

"I release the need to defend myself; in all moments."

"I release habitually attacking others; in all moments."

"I release the burden of my enemies; in all moments."

"I release having enemies; in all moments."

"I heal all my enemies; in all moments."

"I convert all enemies to friends; in all moments."

"I lay down my sword and shield; in all moments."

"I drop all guilt; in all moments."

"I release confusing being empowered with abusing power; in all moments."

"I forgo abusing power; in all moments."

"I release the fear of my own empowerment; in all moments."

"I shift my paradigm from abusing power to empowerment; in all moments."

"I transcend abusing power; in all moments."

"I am centered and sustained in my own empowerment; in all moments."

"I resonate, emanate, and am interconnected with all life in my own empowerment; in all moments."

"I meet all other Souls in their own empowerment; in all moments."

Release the Trauma of Amputation

I facilitated a long distance remote session with a regular client. She had suffered with incredible panic attacks but is much better now. She was having difficulties with visiting a friend at the hospital. Hospitals and medical issues have been a trigger for her and we have addressed layers and layers of the issues that have made her anxious.

She had a dream the night before her session about being in the hospital and being at the mercy of all that that entails. When I heard her dream, an image from one of her past lives came to the surface and I saw the reason for her distress.

It was a makeshift area for tending wounds after a battle. There was chaos all around. Everyone just came through a skirmish and the adrenalin was still high. No one was in a sympathetic state and there was nothing to kill the pain. His (her) leg had to be cut off.

He was adamantly against it. He preferred to just bleed out. No one would listen to him. They treated him like he was not even there. He kept protesting, but the people who knew him were ignoring his wishes. They were about to do something very unnatural to him. He could feel the saw dig through his flesh. When it came to hitting the bone, the sensation was maddening.

As I am seeing this past life trauma, I am explaining it to the client. She is feeling it and it is making her very anxious. I tell her to do a tap: "I release the trauma of having my leg amputated; in all moments." She says that she can't do it! I am firm with her and explain this is what you are reliving when you go to a hospital. This is releasing it so you don't have to keep reliving it. She gets through the tap but the experience intensifies even more.

I ask her, "Do you know when someone is cutting through a board and they want to quicken the process, they push down on the part that they are cutting off so that it snaps off? This is what they did with your leg." She could feel it then and as she is experiencing it for the last time ever, I help her separate from the trauma and remove it from her energy field. Hopefully, she can now go to hospitals without creating such angst in her. We removed another layer.

Here are some taps that may be helpful:

"I release the pain and trauma of being experimented on; in all moments."

"I release the pain and trauma of having my limb amputated; in all moments."

"I release the fear of hospitals; in all moments."

"I release confusing hospitals with pain, torture and imprisonment; in all moments."

"I release the pain and trauma of losing my free will; in all moments."

"I release the belief that hospitals are bad; in all moments."

"I release the fear of being trapped in a hospital; in all moments."

"I release the trauma of dying in a hospital; in all moments."

The most ingrained experiences are the ones when we are alone with ourselves. It is a great form of validation to acknowledge our own pain and tell ourselves it is okay. In this way, we are able to heal ourselves on a very deep level.

Releasing Sleepwalking

A very open research doctor brought his ten-year-old boy to me for a neuromuscular issue. In a session, the whole person is addressed so another issue surfaced. He didn't get along with his much younger sister. They were like oil and water. Because they were both great kids, it was chalked up to sibling rivalry. But the father was concerned about the boy's intense sleepwalking.

In the middle of the night, he would sleepwalk in such a deep state that he could not be stirred. It was unsettling to the parents. As I tuned in, a past life with the two children was revealed. They were in the water together and there was such jealousy and hatred for the younger sister that he drowned her. It was premeditated.

As difficult as it was with the father by his side, I lead the boy through a series of taps one of which was, "I release the guilt and trauma of killing my sister; in all moments." He cried, and it was very difficult. It wasn't until then that the father revealed that the sleepwalking trances would end with the boy just standing over his younger sister as she slept in her bed. It was so disconcerting that they had taken to locking the daughter's door at night so the brother could not get in.

After that session, the father reported back that the sleepwalking was drastically reduced and, as an added bonus, the children were getting along very well together and the tension between them was gone.

Releasing the Spiritual Teacher-Student Dynamic

I facilitated a long distance session with a regular client

who has lost her passion. It has been difficult to break through the complacency that seems to insulate her from her passion. She is intelligent and aware and seems to take every revelation in stride as if she already knows what is uncovered in her sessions. The issue that she wants assistance with is figuring out if she still wants to be a teacher or change to another profession that brings her enthusiasm. She has been at a standstill.

In her latest session, it was revealed from her past lives that she had a spiritual teacher that she truly admired. But the relationship was interrupted somehow. She learned half of the lessons that he taught, which entailed detachment. But she got stuck in one spectrum of spiritual lessons so she didn't get to encompass many of the lessons beyond detachment that would have incredibly enriched her journey.

She confirmed that she had a spiritual teacher in this lifetime who was a disappointment to her. The relationship left her numb and disillusioned. Her being stuck in the role of a teacher seemed to correlate with her disillusionment with her own teacher from this life and even further back.

Here are some taps to assist:

(Say each statement three times while tapping on your heard and say it a fourth time while tapping on your chest.)

"I release being disillusioned by the teacher; in all moments."

"I release the pain and loneliness of outgrowing the teacher; in all moments."

"I release being diminished by the teacher; in all moments."

"I release giving my power to the teacher; in all moments."

"I release being used; in all moments."

"I recant all vows and agreements between myself and the teacher; in all moments."

"I remove all curses between myself and the teacher; in all moments."

"I dissolve all karmic ties between myself and the teacher; in all moments."

"I remove all pain burden and limitations that the teacher has put on me; in all moments."

"I take back all the Joy, Love, Abundance, Freedom, Life and Wholeness that the teacher has taken from me; in all moments."

I withdraw all my energy from the teacher; in all moments."

"I release the fear of outgrowing the teacher; in all moments."

"I release worshiping the teacher; in all moments."

It is difficult to stretch our own wings when we are

bowing our head under the wings of another and supporting their flight with our enthusiasm. The best way to encourage others to grow is by stretching your own wings and showing them what is possible. It is not done by creating a breeze for their flight.

Reliving a Past Life's Dynamics

I recently facilitated a couple's session where the man would go through periods of moodiness and discontent. He thought he was hiding it well from his wife, but he was merely denying it when she made attempts to address it. This was very invalidating to her. He would spend a lot of time alone and in his thoughts thinking he was being a wonderful husband because he was physically present and loyal. His contempt was palpable and his denial left her with no means to address the dynamics. It left her frustrated and disappointed most of the time. While he felt he was being the perfect husband, it read like martyrdom.

In their session, a very old lifetime they shared revealed itself. It was one in which she was royalty. He was a foreigner in her land and was impressed by her level of power. Because of his spiritual immaturity and enjoyment of a challenge, he set out with the intention of winning her over. He did just that. He won her love and devotion, took her from her homeland where she was greatly respected, isolated her from anyone but him, and then withdrew his love from her. He set out to conquer her and he did.

They have been together many lifetimes. Because it was such a drastic shift in her personal dynamics, the scenario replayed itself in many of their incarnations together. It has become such an ingrained pattern that it is at a saturation point in this lifetime. They needed to break this dynamic for the sake of her personal empowerment and for his spiritual freedom.

In this lifetime, this cycle manifested as him having contempt for her for not sticking up for herself. What was revealed in the session was that it wasn't really contempt for her but self-loathing for what he had done to create this neediness in her. She was merely a reminder of his despicable lack of appreciation for the dynamic woman that she was. The neediness that he detected and loathed in her was one that he had consciously developed for his own musings. Her being dependent upon his love was a constant reminder of his own failings as a human being in the need to conquer her. The more she thought she was being loving, he construed it as needy and it only brought more contempt from him.

In the present life, they were clueless to this dynamic. But to both it resonated at such a deep level. They both felt it was their truth. The wife was deeply validated by all that was revealed and her work is to regain her regal stature that is her true nature. The husband thought that when he was going off to be alone, he was being noble. He finally understands that behavior is exactly what caused her to feel even more needy and hopeless.

I explained to him that if he wanted to be free and show

spiritual integrity, he would stay present with her when she needed it and as long as she needed it. He thought being spiritual meant isolating himself and being alone in his thought. But his spiritual work involves using all his skills and talents to pour back into her all that he allowed to be depleted. By empowering her with his love, he was gaining his own spiritual freedom. Isn't this, in a sense, what we do with all our interactions?

Resentment

Resentment is a thin veneer of anger mingled with an undercurrent of feeling wronged and victimized. I am surprised when I feel a layer of it in myself. I know when it shows up. I have a photographic memory for interactions with people. So every time they promise something and forget it, I have not. Every time they say they will do something and do not, I feel it. I do not want to be resentful and wasn't aware of how prevalent it was.

Someone whom I respect told me recently that I had resistance to manifesting my book because of all the times I was killed, tortured, burned at the stake, stoned to death, etc. for sharing my gifts. So I sat down to release it. Now I realize when I was feeling resentful, it wasn't about an afterthought of people I love to help. It was about those times of life and death.

I have the conscious memory of sitting on the side of a hill and welcoming people to come and get healing. I would touch them and the pain would pass into my body and then spirit guides would pull it out of me from the other side. The people kept coming and coming. I could not get to everyone one by one. I took all of what needed to be released into my body and went to lie down to release it all.

Those who came to see me did not understand that I was helping them and got very angry. A few of them worked into a frenzy and stoned me to death. I crossed over with everyone's issues still with me. Those who stoned me were family members in this life. They resented me. Also, while I did the taps that I am about to share, I realized that I was gestated in a pool of resentment. I was the youngest of ten children and was not wanted, or even liked, when I arrived. I have been resented most of my life.

As I did the taps, I realized that this sheath of resentment that I have felt in myself and in other people upon meeting me may not be so personal. It may be like a filter that withholds the light so that it does not blind those who look upon it. Maybe the resentment has been an energetic sunblock for me so others could not read me or use me up in my willingness to please. Maybe I don't need the veneer anymore and maybe neither do you. If resentment has been part of your makeup and if you can even be honest with yourself, stop allotting blame and just release it. These taps may be helpful in finally allowing you to be joyful, loving and free.

(Say each statement three times while tapping on your head and say it a fourth time while tapping on your chest.)

"I release harboring resentment; in all moments."

"I release being a carrier of resentment; in all moments."

"I release being pooled in an underlying current of resentment; in all moments."

"I release being captivated by resentment; in all moments."

"I release saying F#@k you to life; in all moments."

"I recant all vows and agreements between myself and resentment; in all moments."

"I remove all curses between myself and resentment; in all moments."

"I dissolve all karmic conditioning that brought resentment to me; in all moments."

"I remove all the anger that anchors the resentment; in all moments."

"I remove all the pain, burden, limitations that resentment has put on me; in all moments."

"I remove all the pain, burden, limitations and anger I have put on all others due to resentment; in all moments."

"I take back all the Joy, Love, Abundance, Freedom, Peace, Life and Wholeness that resentment has taken from me; in all moments."

"I give back all the Joy, Love, Abundance, Freedom, Peace, Life and Wholeness that I have taken from all others due to resentment; in all moments."

"I release resonating with resentment; in all moments."

"I release emanating with resentment; in all moments."

"I remove all resentment from my Sound Frequency; in all moments."

"I remove all resentment from my Light Body; in all moments."

"I shift my paradigm from resentment to Joy, Love, Abundance, Freedom, Peace, Life and Wholeness; in all moments."

"I am centered and empowered in Divine Love; in all moments."

Sometimes, we can't see our own blind spots. Sometimes, we have been wearing our sunglasses so long we forget they are on. You know how good it feels to take them off and feel the freedom of your own sight? That is what you are doing for yourself spiritually by going through the tedious process of doing these taps.

Save Yourself

(Say each statement three times out loud while tapping on the top of your head at the crown chakra and say it a fourth time while tapping on your chest.)

"I save the 'me from the past' from being abused; in all

moments."

"I save the 'me from the past' from being manipulated; in all moments."

"I save the 'me from the past' from the wrong decisions; in all moments."

"I save the 'me from the past' from the anguish; in all moments."

"I save the 'me from the past' from wasting their time; in all moments."

"I save the 'me from the past' from breathing life into a hopeless situation; in all moments."

"I save the 'me from the past' from abusing themselves; in all moments."

"I save the 'me from the past' from physically, emotionally, mentally or spiritually atrophying; in all moments."

"I save the 'me from the past' from feeding any addictions; in all moments."

"I save the 'me from the past' from hurting themselves; in all moments."

"I save the 'me from the past' from wasting their talents; in all moments."

"I save the 'me from the past' from losing their voice; in all moments."

"I save the 'me from the past' from hiding from life; in all moments."

"I save the 'me from the past' from that fatal day; in all moments."

"I save the 'me from the past' from being abused; in all moments."

"I save the 'me from the past' from all their misconceptions; in all moments."

"I save the 'me from the past' from lying to themselves; in all moments."

"I save the 'me from the past' from trusting the wrong people; in all moments."

"I save the 'me from the past' from not listening to their innate wisdom; in all moments."

"I shift the paradigm of the 'me from the past' from a reactionary state to listening to their own innate wisdom; in all moments."

"I shift the paradigm of 'me from the past' from deferring to others to keeping their own council; in all moments."

"The me from the past is centered and empowered in listening to their own innate wisdom and keeping their own council; in all moments."

Sea Captain

I remember the first time I clearly just knew a person's past life and his fate. It was so obvious to me that I was wondering why others couldn't see it.

A man came into the restaurant where I was working. To me, he looked like a sea captain. He had the ruddy face, beard and smoked a pipe. I could almost imagine him in a captain's uniform. To others, apparently he just looked like a sweet, little old man.

The image was too strong. I had to go talk to him. I blatantly told him that he looked like a sea captain. He laughed and said, "Oh, that wouldn't be me. I am petrified of the water!" But then he went on, "But I love big ships and I love the thought of being on the sea. I am just too scared of drowning."

With that I knew his fate. I could see him falling off the ship that he loved and drowning. It was kind of sad that the fear and memory kept him from what he loved so dearly and that he dismissed it so easily because of the fear. But I realized that this is most likely what many of us do as well.

Short Sighted Wealth

I facilitated a session recently with a woman who loved shoes. I made a light comment about how wearing pumps is the modern equivalent to having one's feet bound, but in her situation, it wasn't too far off.

In this life, she loved pretty things. She wanted to be spoiled and pampered by a rich man who would take care of her. In her past, I saw layers and layers of lifetimes when she was a concubine or a slave to a rich house where the greatest prize was the attention of the master of the house.

To validate this, I questioned her about her relationships in this life. Were you the one giving the most in every situation? Were the men dominant and did you get your satisfaction more from what you gave to him rather than what you received? Were these men emotionally unavailable? She answered yes to every question.

It was a bit difficult to find the right way to release these issues with her because from her vantage point, she didn't feel or think she was unworthy. She was just habitually attracting men that reminded her of the dynamics of being owned. That is what she knew of relationships. Also, when it came to abundance, she expected abundance to come through a rich man. She couldn't fathom it any other way since that is the only way she ever experienced it.

In the overview of all her lives, she was looking for love, as we all are. Her love and validation came through in many lifetimes from the attention she received from being enslaved to a rich man. That is why she desired rich things in this lifetime. It was the closest thing to true love and value that she had experienced. It was her highest pinnacle of love. What she didn't realize was that the material things were preventing her from seeing the richness of love that was all around her. By focusing on material wealth and comfort, she was wearing blinders to abundance and her own value.

Sinus Issues

In one of my private sessions, a core cause issue was revealed for one of my clients who had suffered from sinus headaches. He had suffered with them for years even though his diet and other triggers were eliminated. A past lifetime opened up where he was bashed in the skull with a huge club. On some level, it left him feeling unsafe and vulnerable.

The body's ultimate job is to keep functioning so we can continue to have physical experiences. There are many orifices in the body. Since he was killed by something smashing in his skull, his physical component strives to keep him safer by filling up those orifices so it is harder to crush him when there is a blow.

I have seen past lives where people are crushed in the rib cage. Maybe people who have lung issues caused by past lives of drowning and being suffocated should also look at being crushed to death as well.

During their session, I had them do this tap:

"I release the trauma of having my skull bashed in; in all moments."

When the sinus cavities were hollow, the head was feeling more vulnerable to being cracked open in this life. The only way the body could feel safer from this past trauma was to fill up those cavities with fluid.

It is often this way with our issues. We curse or complain about our body when the thing it is doing is a form of compensating for past trauma. It is defending itself. We show our ignorance and lack of loyalty to ourselves when we show little appreciation or respect for its service to us.

Here are some taps to try for such issues:

(Say each statement three times while tapping your head and say it a fourth time while tapping your chest.)

"I release the trauma of being bashed in the skull; in all moments."

"I release the trauma of being crushed to death; in all moments."

"I release storing trauma in the orifices of my body; in all moments."

"I release the belief that I am vulnerable or unsafe; in all moments."

"I release feeling vulnerable or unsafe in all moments."

"I release bracing against a blow; in all moments."

"I release waiting for the ax to fall; in all moments."

"I release feeling fragile and breakable; in all moments."

"I release overcompensating in rigidity to protect myself; in all moments."

"I drain all the orifices of my body of all negative emotions, thoughts and experiences; in all moments."

Star Planet

I recently facilitated a session with a new client who is a life coach helping many people in her own way. In the first session, some of the releases that came through were the more advanced ones I do with regular clients. She was very responsive and felt that it was right to do one more session.

In her second session, her ingrained detachment and lack of emotional investment in this life came through more clearly. She always felt like she was from another planet. She obviously resented being here to assist a barbarian race of people. We even did one SFT tap that stated:

"I release the belief that humans are barbaric swine; in all moments."

Deeper into the session, we both got a sense of a physical body that she was more comfortable in. I felt the energy at the base of her spine and sensed what it was like to have a tail. The intellect that came through explained how much better it was to have a tail because, along with the legs, it created a sort of energetic pyramid that brought greater balance and grounding.

I also felt the energy below her shoulder blades start to tingle. It was revealed the trauma of having one's wings detached through an explosion during war. Also, when she had to come to earth for the first lifetime, her wings were genetically removed. This created great hostility within her. She never felt comfortable on earth. But in her session, we gave her a sense of healing her wings and we both felt tingling along the backside of her arms where the wings attached.

I have facilitated many sessions with people who felt that earth was not their original home. It was revealed that this is why it is so heavily polluted. People who were seeded here from other planets never fully embrace earth as their motherland. They are, in a sense, like adopted children who never bond with their adoptive mother and expel much energy pining for their original planet. This is why there is such a lack of respect for it by many and why so many do not appreciate the organic beauty of nature.

If any of this resonates, the following SFT taps might be helpful:

"I release hating earth; in all moments."

"I release the pain and trauma of being in a human body, in all moments."

"I release resenting being human; in all moments."

Success

I recently facilitated a session with a very successful businessman. He loves winning. But he notices that when he has a big win, he gets depressed immediately afterwards. The conscious thought process is that he will not be able to maintain such levels of success. The past life unconscious memory revealed how deep those consequences were.

He was a Native American warrior that guaranteed the safety of his tribe. He was very well respected and admired. But then he started to decline. Later in that life, he was abandoned by his tribe. He was left to die because he was a hindrance to their survival. This is what was triggered in the present life every time he felt successful.

Here are some of the taps that we did to help him be able to enjoy success in this life:

(Say each statement three times while tapping on your head and say it a fourth time while tapping on your chest.

"I release associating winning with losing; in all moments."

"I release associating success with rejection; in all moments."

"I release associating success with abandonment; in all moments."

"I release that pain and trauma of being abandoned; in all moments."

"I release linking success with failure; in all moments."

"I release the belief that death follows success; in all moments."

"I am centered in Joy, Love, Abundance, Freedom, Health and Success; in all moments."

Surviving the Titanic

I just facilitated a session with a woman who wanted me to assist her dogs and herself in one session. Working with the dog was easy. But when I turned my attention to the woman, she admitted having walls up in regards to her husband who is a real sweetheart, so it was strange to her. We worked on three areas: jealousy, betrayal and abandonment.

There was a lot of stagnant energy released. But when I began the protocol for abandonment, I started making a shamanic sound that sounded like a fog horn on an old cruise ship. Then images of the Titanic flashed in front of my eyes. They were not images of the aristocrats but of the servants on the bottom deck. My mind flashed to the scene in the movie *Titanic* where the servants were locked in the bottom level. As the ship went under, the young mother, instead of stressing out her children, put them to sleep with a bedtime story. She knew it was the last one she would read to them.

I had the client release the trauma of being on the Titanic. There was a lot of stagnant energy released with that one. She told me afterwards that she never thought she was on the Titanic, but she is afraid of going on cruise ships, being out on the water, being trapped in small spaces and taking her last gasp of air. All of those things were validated in the images that were revealed.

She also treats her dogs with such love and care. She treats them with the tenacity and devotion of the young mother putting her children to bed for the very last time. Being the loving person she is, she chooses love and service to be the experiences she replays in this lifetime. She is lucky not to be stuck in a state of fear but to live in a reverent state of service to her loved ones.

Symbiotic Relationship

I facilitated a session at the request of a beautiful, successful client to help her dear friend whose life was in turmoil. She was recovering from surgery, homeless, and just went through a bad break-up.

I arrived at the woman's home, and she was really attentive to her friend and a bit overprotective. I asked the beautiful woman to sit next to her downtrodden friend and assist her in doing the SFT taps. It was interesting seeing them sit next to each other. They were polar opposites. One had everything and the other had nothing.

It was obvious that the successful woman was feeling the heaviness of the work we were doing. I was concerned that she would be affected by the session, so I turned to her. I had her release the guilt of surviving when her friend was destroyed. She broke down and could not speak. It came to light that they had a symbiotic relationship. They were twins in one life where the one sacrificed everything for the other to survive. In another life, the woman was the mother and threw her child, (the client), away. There was also a life where they took a blood oath together. All these dynamics needed to be released.

Their core belief was that the one was more important than the other. This played out lifetime after lifetime. As I had them BOTH do the SFT taps to change the dynamic, there was a change in both of them. The burden was lifted from both of them and they both looked joyful and abundant. They were no longer polar opposites, but both were centered in Joy, Love, Abundance and Freedom.

Technique to Right Past Transgressions

You know all those interactions and scenarios that bring anxiety when thinking about them? Remember the times that you were wronged, rejected or diminished in some way. Or, the times that you weren't as kind or loving as you could have been and hurt someone? They cause a heaviness that is difficult to carry around.

During a quiet time, comb over all the experiences that have caused anguish. Visualize taking snapshots of them. As you take a snapshot of each one, take the photo and toss it in a pile. Take as many photos as you need in as many different scenarios as possible. Make a big pile.

When all the scenarios are exhausted and there is a huge pile of photos, visualize taking a spark of divine love and setting the pile in a blaze. Know that divine love is burning out all the energy of the experiences. Visualize the fumes going back to whatever person was wronged and giving them back what the experience took from them. Don't focus on any one individually. Just know that everyone is coming to balance as the experiences are cleansed out of your causal memory banks.

After the whole pile has burned and cooled, see that all that is left is a pile of ash. See a breeze blow in and sweep away the ashes to reveal little nuggets of gold. See that nothing is left but the beautiful little nuggets. Visualize picking up each little piece of gold and placing them against your heart. Have them melt into your heart. Feel them dissolve from your hand and absorb deep into your body through your heart. Feel uplifted by the process. Be energized by the awareness that you have righted deep wrongs. Feel the happiness and freedom.

The Altantis Jewelry Shop

In a different time, jewelry was not merely a decoration. The people of different lands realized that gems, minerals and crystals all had different properties. They were allowed to wear only the properties that reflected and complemented their skillset. Everyone would know what a person was worth by what jewelry they were able to wear. People in power would wear many items to instill awe in their people. That is why jewelry was considered so valuable then; it reflected one's abilities and talents to the community or displayed power. In the present day, the importance of jewels is remembered but has digressed to being a relatively crude display of accumulation of wealth.

I went into a local jewelry store last year. They were located in the basement of an old house that was set up as a mall. They had pieces that were designed to compliment the energy of a person. When I walked in, it felt like I was back in Atlantis. There was a feeling of Lemuria as well. I saw the past life memories of the shop. The shop had no people in it and it seemed secretive. In Atlantis and Lemuria times, it was a shop that catered to empowering everyday people with the energetic stones that reflected their abilities.

It existed as an underground place in those societies. It was serving humanity by giving the jewelry to those who had the gifts and abilities to use them to assist others. It was supplying a great service. It was empowering truth and divinity in its own way. I saw that in both societies, the shop was closed down and the owner and workers were dealt with harshly. This fear and a slight paranoia were reflected in the present day scenario.

I wanted to share my insights with them so that they could move on from the past experience and be successful. I explained to the shopkeeper how the energy was blocked from people finding the place. She got very reactive and fearful and did not want to hear it. She became terrified that I would assist. I reassured her that I would not. Her reaction reaffirmed the past life images that were shown to me. It was too bad. The shop, like individuals, can move beyond its old conditioning to have new and enriching experiences.

I believe the shop has closed since then.

The Cause and Relief from Fibromyalgia

The following is a passage from the Daily Letters of Accord that I share with anyone who wishes to receive them. They are mostly private because I consider them a message from the heart of truth to the reader's heart. In today's letter, I was given the intangible reason for fibromyalgia and why the sufferers are in their own private hell because an aspect of themselves is literally, in hell. If the following information helps anyone, then it was worth sharing. If you try this technique, I will be assisting you in your desired results regardless of whether we know each other or not.

If you would like to receive the Daily Letters of Accord that I write, simply provide me with an email of where to send them on my website. (www.jenward.com)

There are people who are on earth today that think of this life as a constant hell. Part of them energetically actually is still in hell. Remember those puritanical depictions of a fiery existence of brimstone? Those depictions, coupled with fear and deep devotion, created a landing site in the afterlife that matched those hopeless scenarios. It is where many have gone who believed that is where they belonged. There are many people alive today who have a subtle aspect of themselves burning still in a fiery hell forever. They created it because it is what they were taught.

I have rescued clients who created this fate for themselves in a past life as they crossed over. Perhaps those who are dealing with fibromyalgia still have an aspect of themselves burning in a perpetual pit of hell. Perhaps as we all come to terms with a higher consciousness, these subtle fates that we created in a past existence are playing out in our present life.

What is happening now in the world is all our past lives and experiences are coming together in the same time and space of the present moment. We are no longer going to be having all these parallel existences. We are all coming together in the moment of now. That is what the energetic shift entails.

Perhaps a way to deal with the incredible pain of fibromyalgia is to get a sense of whether a part of yourself is suffering in an eternal hell that you were sentenced to in a past life. It would have been a reality you created as you crossed over in correlation with your belief system of the time. If so, the way to end your physical suffering is to end the emotional suffering of you in a past reality.

See yourself suffering in an eternal hell. Sense your anguish and hopelessness. Then simply, with your pure intention, do what I have done for some clients. With your visualization skills go into the experience and simply pluck yourself out of the hell you were experiencing energetically.

Cool yourself off, nurture that aspect of you, perhaps apply a loving balm to it. Heal it. Then simply place it back within your own body and feel the completion, peace and the deep serenity of having it returned. You may very well end the suffering that you have endured in your physical skin. Doctors have not found a cause. Perhaps this is it.

The Connection

The beauty of my sessions is that sometimes they can uncover answers to questions the client didn't realize they were asking.

One of my clients is adopted. She loves her parents but doesn't understand why the Universe put them together. She has a great life and their love has given her much opportunity, but she feels so different from them. It has always been one of those questions within her that settled as uneasiness within herself.

In one of her sessions, I sensed her past life as a soldier in Vietnam. I asked her directly to see if it was something that resonated, "Were you in Nam?" I asked. She told me her father was. From that statement, her truth revealed itself.

The bond between soldiers is very strong. There is a connection that is forged in life and death situations that is not understandable by anyone else. Soldiers come together from all walks of life and are leveled by the life and death scenario that they are thrust into. These two soldiers were thrown together and became dependent on each other to survive.

My client died in that war scene. The guilt of leaving her buddy and the connection that they forged was enough to bring them together in this lifetime. Her loyalty and her desire to protect him carried over to this life as well. She finally had the answer to why she was connected to her adoptive parents. The Universe was not random. It was specific.

The Cycle of Power

Clients come to me for private sessions, many times, because they are feeling victimized. Since I am able to see glimpses of their past incarnations, I can see the cycle of the power plays in their interactions. For example, if someone was abused by a relative, many times it is revealed that in past lives, they were also the abuser of that person. This happens with organizations as well.

If someone was abused by a certain group, like family, religion or social group, it is revealed that they were in a position to set up the rules of that group in a previous life. While they were in the position of power, they instilled the "law of the land," and many lifetimes later, they are reaping the ill effects of those same rules. This is how souls, in the classroom of life, learn.

When we instill laws and rules, we would do well to know that, at some point, we will be the victim of those exact rules. The more we can see ourselves in the position of those that depend upon us, the less we will be cutting off our own freedom later down the road.

The Fighter

I made a house call to a woman who had received a diagnosis of cancer. I had never met her and knew no details about her. When I met her, she seemed vibrant. This was interesting because usually it is obvious to me in a person's energy when they are struggling with dis-ease.

The first thing I saw in her was how her son was struggling with her diagnosis. He held in his feelings, but she and I both knew that it was affecting him. As we talked, she confirmed this.

There were several dynamics in this situation. The first was that she had a sense of being a martyr and was resisting my help. The second was that she knew that my work could benefit her son, so she was receptive. I explained this to her and we did an SFT tap to help: "I release being a martyr; in all moments."

I saw a few of her lifetimes and knew what she needed to release. She was tortured and killed for secrets that she did not give up. This reinforced her belief that death was a way out. She also was very good at keeping everything in. She needed to release all the energy from all the scenarios where she held it in, literally, to the death.

She had a great love for her husband, but in past lives she had been forced to marry him and felt like a prisoner. These feelings were an undercurrent that was not clearly expressed in this lifetime, but they were bleeding through. She felt pressure to work even though she wanted to just be a mother. This contrast between her life now and the great traumas she endured in past lives set up dis-ease in her.

She released as much as she was able to handle. During sessions, people get very tired because of the great energy shift that is happening within them. I instructed her through many SFT affirmations that seemed contradictory to her present relationship with her husband.

Some were:

"I release hating _____; in all moments."

"I release being imprisoned by _____ ; in all moments."

"I release being raped by _____; in all moments."

These were all validating at a very deep level. The other thing that she released is a common one for people with a diagnosis:

"I release the belief that God is punishing me; in all moments."

From the vantage point of a facilitator, it was obvious to see that God did not have a hand in her condition, but it was a self-created escape valve. The great thing about that awareness is that it takes her out of defeat mode. It allows her to use all of her resilience and fighter qualities that she has to get herself well again.

The Game of Thrones

The Game of Thrones is a pretty accurate depiction of the barbaric and insidious things that have played out in our past lives. The show, *The Vikings*, is pretty accurate too in many ways. We like to look at these things out here as a safe form of entertainment without having to subscribe to the belief system of past lives.

It is helpful to see what we have been capable of doing to each other and what we have endured. It gives us a better sense of why we are so terrified to show up as dynamic and so terrified to speak our truth. The Akashic records I read of people look like a scene out of one of these barbaric shows.

If you get nothing else from the show, be grateful of the times that we live in now, feel a sense of pride at how much you have endured in the past and how strong you must truly be. Mostly, recognize how important it is to be kind to yourself for all that you have endured. Also, please extend that kindness to others. So many are licking their inner wounds as they try to maneuver this life.

Everything that I share is about healing those inner wounds so everyone can be whole again. For so many, it has been a very long time. We, as a whole, are well overdo for it.

The Heart Chakra of the Universe

The fluidity of humanity is in its creativity. It is also in its Joy, Love, Abundance and Freedom. Those with an agenda have us fixate on problems of the world to prevent us from enjoying the fluidity of life. Humanity is all coagulated. The stringent moral beliefs of different sects dry up the sap of humanity's creativity. We are all aware enough now to be a witness to that.

Many people question what they have been told about the hereafter. But they also are forbidden by their doctrine to believe in alternative worlds or reincarnation. They are paralyzed in an indifference of denial. If you can honestly talk to someone about what they truly believe, they will tell you they don't believe in the traditional heaven. But when you press them further, they will shrug and get defensive. They are terrified to go against the conditioning of their sect.

This is the behavior of someone who is trapped between a rock and a hard place. That is what society has done to all its inhabitants. They are not free to express their inner promptings of what its innate intelligence is telling them. They are not free to delve into all the experiences they carry within the memory, like a treasure trove.

Universal peace can't happen unless a majority of

individuals attain inner peace, for we are all a mini-schematic (microcosm) of the whole (macrocosm). Having everyone fixated on outer problems and turmoil is actually a calculated intention of keeping people enslaved to the turmoil. All of humanity is like a self-holding trap. The more we struggle, the more we hold ourselves trapped. The escape is to totally relax and allow your energy to drop out.

What is interesting about humans is they share more information than they realize. We are all symbiotic that way. An energy field is not dead energy. It is emitting frequencies and information faster than the human brain can receive it. That is all being psychic really is, being able to read the energy signals that an energy field is putting out without having to wait for it to be translated into language. This is slow and clumsy. We are all outgrowing the need for such cumbersome communications.

If you want to facilitate the advancement to Universal peace, gain peace within yourself. Honor peace as if the sanctity of all of life depends upon it. Because it does. What you choose for your thoughts, feelings, speech and actions is averaged into the collective. The more individuals can choose positive and productive thoughts, feelings, speech and actions, the more all of humanity will respond. Better yet, if one can practice the neutrality of Divine Love without putting a judgment or spin on it, the quicker this world will flourish into a blossoming, universal expression of truth and love.

I was explaining this process to one very advanced soul.

He was indifferent. I could see his thought energy. He was reading indifference. He did not care. He could travel to any of a few wonderful planets that were better suited to him than earth. He had little investment in earth and resented being here. Here was this spiritually advanced individual, and he was as indifferent as people immersed in the indifference of thinking they only live one life.

I immediately tuned into the Ancient Ones and asked them how to make him understand that earth mattered. They revealed a new truth to me. Earth is very important to the wellbeing of all the planets he visited. There was a reason so many advanced individuals had incarnated on this planet. It is the heart chakra of the Universe. To open all the lower worlds to love, the earth needed to be opened up unquestionably to love.

Many spiritual beings were led into indifference by the belief that this is a warring planet and there is no point in trying to uplift the consciousness. This was an intentional attempt to enslave all the lower worlds in indifference. They were taught to focus on themselves because spirituality is an individual experience. They were given half-truths to enslave them in indifference. It has been a means of putting a glass ceiling on the most advanced spiritual beings and trapping them in the mental realms.

I see many people that I respected as dynamic energy years ago, now milling around in the mental realms. They scan social media for anyone who believes differently than they do and engage them in a hearty debate. They are intending to lure people to their belief which they have been taught is the way to truth. But as anyone spiritually can tell, it merely leads to a cul-de-sac in the mental realms.

These dynamic individuals are seen as ineffective as spiritual mavericks, and they do not see it within themselves. But if they are capable of being honest with themselves, they see it in other members of their belief system. In a way, it is more tragic than pure ignorance because there is little way to reach these individuals unless love and truth are able to bore through the mental trap.

So the Ancient Ones feed truth into someone like myself who no one listens to, no one respects and no one values. Someone who clearly is removed from all that brings anyone esteem in this world. They hide truth in plain sight. Then they observe who is able to get past their own objections to find it.

This guise is brilliant to be able to write all the truths that have been sieved out of humanity with none being the wiser--except those who can get past their own ego. When someone first comes to my page, they may have such contempt for me, that it is painful to tolerate. But once one truth gets through, it shifts them a little and then they are easier to engage. This happens continually.

There is a reason that I am in a female body. It is true; it is much easier to catch the attentions of others in a male body, and anyone in a male body will tell you that a male body is necessary to assist others to their empowerment. It has better defenses against the blows and onslaught of contempt. But male energy is not the only embodiment to serve in. This we now know is a lie because many have been led to their empowerment through my assistance.

It is much more difficult in a female body though. It is excruciating. It takes a strength and endurance that a male body cannot fathom. The sensitivities to what a female body can endure are so much more extreme than a male body could even withstand. A male body would wave it off and be done with it. That is its grace. A female energy must expand herself even further to endure the coarse thoughts, feelings and actions of all that are within her realm. She does not dismiss anyone. All are worthy. No one is a throw away.

It is not her nature to turn anyone away or to dismiss them. It is not her nature to influence where they go energetically. She does not collect followers to sit at her feet. She gives all of herself to all that she loves and blesses them in every direction with her loving protection wherever they go. She does not collect followers at all like marbles in a jar. She expands her consciousness as far as necessary to love everyone where they are.

When I was imprisoned, starved and tortured that year, I went through enlightenment. I was fascinated by the depths of my connection to something I was not able to formulate because of the conditioning of the torture. But I knew I was connected and protected somehow. I remember burning my arm on the side of the iron furnace every night. I watched as my arm formulated a welt or blister from the furnace and I didn't feel a thing. I felt no pain.

That is the level of pain and diligence it takes to pour truth and love into the world. I didn't realize at the time what an analogy that was for my future. I tend the world day and night, fueling it with love and truth so that the last embers of such do not die out in the world. I try to ignite flames of empowerment with my writings and posts continuously watching them catch flame and then dampen with indifference. All the while, being protected and numbed of the excruciating pain associated with the process.

Want to hear the most ridiculous part? No one takes me seriously. Not even anyone I have assisted, healed or proved myself to unless I preference truth with saying that I am speaking to my Guides which, of course, people construe as a panel of men. Think about it. That is how deep the conditioning away from the empowerment of a balance between male and female energy goes.

Even a dynamic healer needs to defer to a panel of men to be deemed legitimate. This is how deep the conditioning goes. This is why it is so important to live, see, breathe and sleep truth. But most of all to speak it. So that others may know truth without having to suffer for the privilege.

The Lost Lamb

I facilitated a session with a woman who was at the end of

a committed relationship with a great guy. They loved each other but could not reach a level of passion that they would like. It was perplexing because he was so drawn to her, the connection was instantaneous.

In a session, a scene opened up to a past life in a sheep herding arena. Sheep were being sheered and separated. It was very chaotic. There was a little lamb that was usually glued to his mama's side. But mama got pulled away from him and his cries were lost in the chaos. He felt empty and alone. That feeling may have stayed with him all of his lives until they were reunited in this life.

My client was the mother sheep in that scenario. The baby lamb was her devoted boyfriend in the present. Now she realized why he was so drawn to her. We released the dynamics pulling on her that were creating such conflict within her. She was now free to accept the beautiful connection without having to define it as a win-lose scenario that relationships fall into. They were free of the conflict but the love remained.

The Mule Hearted Client

Recently, I facilitated a session with a client who was very frustrated and confused at her own ambivalence. She was aware that she had many talents and gifts but seemed not able to share them. She seemed to have a very subtle contempt for the incompetency of others and yet seemed to seek their approval. Even though she felt manipulated by their compliments, she seemed to allow them to appease her. The dynamics of it seemed to leave her feeling helpless and not in control. She also felt very burdened.

In her session, a past life image of a donkey came through. She was really stubborn and made to carry such a heavy load. Beating her did not get a response. The only thing that would motivate her in that life was sweet talk. To her in that life, sweet talk was the closest thing to love that she received. On a subtle level, she was still registering sweet talk as a viable form of love. It was so ingrained in that past life from the loneliness and pain of the beatings that it had imprinted on her and was affecting the present life.

After I led her through a bunch of taps, she felt the heaviness of this invisible burden lift from her. She was much lighter. Hopefully, she will be less vulnerable to shallow praise.

(Say each statement three times out loud while tapping on your head and a fourth time while tapping on your chest.)

"I release being manipulated by praise; in all moments."

"I release craving validation; in all moments."

"I release seeking approval; in all moments."

"I release the need to be appeased; in all moments."

The Past

You are a different person now. There is no need to

identify with the past experiences at all. All of those words used to describe the past are vibrations of the past. Simply by saying them, the vibration of them is stirred. It does not serve you to give life to them. Stand by the beauty and conviction of yourself in the moment. That is where your magnificence is. The best thing you can do for someone is forget the descriptions they give you of their past so as not to stir something in them that they are releasing. May others that you describe your past to be as conscious so as not to link identifying you with such things. You may let go of the identification of you so they don't have to do this for you. That you have conquered such a devastating experience is amazing. Now you may want to let the vibrations of it be dormant until they turn to dusty wisps and blow away.

The brain doesn't hear the negatives. It does not register them. So instead of hearing one has survived a certain disease, it only hears the disease in identification with the person. See? One must be as diligent with their verbiage as they have been with their treatment. In fact, it is a great tool in self-healing not to identify with past experiences.

You have so much to be proud of. Surviving your past is not your only benchmark though. You are an amazing person that is multidimensional. That is your mainstay. By using your past to define your present, you are staying tethered to the past. The less you use the words with a coarse vibratory rate, the more you will realize that you don't need even the benchmark to define you.

It may be challenging to you a bit to do this, but the

payoff is in being seen as a healer, teacher, leader and inspiration to others without the remnants of the past to use as contrast. By defining yourself in only the broadest strokes, you are kicking the crutch of the past away.

The Pilgrimage

I had a session with a client who was having some conflict with her husband. It centered on finances and trust issues in regards to their security. People try to tell me what is going on in the present, but I really don't need to hear it. They are already showing me energetically the past life scene that is playing out in the present day. I can get to helping them much more efficiently if they don't try to micromanage the session because if they consciously knew, they wouldn't need assistance.

There is a definite energetic difference between people who have had Christian lives and those who have had Jewish lives. With Christian clients, there are definitely more oaths and martyr experiences to release. With Jewish clients, there are more unnamed currents of suppression, mother issues, and duty to the group to release. Of course, this is a gross generalization.

In a scene from my client's past, I saw a huge caravan of people walking across a desert-like setting carrying everything they owned to a new land. She and her husband were amongst them. It was only the two of them in the group together, meaning they had only each other to rely on. It was a very difficult journey, but it delved such incredible love and trust between them that it secured a bond between them that could endure anything. For some reason, I saw her carrying a chair.

The client chuckled and said that when they first started living together, they acquired their furniture from others' refuse and it was a special memory when they carried it home. I explained to her that the caravan life was a time when she and her husband became as close as two people could become. In her present life, she was trying to reenact the bond by creating the drama that they endured in the past lifetime. She had explained that she did this with all her relationships. She was testing them to see if they were the ones who endured with her in those times.

Here are the taps I gave her:

(Say each statement three times while tapping on your head and say it a fourth time while tapping on your chest.)

"I release creating struggle to feel loved; in all moments."

"I release equivocating struggle with intimacy; in all moments."

"I release equivocating intimacy with struggle; in all moments."

"I release creating upheaval; in all moments."

"I recant all vows and agreements between myself and the pilgrimage/exodus/migration; in all moments."

"I remove all curses between myself and the

pilgrimage/exodus/migration; in all moments."

"I dissolve all karmic ties between myself and the pilgrimage/exodus/migration; in all moments."

"I remove all the pain, burden and limitations that the pilgrimage/exodus/migration has put on me; in all moments."

"I take back all the Joy, Love, Abundance, Freedom, Health, Success, Security, Companionship, Peace, Life and Wholeness that the pilgrimage/exodus/migration has taken from me; in all moments."

"I withdraw all my energy from the pilgrimage/exodus/migration; in all moments."

Sometimes freedom and love will strike the human consciousness as a pronounced emptiness. If one can train themselves not to react and to remain at ease in the emptiness, they will be able to then experience a satiating of their whole being in a more subtle way.

The Professional Singer

I facilitated a group session that led me to single out a very talented singer. The only problem was that she conveyed such shame in singing. Even in talking about her talent, her demeanor furled up. We explored why.

A lifetime opened up in a very poor part of England. It seemed like a city from a Dickens' classic. She and her friend in that life were as they are in the present: sparks of potential and optimism. They saw opportunity everywhere and stayed honest. Although they were very poor, they would clean themselves up and sing for he rich. They were valued for their talent, but there was always a drastic class division that carried over for the girl in this lifetime as shame.

As I was sharing the scenario with her in the group, it resonated with her and she could connect with herself from the past. She could feel the shame. I instructed her to sing right then within the group. She resisted. I argued with her that if she is a professional singer, she should not mind singing. As she performed, I released all the shame that she was reliving over and over by expressing her talent. Her energy and voice opened up. The notes were round, perfect and pure. She was no longer conveying shame.

She is now a very promising professional singer.

The Raging Bull

We accrued much of the trauma of our existence during times when we lacked a thinking mind to process it. This trauma is just stored as a confusing turmoil of angst, frustration and even blinding rage.

When we store trauma without it being processed by the mind, then it is difficult for the mind to recall it cohesively. So to try to deal with it, we either process it through our emotions or through physical pain. With awareness, however, we can go back to the experiences we've had and look at them with a clear mind. We can understand them in hindsight as a way to release the dis-ease they cause. Here is an example:

My client was feeling incredible emotion at a very deep level that he was unable to articulate. In my mind, I experienced the scenario where some of this emotion was created. I found myself in a raging bull's body. He was bucking fervently, boxed in a small wooden fence with two men jabbing skewers in him. He didn't know why. He was relatively young. Just a few months ago, he was a playful little calf dancing in a meadow. But then he grew big and he was treated differently, and now he was being tortured and ready to be sent to his death for the amusement of others.

This type of experience, where our innocence is murdered, happens again and again in our experiences. It is these kinds of things that we have stored in our psyche. We were unable to help ourselves in the scenarios so we may feel helpless in the present. The way to fix ourselves is to look at what is uncomfortable in our past and give ourselves incredible love and compassion back then and in our present. It also is a good practice to nurture innocence everywhere and in every form. In return, we will connect to that sacred place within ourselves and make it whole again.

The Self-Serving Reason to Stay in the Moment

We just got off a powerful group phone session. It was so powerful that we were all knocked off the call before we were finished. A great truth was revealed during the session. I saw the trauma of one participant where she had struggled many times with crossing over and what it entailed. Crossing over etches deep engrams into our energy field as we struggle for that last breath and then suddenly are shifted into the other side.

I was shown that the struggle of crossing over is a huge part of the fear that keeps us locked in the physical body. To release that one moment of struggle is to unlock a key to our own expansiveness. To release that experience from our repertoire is to remove a huge driving force of primal fear.

My Guides showed me what the struggle at the end of the life is really about. It is shaking the undisciplined human consciousness into the moment so that it can cross over. That is the purpose of the struggle. If one wants to bypass that struggle at the end of their physical life, the way to do that is to practice being in the moment as much as possible. That way the shock of being forced into the moment is not so severe.

Being in the moment blurs the line between shifts in awareness. Being in the moment regularly makes it easier when one crosses over to waft away from the physical realm as opposed to being ripped out of it. That is the best reason that some may find for themselves to practice being in the moment.

(Say each statement three times out loud while tapping on the top of your head at the crown chakra and say it a fourth time while tapping on your chest.)

"I declare myself a surrogate for humanity in doing these taps; in all moments."

"I release the fear of transcending; in all moments."

"I release the trauma of being a carbon-based unit; in all moments."

"I release reliving the precipice of crossing over; in all moments."

"I remove all vivaxes between myself and the precipice of crossing over; in all moments."

"I remove all tentacles between myself and the precipice of crossing over; in all moments."

"I remove all the trepidation that the precipice of crossing over has put on me; in all moments."

"I remove all programming and conditioning that the precipice of crossing over has put on me; in all moments."

"I release confusing the precipice of crossing over with death; in all moments."

"I release the fear of being separated from my consciousness; in all moments."

"I remove all engrams that the precipice of crossing over

has put on me; in all moments."

"I send all energy matrices into the light that paralyze me in the precipice of crossing over; in all moments."

"I send all energy matrices into the light that induce a catatonic state on me; in all moments."

"I recant all vows and agreements between myself and the precipice of crossing over; in all moments."

"I remove all curses between myself and the precipice of crossing over; in all moments."

"I release being locked in the precipice of crossing over; in all moments."

"I remove all blessings between myself and the precipice of crossing over; in all moments."

"I remove all strings, cords, and wires between myself and the precipice of crossing over; in all moments."

"I dissolve all karmic ties between myself and the precipice of crossing over; in all moments."

"I release being trapped in the precipice of crossing over; in all moments."

"I release being trapped in choosing between staying and going; in all moments."

"I withdraw all my energy from the precipice of crossing over; in all moments."

"I strip all illusion off of the precipice of crossing over; in all moments."

"I remove all masks, walls, and armor from the precipice of crossing over; in all moments."

"I remove all the pain, burden, and limitations that the precipice of crossing over has put on me; in all moments."

"I remove all the fear, futility, and helplessness that the precipice of crossing has put on me; in all moments."

"I remove all the shock, linear perception, and illusion of separateness that the precipice of crossing over has put on me; in all moments."

"I release resonating with the precipice of crossing over; in all moments."

I release emanating with the precipice of crossing over; in all moments."

"I extract all of the precipice of crossing over from my sound frequency; in all moments."

"I extract all of the precipice of crossing over from my sound frequency; in all moments."

"I extract all of the precipice of crossing over from my light emanation; in all moments."

"I collapse and dissolve the precipice of crossing over; in all moments."

"I shift my paradigm from the precipice of crossing over to perpetual expansive freedom; in all moments."

"I transcend the precipice of crossing over; in all moments."

"I am centered and empowered in perpetual expansive freedom; in all moments."

"I resonate and emanate perpetual expansive freedom; in all moments."

The Truth About Fear

If you have a fear, that means it was instilled. You only fear what you have experienced. If you have already experienced it, there is no need to experience it again. The logical choice is to experience whatever you have feared in the past, easily conquer it, and be empowered by it. That is a new experience and that is what growth is, new experiences.

The Unconscious Memory of the Stripper

I have facilitated a handful of sessions for different exotic dancers. None of them felt shame in dancing. In fact, it was spiritual for some and a means of connecting with something greater. What I have experienced is that dancing may be a way to preserve an ancient ritual of worship. Tuning into a few of them, I was able to piece together an ancient history.

In ancient times, man was not considered superior to woman. They both were known for different strengths.

While man seemed to focus all his energy on an objective goal and "target" it, woman was able to "relax" her energy field so it encompassed all. She would "sense" all the subtleties that were lost on man.

Lands were ruled with great wisdom and compassion. Women were groomed in great lineages just as men were as kings. The wisest and most gifted seers were groomed to be wedded to their male counterparts. There were temples to teach women the intuitive arts and the greatest priestesses were wedded to the greatest kings. They were the most successful sovereignties.

Barbarians grew jealous of the wealth of the great kingdoms. They were not strong enough or smart enough to battle the kings so they destroyed the wisdom schools where women were trained. They raided and desecrated the temples, raped the women and scattered them to the ignorant. They forced them to wed to improve their status.

When they still lacked the success they desired, they grew angrier at the women for withholding their gifts. They used the women as showpieces for their conquest. They forced them to perform their rituals as a way to show off their skills and retell the tale of their conquest. Women would go through the motions with the rituals which became a form of dance.

The priestesses desperately missed their homelands. They were isolated and defeated. When they danced for the barbarians, it was a way to stay connected to their sisters and was their plea to God to rescue them. For men, the dance symbolized his conquest of her. Without an understanding of her gifts, and she without physical strength, he deemed her weak and useless. She became a showpiece for a conquest and not much more to him.

In the generations to follow, the women tried to remember the ways of the seer and pass them down to their daughters, but they were not able to preserve technique or purpose behind the dance. It became a means to pacify their mates. The subtle arts were lost and replaced with the art of seduction.

Many exotic dancers hold the memory of these ancient ways and are attempting to connect with a greater aspect of themselves through stripping. Maybe the men who attend the strip clubs, too, are remembering an ancient time of the conquest.

Transcend Your Akashic Records

Powerful Taps from a Group Session:

You know how you have been driving yourself crazy lately running the things in your head that you regret? Have you been playing out scenarios of when you have been disappointed in life? That is you running through your Akashic records. You are not alone in doing that. Universally, we are moving beyond the astral plane and into the causal plane. The causal plane is where all our Akashic records are kept. All of the images, memories and experiences that we have ever had are documented in the Akashic records. These are what I read when I tap into your past lives.

But because we are all evolving, we are all ruminating through our Akashic records and reliving old disappointments. You may of thought you were the only one doing that, but no, many of us are. These taps will help give you relief from the anguishes you have been replaying in your memory banks. In fact, knowing that you are not the only one may bring you some relief already.

(Say each statement three times out loud while tapping on the top of your head at the crown chakra and say it a fourth time while tapping on your chest.)

"I extract all the memories of disappointment from my Akashic records; in all moments."

"I extract all the memories of torture from my Akashic records; in all moments."

"I extract all the memories of being humiliated from my Akashic records; in all moments."

"I extract all the memories of abusing power from my Akashic records; in all moments."

"I extract all the memories of being abandoned from my Akashic records; in all moments."

"I extract all the memories of being rejected from my Akashic records; in all moments."

"I extract all the memories of being defiled from my Akashic Records; in all moments."

"I extract all the memories of being unloved from my Akashic Records; in all moments."

"I release the fear of transcending the Akashic records; in all moments."

"I released being enslaved by the Akashic records; in all moments."

"I remove all vixaxes between myself and my Akashic records; in all moments."

"I remove all tentacles between myself and my Akashic records; in all moments."

"I remove all emotional attachment to the Akashic records; in all moments."

"I remove all mental attachment to the Akashic records; in all moments."

"I remove all physical attachment to the Akashic records; in all moments."

"I remove all spiritual attachment to the Akashic records; in all moments."

"I remove all the engrams that the Akashic records have put in me; in all moments."

"I remove all the programming and conditioning that the Akashic records have put on me; in all moments."

"I send all energy matrices into the light that prevent me from transcending the Akashic records; in all moments."

"I remove all limitations that the Akashic records have put in me; in all moments."

"I recant all vows and agreements between myself and the Akashic records; in all moments."

"I remove all curses between myself and the Akashic records; in all moments."

"I remove all blessings between myself and the Akashic records; in all moments."

"I sever all strings, cords and wires between myself and the Akashic records; in all moments."

"I dissolve all karmic ties between myself and the Akashic records; in all moments."

"I remove all the pain, burden, and illusion of separateness that the Akashic records have put on me; in all moments."

"I take back all the Joy, Love, Abundance, and Freedom that the Akashic records have taken from me; in all moments."

"I release resonating with the Akashic records; in all moments."

"I release emanating with the Akashic records; in all moments."

"I withdraw all my energy from the Akashic records; in all moments."

"I strip all illusion off of the Akashic records; in all moments."

"I collapse and dissolve the Akashic records; in all moments."

"I extract all of the Akashic records from my sound frequency; in all moments."

"I extract all of the Akashic records from my light emanation; in all moments."

"I shift my paradigm from the Akashic records to Joy, Love, Abundance, and Freedom; in all moments."

"I transcend the Akashic records; in all moments."

"I am centered and empowered in Joy, Love, Abundance, and Freedom; in all moments."

Trapped in Death

I facilitated a session recently with a woman who had severe panic attacks. In the last couple of years, we have chipped away at many of the issues. The panic seemed directly related to the trauma that she has experienced in past lives. It is not an elusive intangible. There is a direct proportion between panic and the Akashic (past life) images she carried. The images didn't need to be conscious to cause a reaction to them.

When she recently had another bout of panic, I was curious what was to come next. Some of her unconscious memories have been pretty horrific for me to be privy to. So I was curious what I would perceive on her behalf next.

What was uncovered is something that I sense is more common than people may realize. I personally have had the experience of dying during wartime, and when I should have crossed over, I stayed with the body. I wondered why my fellow soldiers were just stepping over me and not helping me. I didn't realize to them I was dead.

My client has struggled many lifetimes with conventional beliefs. To her, the concept of heaven and hell didn't make sense. She had no emotional connection to heaven and a cynical resistance to the belief system. In her records, she held the memory of dying, but because she did not believe in heaven, she stayed with the body. In her psyche, she was trapped in a coffin.

The astral world looks a lot like the physical world and when one crosses over, it feels as solid and real as the physical world. In her experiences, she was in her astral body but felt that she was still in the physical body. I do not even know how long she stayed trapped in that belief system before the experience played out and she shifted. But it was the source of the terror that was seeping into her present life.

To counter these fears, I gave her some techniques and visualizations to teach her how to leave her body while she is still in the physical body so that she knows she will be able to get out when it is time to cross over. Some people call this soul travel or astral projection. We also, as a technique, went to her that was trapped in the coffin and we visualized helping to pull her out and to cross over.

If anyone is suffering with panic attacks, I suggest they look for similar clues that will help to free them. What they need to know is that it may be caused by something from the past that doesn't need to be part of their present.

Unconscious Patterns

I recently facilitated a session where the client was in the midst of change sweeping through her life. Every aspect of it was affected. From her vantage point, life was messing with her. This pattern seemed to happen every few years and even though it was exhilarating in some ways, she had grown weary of it.

In her session, I saw a Phoenix rising out of the ashes. It was as if this were a symbol that she identified with. She seemed to draw inspiration from the symbol.

In her past lives, I saw her surviving great catastrophes. It wasn't the devastation that came through as significant, but what happened afterwards. Some of her best lifetimes were in the aftermath of great turmoil. This is when the human spirit showed its resiliency to thrive. This is what imprinted upon her and this is what she was recreating in her present life over and over. It was in rebuilding a new life where she felt the most joy and plugged into a purpose.

We released a lot of the unconscious behavior around this pattern to free her from creating such turmoil in her life. She left much lighter and exhilarated after her session.

Here is a tap to assist in interrupting the patterns that we have set up in our life.

(Say this statement three times while tapping on your head and say it a fourth time while tapping on your chest.)

"I release creating drama; in all moments."

Uncovering Our Own Past Lives

Someone asked me how to know what their past lives are. It is a great question since it is more empowering to figure it out for ourselves than to have someone else just tell us.

So here is a homework assignment to help you do that.

First, make lists of all the things that:

- You are afraid of,

- All of the things that you dislike, including climates, people, customs and time periods,

- All of your character weaknesses and prejudices.

Second, cross-reference your lists to see what things seem to go together. It may start to stir images or ideas in you of why you have an aversion to these things. These are the lifetimes where you may be holding trauma, and you may even uncover the ways that you have died in the past.

Third, do the same thing with the opposite side of your life with all of the things you like. Make a list of:

- The people you are receptive to,

- The cultures you wish to visit,

- Look at movies which are time period pieces and feel which ones seem comfortable,

- Think about the times in history that you could have lived comfortably.

Fourth, use your imagination:

- Who did you love?

- What did you eat?

- What was the climate?

- What were the customs?

Discovering who we are and who we have been is a great adventure. It is our own personal mystery to unravel. And we are the key.

Untangling Misconceptions with Core Beliefs

I facilitated a long distance remote session with a client who has endured many lifetimes of slavery. She wanted to work on the issue of low blood pressure. The doctors felt it was better than the alternative, but it left her lethargic and weak feeling. When I tuned into her, I could feel the lack of zeal within. It wasn't that it wasn't there; it was more like it was being suppressed by something intangible.

During her session, we uncovered her core belief about freedom. As we stripped down what it would feel like for her to be free, she got an overwhelming sense it would leave her helpless. That was the issue that we needed to address for her to get out from under that intangible pressure. She felt free and expansive with doing the work around the core issue.

There are many inconsistencies between what the concept of a word is and what they mean to an individual. There are a few of them that show up in private sessions. Here are some taps to untangle the core beliefs around positive words.

(Say each statement three times while tapping on your head and say it a fourth time while tapping on your chest.)

"I release the belief that being free will leave me helpless; in all moments.'

"I release defining freedom as helplessness; in all

moments."

"I release the fear of abusing power; in all moments."

"I release relinquishing my power in the fear of abusing power; in all moments."

"I release the belief that being rich entails overwhelming responsibility; in all moments."

"I release the aversion to being rich; in all moments."

"I release using dis-ease to escape responsibility; in all moments."

"I release using illness as an excuse; in all moments."

"I release using illness as a call to be nurtured; in all moments."

"I release the fear of being attractive; in all moments."

"I release defining being attractive as unsafe; in all moments."

"I release defining relationships as a form of enslavement; in all moments."

"I release confusing love for power; in all moments."

"I release the belief that security is boring; in all moments."

"I release buying security with my freedom; in all moments."

"I release the belief that creativity is frivolous; in all

moments."

"I release defining peace as complacency; in all moments."

"I shift my paradigm to Joy, Love, Abundance, Freedom and Wholeness; in all moments."

More often than not, it is the unconscious beliefs that prevent us from our desired goal. To take total responsibility for our station in life is a sign of a mature soul. The more we do this, the more we can also take the steps necessary to make the shifts happen so we can be where we choose to be.

Untangling the Psyche

Sometimes during private sessions, my clients and I discover connections between past life experiences and events in the present that don't really make sense. The psyche tangles and associates negative emotions with something pleasant due to overwhelming trauma in a past lifetime. It even changes perceived definitions of a word for some people. For instance, someone who was sacrificed during a celebration in a past life may meet going to a party in this lifetime with dread. Here are some taps to untangle some of these responses.

(Say each statement three times while tapping the head. Say it a fourth time while tapping on the chest.)

"I release confusing marriage as imprisonment; in all moments."

"I release associating dread with special occasions; in all moments."

"I release associating being beautiful as dangerous; in all moments."

"I release hating children; in all moments."

"I release the trauma of being a parent; in all moments."

"I release associating parenthood with death; in all moments."

"I release confusing success with shame; in all moments."

"I release confusing natural hunger signals as starvation; in all moments."

"I release the fear of starving to death; in all moments."

"I release defining being obese as healthy and safe; in all moments."

"I release associating holidays with sadness and lack; in all moments."

"I release defining nonconformity as dangerous; in all moments."

"I release confusing sugar for love; in all moments."

"I release confusing fatty foods as security; in all moments."

"I release confusing being self-centered and abusing power; in all moments."

These are a few of the ones that came through to help uplift the consciousness of the readers this morning.

Uplifting Humanity by Releasing the Vanities

It is fortunate that I am able to see the Akashic records of a client and know what their issues are so that I can address them. A recent client had been an abuser of power on a grand scale. It is a very important lesson to knowing compassion. In the present life, I could get a sense of her records and how she has made life difficult for others in her stubbornness.

In her first session, she really compartmentalized my work and it was a bit off putting. She seemed to value only the components of it that she had a strong reaction to. The other parts we seemed to dismiss. In her session, the images that I was seeing were all of Nazi Germany during the Second World War. They were more than an abuse of power; they were a disregard for human life. I perceived her as a high-ranking official in the Nazi regime. Her whole session was addressing this issue. When her session was over, the exchange was as cold and thankless as if I had handed her some dry cleaning. But I was comforted by knowing that this session benefited humanity in some way. Releasing her dynamics with the world released the world from whatever she had unleashed on them. This is how I approach every single session, as if it unties some of the karmic strings on some and loosens the ones in all others as a byproduct.

I was surprised when she contacted me for another session. I refused to give it to her before we talked about the first session. I was surprised that she actually knew she had benefited greatly from the session because of her lack of gratitude. I explained how she left me feeling and she seemed genuinely surprised. She thought I was hard on her in the first session. She had no idea what was to come in the second session.

Because I am releasing issues that people would otherwise have to experience, the client still needs to absorb the lesson that they would have been learning on their own. With this woman, I had to be really direct to help her to compensate for her denial. In other clients, it can be a process that happens within them and is none of my business after the session. I will support them, but I don't even remember sessions or many of the clients after a session.

There is a subversive exchange that happens between people on an energetic level. To understand this, think of talking to a teenager and they are saying what you want them to say, but you know that they are holding contempt for you. Since I perceive mostly in energy, this is the dynamic I address in people. They seem confused at first, but I let them know what they really are doing. To be called on it is confusing yet refreshing to them.

On the surface, she was very polite, but energetically she was seething with contempt. Those layers that were being released did not want to go. It was them that I was addressing with my strong tone. It was the thick layers of facade that I was stripping off that I was addressing. Clients know this somewhat because I will toggle between very harsh tones and my usual kindness. Also, what clients may not realize is that while I am addressing them, I am also moving energy with an energetic intention.

At the beginning of her second session, I was surprised by this woman's voice. She was warm and kind. I was very pleased about the change from the first session. Still, I honestly explained to her how she was the only person who left me feeling so unappreciated after a session that it felt like an abyss. I also explained that after her session I checked out her Facebook page to see if I could tell which member of the Nazi party she reminded me of. I told her how when I saw this one photo of her, that it left me cold. I asked her if she were Hitler. This seems silly to say out loud, but I wanted her to get a sense of the magnitude of the abuse of power that I was tuning into.

From the beginning of the session to the end, she convulsed in huge sobs. I gave her no sympathy. The image of the plights of the world that were devastated by power left me unwavering in compassion. Energetically, she needed to experience the lack of compassion that power plays had subjected the world to. If someone did not know the inner dynamic that was playing out, they would have thought I was ruthless. But it was what was necessary for this session.

I was actually very pleased with her that she was so receptive in the session, but I did not allow her to know that. When bringing up the photo, she admitted (with a hint of pride that she was not aware of) that she had an evil streak in her. That needed to be stripped from her. The fact that the session was so difficult for her was evidence of just how deep the session was.

She wanted to address her judgments and jealousies. When I facilitate a session, I am conscious of how the victims of my client are going to benefit from my client energetically giving back all they have taken from them. I am also aware of the benefit all their victims receive by them erasing all their transgressions. I performed this session from the point of view of what would people who were affected by the abuse of power want it to look like. They would want her to feel a hint of what they have experienced. They would not have been disappointed. This was an incredibly intense session and I am so proud of her for allowing me to share this with everyone.

Here are some of the taps I shared with her. There are some that brought her into convulsive laughter. You may recognize which ones. I handed out the taps as if I had Hitler himself complying to do a session. That is very harsh, but it describes the level of responsibility I take in doing these sessions. It is incredibly effective. That analogy gives a good perspective for everyone doing the taps. Do them from the vantage point of abusing power and be a surrogate to release deep injustice in the world and regain balance. They began with releasing the vanities. These are anger, greed, lust, attachment and vanity.

(Say each statement out loud three times while tapping on

your head and say it a fourth time while tapping on your chest.)

"I declare myself a surrogate for humanity in doing these taps; in all moments."

"I release abusing power; in all moments."

"I release giving my free will over to the vanities; in all moments."

"I release succumbing to the vanities; in all moments."

"I release worshiping the vanities; in all moments."

"I release being enslaved to the vanities; in all moments."

"I release wielding power for the vanities; in all moments."

"I release craving world domination; in all moments."

"I release perpetuating the vanities; in all moments."

"I release choosing the vanities over love; in all moments."

"I release the relentless pursuit for the vanities; in all moments."

"I release an allegiance with evil; in all moments."

"I release endorsing evil; in all moments."

"I release being or personifying evil; in all moments."

"I withdraw all my energy from evil; in all moments."

"I recant all vows and agreements between myself and the vanities; in all moments."

"I remove all curses between myself and the vanities; in all moments."

"I dissolve all karmic ties between myself and the vanities; in all moments."

"I remove all the pain, burden, limitations and engrams that the vanities have put on me; in all moments."

"I remove all the pain, burden, limitations and engrams that I have put on the world due to the vanities; in all moments."

"I release endorsing Putin; in all moments."

"I release providing a blueprint for war; in all moments."

"I release creating war in the world; in all moments."

"I release being responsible for the conflict between Palestine and Israel; in all moments."

"I withdraw all my energy from the vanities; in all moments."

"I withdraw all my energy from war; in all moments."

"I take back all the Joy, Love, Abundance, Freedom, Life and Wholeness; in all moments."

"I give back all the Joy, Love, Abundance, Freedom, Life and Wholeness that I have taken from the world due to the vanities; in all moments."

"I release resonating with the vanities; in all moments."

"I release emanating with the vanities; in all moments."

"I remove all of the vanities from my sound frequency; in all moments."

"I remove all the vanities from my light body; in all moments."

"I shift my paradigm from the vanities to Joy, Love, Abundance, Freedom, Life and Wholeness; in all moments."

"I transcend the vanities; in all moments."

"I remove all masks, walls and armor; in all moments."

"I repair and fortify the Wei chi of all my bodies; in all moments."

"I am centered and imbued in Divine Love; in all moments."

"I emanate and resonate Divine Love to every corner of the world; in all moments."

"I dissolve everything that is not motivated by Divine Love; in all moments."

This exercise is an incredible gift that my client allowed me to share with everyone. The taps may seem really harsh. But on some level, if we are not doing everything in our own lives to overcome the vanities and are abusing power, then we are adding to the conflict of the world.

This life is the tipping point and what we do here, although no one will pat us on the back for it, is us doing our part to uplift the quality of life for everyone on the planet. We are not bystanders in life. The more people do these taps, the easier it will be for others to recognize their importance. I encourage everyone to do them and to share.

War Buddies

A woman called me to help her dog who was traumatized by fireworks and thunder. It would send him into the closet shaking with fear. She was a born again Christian and I wanted to show respect to her beliefs. She not only was open to my help, but it seemed to answer a prayer about a bigger issue.

I tuned into the dog. I asked her if she had a son. It was obvious that the dog had been a soldier in past lives and because of an incredible connection with her son, he had returned. In fact, it came through that he had an incredible connection with the son's group of best friends as well.

Hearing this was out of her comfort zone, but something about it resonated. She told me that the boys were all closer than brothers and they all loved the dog. In fact, when they came over to the house, the dog was included as one of them and they were always sweet and respectful of him.

The boys were all army buddies that had been in war

together. It made them very close and they had taken a pact to come back together. The dog was a part of that pact. He died in war and trauma, possibly saving their lives. It was too devastating to come back as a human, but he honored the pact by coming back in a dog body. On some level, they still recognized and respected him as an equal.

This may have seemed very farfetched to the woman's belief system, but she told me more background that helped her believe. She said that her son was fascinated by the military and plans to enlist as soon as he is old enough. She had a bad feeling about it and asked me to talk with him. I agreed.

She brought the dog, the son, and three other siblings to see me. We sat around in a circle and I released a lot of angst from the dog. We prayed. I talked with the boy. I explained to him that he was romanticizing war because he had a good experience in a past life with it. In a past life, it served a purpose of connecting him with great friends and important experiences. But those were in the past and the war he would be enlisting in was not the same.

I don't usually interfere with someone's freedom of choice, but his mother had prayed for my help and she was out of her comfort zone yet receptive to my help. He was her charge for a few more years. I did not tell the boy what his mother and I both knew, that he would have a short life if he took this path. I just told him that the war lives that he enjoyed had already happened and that he would have a happier life if he went to college and pursued his talents. I cost the Bush-era one soldier. His mother was very grateful.

What's Your Shtick?

I recently facilitated a session where the client had many health concerns. But the first issue that showed up in looking through the pictures of his life was the issue of not being listened to. When I mentioned this, he didn't think it was an issue at first, but then he started to think back to all the times when he was dismissed and realized it was an issue.

In his past lives, I saw layers of lifetimes where he was considered so ill that the only time he was listened to was when he had another devastating symptom. I saw a particular lifetime where he was a child in an affluent family and both arms were tied to a bedpost. His family was leaving the room after a consultation with the doctor and he was screaming for them to stay or to untie him. The father's face had such concern on it, and that look of concern was the only love the client was privy to. That look of concern translated to love in my client's mind.

In this life, the client unwittingly was still trying to get that look of concern from people. He didn't understand that people only listen to problems for so long before they shut down. So the way to get that look of concern is to up the ante on the symptoms and, unfortunately, the pain and discomfort that go along with them.

Here is the tap we used. There were many, but it boiled down to this:

(Say this statement three times while tapping on your head, and say it a fourth time while tapping on your chest.)

"I release using illness to be loved; in all moments."

For many people, illness is what they use to get love. Most of us use something to get our need for love met. It could be beauty, intelligence, sex, giving, drama, helping, money, laughter, skills, gossip, superiority, etc. Whatever it is (it will be healing just knowing what it is), replace that word with illness and do the tap. You may be amazed at how good you feel.

When pets cross over, they take their cues from us. If we can be happy and excited for their new adventure, it can ease their transition. Have a contingency plan in place. Tell your pet that you welcome them back in a new body. Tune into them before they cross and get a sense of what sex they will come back as and what they will look like. They will recognize you when they return.

Look for a baby that is born after your pet transitions. They may turn around and return right away. There is no need to look too hard. Just ask your pet and the Universe to arrange things and then stay open.

Why Reincarnation? Or...Flowering into Peace

Once you have felt the gnawing grip of starvation,

You cannot stand to see anyone go hungry.

Once you have helplessly watched your babies suffer,

You can't stand to hear the cries of a child or know one is in pain.

Once you have been hunted down as prey in either human or animal form,

You can't tolerate hunting for the sport of it.

Once you have been beaten up and discarded,

You wince at the hint of anyone being bullied.

Once you have cried in the night unattended with no solace,

You cringe at the thought of anyone living in despair.

Once you have been trapped and kept in a cage,

You can't help but ache for the multitudes locked up with little regard.

Once you have felt your mind race out of control with no brake,

You are able to understand the torment of mental illness.

Once you have felt your body decay from within as you helplessly watch,

You truly understand the devastation of disease.

Once you have carried the weight of many battles and multiple wounds,

You no longer have a taste for war that needs satiating.

Once you have put all your heart, soul and wishes into being prosperous to no avail,

Do you truly understand the futility of being impoverished.

The longer your memory, the more these things bleed through. People ask why there are such horrible things happening in the world. It is because people have such short memories. They disconnect from their own suffering. Perhaps that is the design to allow power and control to flourish.

The cure is to awaken to one's own depth. Rip through the denial and dust off the book of your own hidden memories. Perhaps then compassion can truly take root and flower into peace.

Cleaning Out the Barn

It seems that there are so many people experiencing the loss of someone right now. It is a shame that death has to be marked with such negativity and drama. Death is a natural cycle of life that needs to be celebrated. It is a time when a person is supposedly able to gather up all their energy and naturally slip out of the physical realm into a vibration of existence that is more refined. This vibration is called the astral plane by some but heaven by others.

When one leaves the physical realm, they are merely dropping a coarse casing of themselves that is worn out or diseased. They then will be operating from their astral body which is a youthful, healthy version of the physical body. The astral body is the same vibration as the astral plane, so when you are existing on the astral plane, it is as solid and tangible as the physical realm except it operates by different laws. Strange things may seem to be there. For example, the law of gravity is not the same as the physical realm so people can appear to be able to fly.

People visit the astral plane all the time when they sleep. That is why they fly in their dreams. They visit their friends who have crossed over and now reside there. They actually can have the whole experience of continuing the life they have had on the physical realm if that is what they wish to do.

For instance, a married couple that always fantasized about having a dream home can manifest that on the astral plane. If one partner goes first, that partner can seem to be living in that dream home and waiting for the other partner. But the truth of the matter is that they both live in the dream home in their astral body. The one person who has crossed permanently is withdrawn from the physical realm. The one person who is so called "alive" just happens to hold some awareness and do some time in the physical world still.

They both have an astral body still so they are always together there. But because of such heavy conditioning on the physical realm, that person feels lost to the one who has crossed. They are with them in the dream state. They slip off their physical body and visit them at night. They understand the process on the other side and both can even have a good teasing laugh about how dramatic the one partner is who is in the physical world and trapped in the illusion of loss.

The truth of the matter is that it is very pleasant to cross over. It is like a celebration, graduation and revitalization magnified a thousand percent (when done by natural means and not self-inflicted). There is no trauma in crossing. The trauma is held in what happens to bring one to crossing but not the actual experience. It is very pleasant, like shedding old skin, being freed from a sarcophagus or inhaling a delightful fresh breath of spring. In fact, it is much more traumatic to be born than it is to "die".

Our concepts of birth and death were formulated in the Dark Ages when fear was the optimal form of control. Unfortunately, we have never come out of the Dark Ages with many of our beliefs. We have just become savvy in our ignorance. We have created so many upgrades in technology that can give us a better life, but aspects of our development have been purposely thwarted to keep us seeped in ignorance. We see this blatantly played out in how different factions insist that there is no climate change and will mandate laws to perpetuate the myth. The same technique was used to phase out the understanding of reincarnation. In fact, the Dark Ages were marked by the genocide of all those who accepted reincarnation. That is why it is so fearful to talk about or accept. Many of us hold the memory of being viciously murdered for our simple beliefs. This same fearful memory is held in the silly demonization of tree huggers.

This is the same form of manipulation that has been used to formulate our concepts of death and the belief of only living one life. Power factions force feed us one life doctrine to maintain control on society. Even though many people are remembering their past lives, they are demonized if they accept this level of awareness instead of adopting the fear based rigidity of their faith based religion. Many children are coming back to the physical realm with vivid memories of their past lives. They KNOW who they are. That is because our past life records are stored in a vibrational aspect of ourselves that is more refined than the physical body.

Everything that we have ever experienced is kept in records in a vibrational aspect of ourselves called the causal body. Since it is an aspect of us that we don't lose when we cross over, we have the same causal vibration as we always do. It is merely our physical body that we drop out of when we cross. Everything that we have ever experienced is stored in our retrieval component called our Akashic records. If you ever have dreams of looking at photos in a book or a catalogue of pictures, your higher self is telling your physical self that you have been reading your Akashic records.

Every event that we hold as emotional trauma is stored in our Akashic records. The events that seem to happen in your physical life are habitual experiences caused by something that you stored in your Akashic records. That is why the vibration of the past life realm is called the causal plane. When someone comes to me for a session, I will read their Akashic records to see what the initial cause of the physical dis-ease is. Then I can walk the client through how to release the issue by erasing the Akashic record of the trauma. Your physical body is a reactionary to what is held in your causal body. This is the true meaning of the expression from the Bible, "as above, so below."

This information should be common knowledge to anyone who is interested in such things. Many groups have taken much pain to withhold it from the mass consciousness. They have collected it and doled it out in tiny amounts and have charged a fee for the right to know it. Their reasoning is that man is not capable of handling the truth. But in fact, this has created a warped sense of the world that has left people living in fear and creating a lot of drama around the cycles of life when, in fact, every aspect of the cycle of life should be celebrated as worthwhile as the birth of a new baby.

The drama and sadness that is collected from the crossing of a loved one creates this psychic sludge of energy that people have been used to creating and living in. It is like having livestock and never cleaning out the barn and walking through it like it doesn't exist. This is what is created in the heavy balm of someone passing with the loved ones lamenting and carrying on like it is a natural thing to do. But it is not. The drama of being overwhelmed when someone crosses over is a conditioned response.

Deaths are traumatic when the person was the breadwinner of the family and their death meant the whole family would be turned out into the street and forced to beg for food. A death of someone was traumatic in the past if you were a woman and your husband died and everything you owned was taken away from you because women could not own property. A death is devastating if you had one strong healthy son who was caring for the farm and he was struck down. It meant the whole family was doomed.

These are examples of devastating reasons that someone crossing over would be traumatic. These tragedies are stored in our causal body and are triggered upon a present death, even if it is a good death, meaning someone who is ready to go. This person is going to a better life but is not quite allowed to know it because of societal conditioning and just has to trust that it is so. This kind of death can be a little sad but mixed with relief for the one who is free.

Native Americans have the right idea of the cycles of life. They don't talk about those who have crossed out of respect for them and because they don't want to hold them back on their journey. They accept children back into this world realizing that they are their mothers and fathers who have passed and are coming back into to the family in a new body. This is a form of acceptance that is so clean and freeing because it doesn't create the pulling and drama on any person's soul journey. It allows them to more freely walk through the cycles of life without any heavy psychic mandates on them.

One of the best gifts you can give someone who is ready to cross is the freedom of your blessings and allow them to go. Many people are held in the nightmare of dis-ease by a selfish or ignorant loved one who won't allow them to go. They inflict their self-will over the person and keep them trapped in the hellish experience of dying because they are triggered by a past life trauma in their own causal records that brings up a devastating consequence of losing someone. The drama of those who mourn can create angst in those who have crossed and distract them from their new found freedom. It is like being the guest of honor at a wonderful celebration and all the guests make it about them or spoil it by being in bad moods.

Many people can experience the cycles of reincarnation through their pets. People will lose a dear furry friend and then have another pet show up in the future with a strange familiarity and similar personality to the one who crossed. Because of societal conditioning, this reunion is not acknowledged as a reunion but a pleasant coincidence and nothing more. The original loss is not allowed to be erased by the return of their loved one. This is true of babies as well.

This post may be difficult for some to digest. But the absence of fundamental truth has left this world in a twisted state of confusion devoid of any sense of peace. If this understanding is absorbed by anyone and it brings an end to anyone's suffering from loss, then that is less psychic energy for us all to wade through or, less for some of us to clean out of the barn.

SECTION TWO: DREAMS

Absolutes

I just awoke from a dream that was showing me something that I needed to know. The dream looked nothing like the lesson that I construed from it. The thing about dreams is that they are personal lessons for the person who is having them. Every dream symbol is forged from your own experiences. The same subjects that show up in my dream may mean totally different things to someone else.

When one wants to learn to interpret their dreams, they take all the information that they can retrieve from the dream and list it as clues. People say that they don't remember their dreams. That is because the higher self isn't going to feed you truth unless you are interested in receiving it. The moment you make it a priority to write down the wisps of your dream, the more information your higher self will feed you.

Just saying you don't remember your dreams shows your higher self that you want to stay in the ignorance of not knowing. Many people consciously choose to be ignorant. It is because they have been conditioned lifetime after lifetime of what happens to the person who stands out from the crowd. The person who knows too much has been targeted by controlling power factions since modern history began.

In the dream, I was in a warm loving kitchen that I was familiar with. But it was not my home. It was the home of a friend of mine who had extended family. It looked like my another friend's house where we have collected through the years, but the owner was the friend of mine who has a big loving family that she feeds a lot. The dream used two strong images to get the point across of extended family: the friend and my other friend's kitchen.

There were a lot of relatives milling about having a good time. But none really stood out. For some reason, I took it upon myself to feed them. There was a small conventional oven and many relatives. I was also limited on the menu. I used the ingredients that I had. All the people were my friend's family. I was feeding them for the day and trying to make it special.

What I had to use was bone marrow, okra and whatever someone brought over. But anyone who brought something to share did so in an indifferent way and never brought enough to feed everyone. They just plopped it on the counter and expected me to add it to the meal. I did not know what to do with most of it. With some of the ingredients, I broke them apart and made little salads. But there wasn't enough to go around and people were not happy with the choices.

In fact, people were happy that I was cooking, but they all had an opinion how I was doing it wrong. They got annoyed with me for not using their ingredient or what they brought to the table. They also were an Italian family and wanted to be gorged on the meals that they were accustomed to eating. They brought none of the ingredients with them. What they ended up bringing over was desert. (You know how people bring desert as an after thought?) It was a day old and not enough to serve everyone.

The things that I was given to serve were the items that no one else wanted to claim for their own. The bone marrow is what I feed my dog, but I know it is served in fancy restaurants. The okra was bitter and hard to cook. I baked it and squeezed mustard into each one to make it tasty. Mustard is the item left over in the refrigerator that no one thinks to throw out.

The meal I was cooking was me serving up truth. I was serving in the kitchen of someone else because I have no family of my own. Family represented a group of people with similar vantage points on life, people of a certain belief system who assimilated truth in a similar way. However, there was little left to serve them because everything of life that is palatable was gobbled up by the doctrines and beliefs that different groups engaged in believing. Truth had nothing of substance to use that was not tainted by dogma or limitations.

The family milling around were all waiting for me to serve them truth. Yet none of them assisted in putting the meal together. The family members vested the most in eating were the ones who heckled and criticized me the most. They were the ones that were annoyed that they were not getting a huge plate of pasta. People say they want truth but when you try to give it to them, they are annoyed because it doesn't look like the banquets that their particular belief system serves up. They resented me for not serving them truth in the way they wanted it to look. If I talk about reincarnation, for example, they are put off. Yet they were all starving for truth and I was the only one who took the initiative to create a meal for them.

The friend whose house it was in belongs to a spiritual group that believes they are above reproach. The members have taken what was at the beginning a viable means for the individual to achieve higher consciousness and created concrete doctrine around it that merely captures those with a hunger for truth in a new set of rules that seem less limiting than the old set of rules that they have outgrown. But the rules are indeed very similar.

It has become a limitation that has morphed into a replication of the old doctrine they rebelled against to find truth. Yet they are too afraid to leave in case they are wrong. It is like the young person running away from home to find freedom and meets up with someone with more guile who says all the right things and entraps them more than the home they ran away from. They are then apt to stay in fear of meeting a worse fate.

Anytime there is a set of absolutes that one must heed and something is hung over the individual's head, then there is a limitation. In the "spiritual" group that my friend belonged to, there was a central figure that was a benevolent man that assisted them from harm and led them to truth, but they had to pay allegiance to the group annually to belong or they would risk being bombarded with so much more karma than when they first came into the group.

Anyone that induces fear is limiting your freedom. This is true especially when peer pressure is introduced. Fear of going to hell or fear of taking on so much karma that you feel like you are in hell are merely subtle different hues of the same color. This group started out with an individual at the center who had abilities to assist others who were struggling in the inner realms. He set himself up to assist everyone who needed his assistance. That is how great his love and abilities were.

But I will do the same for anyone. I assist people in the other realms constantly. It is done without fanfare and most people don't know who I am. But it is not important. What is important is that it is possible to assist those around the world who are suffering in their own private hell and pull them out of the anguish of their experience. Our karmic situations are like a spiritual catch and release program.

Sometimes it works well to help others, and these people now assist others. But sometimes these people, when freed from their anguish, will use their freedom to judge or control others. Some will go back to being a pest to others again. That is okay because the love generated in assisting others is the real "take away" from the experience, not the results of whether this person is totally free.

The leader of this spiritual group put a cap on spirituality in a big way. He taught the group that he was like God on earth and set himself up to be worshiped. Even though they said it was not, worship was inevitably what they do with the man who found himself in the position of his predecessor. This wonderful man put a cap on humanity by telling all these spiritual seekers that you had to be born male to be as empowered as he. This is, of course, a lie that there was only one who could serve in this capacity. Perhaps back then, but not now.

The truth he shared was very compelling. It was a collection of truths that he had accessed through others who had done the footwork. Madame Blavatsky spent her life collecting the truths from all religions. This is the information that this man drew upon. The problem was that she did not set herself up to be worshiped. Her intention was more pure. She wanted to help people to access truth for themselves without being limited by doctrine. She gave them all the doctrine so they could discern truth for themselves.

The central character of this spiritual group took her truth and claimed it as his own. He borrowed many charged words that were sacred to many groups through the ages and copyrighted them as his own. He tried to copyright and own truth. I still vacillate between whether this man is a wonderful enlightened soul who entrapped others in a limited state of consciousness by his desperate need to be validated or was sincere in all his intentions. Perhaps it is somewhere in between.

But what he did is entrench humanity further into slavery by a few tenants that all of his group were set to believe: That you needed to be a man to reach the pinnacle of spirituality, (this is not true as I have proven through my assistance to others), and that this is a warring world and you shouldn't bother to wish for peace (this is a load of crap that makes me question his intentions). Either he was gullible as a spiritual adept, or he was influenced by negative power mongers in the truth that he shared. World peace is ours to realize.

What he left behind in the few tenants that his group follows, left the world so immersed in apathy that it is appalling. While he was alive, he was a gateway for truth. But after he crossed, men of less aptitude were put into his position of reverence without having the abilities that he had. This has left the world in believing world peace is not possible and that you shouldn't help anyone who is struggling because they need to strengthen themselves through the struggle. Struggle does strengthen someone when there is a chance. But the deck has been stacked against anyone finding truth through the limitations of current belief systems.

Every single belief that he left the group of his followers with should be challenged because there is always another step in the understanding and owning of truth. Limiting one's self to what was believed decades ago is a dishonor to your own journey to truth. I know because I connect to the same Guides that this man was introduced to by Madame Blavatsky. They tell me the limitations of how he spun truth and how now it is holding humanity back from realizing their own empowerment. The beliefs held by the current man in charge have led to the imbalances that we see in the world today.

People are starving for truth. Since he took so many spiritual truths and twisted them with his own limitations, he has left humanity starving for truth. I have taken it upon myself to feed them because no one is really stepping up to be the chef, but all that I am left with is bone marrow, okra and mustard packets. I am not accepted by any group. I am mostly resented by them. But it sure would be better if everyone rolled up their sleeves and pitched in to feed truth to the masses.

Of course you don't have to be in a male body to be God realized and be able to assist others. Of course there is the presence of God walking among us. Why does it have to be just one person who is empowered in this way? No. Humanity awakens when all are validated as the God beings that they are. If one person is on a pedestal that means everyone else is diminished. This is a core belief that needs to be challenged.

Any absolutes, limitation of gender, beliefs or any other requirements that are creating a spiritual tribalism are limiting the amount of truth and love available to all. The more people can see the limitations they have on them and crack the glass ceiling, perhaps we can generate enough love and truth to uplift all of humanity. As silly as worshiping a cow or being rewarded with seventy-two virgins in the afterlife sound, that is how silly it sounds to me to believe that we have only one short life on earth.

Just look at all the limitations that belief brings to the table.

If you want to be served truth, you need to be willing to come to the table. Some of the controlling belief systems are intended to prevent you from coming to the table. I can make the bone marrow and okra as tasty as possible, but it would sure be helpful if others would be receptive and share what they can in truth and love to bring more ingredients to the table. What are your talents? How can you serve?

Comforting a Loss

Hi Jen.

I hope you're well. I am having trouble coping with the loss of my dad. He passed unexpectedly two weeks ago today. I woke up sobbing this morning but unable to remember the dream. I was hoping you might have a tap that could help me. I know that death is just a rebirth and I'm well clued in to the spiritual world, but I'm having a really hard time right now. I would appreciate any help you can offer.

With my sincere thanks, xoxo.

Jen: You are crying because you were with him last night. You spent the whole night with him. You had fun and you did some outside activity that you have enjoyed together. The crying is the shock of the two opposing worlds. Just on the other side, you are laughing and enjoying each other and as soon as you wake up, you are the one who is separated from the joy.

It is a silly thing that those on the other side watch us do as we slip back into the physical body. We do it again and again, morning after morning. So the taps would be:

"I release forgetting being with my dad; in all moments."

"I pull back the curtain between here and there; in all moments."

"I shift into my higher awareness; in all moments."

The Nightmare Epic

I woke up from a dream that I thought was a nightmare, but what I was being given is understanding. Those who don't understand concepts of a higher vibration may be afraid of them at first. So I received this higher truth in the form of a nightmare. It was a means of absorbing the fear for others who needed to accept higher truths without it wreaking such havoc on their nervous systems. People have been induced to fear too much. They are saturated with it. It is time for them to experience the love and awareness that dries up all fear.

In the dream, my home was very peaceful and calm. It was the haven that it is for me. Outside the window was a deep trench with a fence built up on the other side. It was beautiful nature. There were little animals that seemed different than anything you can see on earth. They looked like a cross between a koala bear and a squirrel. They were fine to look at from afar.

But in the land across the fence, the animals began to be more prevalent. There was a huge, blue, birdlike reptile. It looked like half dragon and half horse. But it was erect like a seahorse. It was beautiful. When it landed, it pounded the earth so hard it created a big trench in the rolling hill beyond the fence. It was a real experience. Not a dream. It was real.

More and more of them came, animals of all different kinds. There were so many that they compromised the fence and were getting into my house. I was scared and woke up a little bit shaken. But as soon as I awoke, I was given a greater understanding of the dream experience.

When one of us taps into higher truth, we feed it to the whole through osmosis. The beasts that were inundating my home were actually truths I had tapped into by expanding my understanding of inanimate life. To many who believe in archaic beliefs, my understanding of the world would terrify them. But this is what is happening. Everyone is being upgraded in understanding. It is scary to them.

So in the dream, I was absorbing the fear for them so that they could get comfortable getting used to it without being paralyzed in fear. It is so much easier to love than react and lash out in fear and hate. This is what I am allowing them to do by absorbing the fear.

Inanimate life has a lot to teach us. If you want to enhance your awareness, speak to it, respect it, listen to it. A way to do that in a way we are familiar with is to adopt an inanimate friend. It may be a way of getting you comfortable with all life speaking with you. As you listen to the inanimate world, you will realize that all animals, nature, trees and bees can have more access to speaking with you. The payoff is very rewarding. The side benefit is that you will be stretching the capacity of awareness in humans and diluting the ignorance.

Don't Eat the Peas!

One of my clients had an interesting dream last night. She and I were going to a huge cathedral. There was a Christmas chorus singing songs very loudly and off key. No one seemed to notice. Everyone sat down to a huge meal, but I wouldn't touch it. I was really loud and caused a bit of a scene. I refused to eat the peas because the sauce they were served in was poisoned.

I yelled pretty loudly that the sauce the peas were in was poison. People around me stopped eating their peas and eventually everyone stopped eating their peas.

This is what I do here on my page. I try to help people from being duped by a certain concept or belief. The belief itself may be based on a spiritual truth, but it is being fed to everyone in a poisoned base meant to control them, limit them or cause spiritual sickness. People are so used to giving away their power that they will accept anything that is served to them. They so desperately want to have things to be good that they accept what is not as a form of denial.

Well it is time to stop believing that anything that doesn't resonate well within your own energy field is still okay. It is time to serve up your own truth and stop eating poisoned peas. The songs being off key is the sound frequency being distorted and no one else noticing. It is time to start resonating with truth. It is time for truth to ring pure and clear.

Dream Help

This is a cool message I received this morning. It was funny because there was a castle turret in my dream too.

Jen, I have to thank you so much. You just came in one of my dreams. I called you because I was so afraid. You protected me from that scary situation, and then you made three noises and I woke up.

I was in a big old house, like an old castle. The weather was severe; some big event like a hurricane was starting. My mother was with me, but she left the house to go hunting wearing green armor and guns. Teddy, my cat, was with me in this big empty house. Then a black cat tried to get in the house. He was looking for shelter. I wanted to let him in, but he was like bad. He snapped at me.

When I closed the doors, let the black cat out, and I was alone in the house, I felt so much fear. There was the presence of a woman calling me, a scary, bad woman. The hurricane kicked in, and I was so afraid of this woman and her call.... That's when I called you, Jen.

I said, "Please Jen come and help me, I am so afraid."

You came, but not physically, and took me away from that presence of that woman. Then you made three sounds like snapping fingers, and I woke up. It was so cool! Thank you.

Dreaming is such a blanket statement. We do so many things when we slip out of the physical realms to wander at night. And when we match the same vibration of the world we are in, it is not wispy like a dream, but solid matter to us. Every night is an adventure. Every adventure is a key to our infinite self beyond the physical world. Fear and drama fall away and Love fuels our lives. We become awakened in the true sense.

Harvesting the Fruit of Humanity

I received an emergency message from a client who was disturbed by a dream she had. She felt very bad and wanted clarity. She is very open to my work but is also concerned about the way she is perceived if she endorses me openly.

In the dream, her basement was slightly flooded. She tried to find the controls on the right side, but when she did, a sheriff from her old house came in and restrained her. She was helpless and begged the officer to let her go. She swore on her husband's life that if he let her go, she would be complacent. (This is the part of the dream that disturbed her.) Then she saw millions of tomatoes rotting and was thinking of what a shame it was. The dream left her very sad.

Here is the interpretation. The basement flooding was the flooding of the world issues into her home. She is one that does not like to speak her truth because she doesn't want to provoke anyone. But in not speaking her truth, she thinks she is safe. She confuses speaking her truth with being confrontational, but by not speaking her truth, she is agreeing to the terms of power. She retreats within herself, which is her haven, and believes all will be well. But she also gets an uneasy feeling that it will not be.

Her looking for the controls is her using the ego to fix the situation. The controls being on one side symbolize that she is not centered. Since she identifies strongly with being a female, she relinquishes embracing the male counterpart within herself which creates an imbalance. The officer represented the old paradigm of male dominated power. That old paradigm is making one last ditch effort to restrain female energy, which is evident from the current events of atrocities inflicted upon women and female children.

Her begging on the life of her husband was actually her being pushed up against the wall to finally embrace her male energy. It is the position we are all in. We can either concede to the current treatment of women in the world or we can "man up," literally, by embracing the balance between our own female-male energy. We can take a more balanced stance in our own empowerment.

Her seeing the tomatoes everywhere and watching them rot is symbolic of seeing all the wasted potential in people everywhere rot from lack of use. Tomatoes are a fruit that is not considered a fruit. The hearts and intentions of all the individuals in the world are also fruits that are not considered. She was scanning the world and grieving that the fruit of humanity was being wasted. She saw the decay of wasted potential.

So many people say they like my posts and say how I have miraculously helped them, but they do not share this truth with others. They even go to lengths to hide it, even from themselves. They are like my client in the dream. They feel the truth of my posts and my purpose, but retreat within themselves and hide it as a secret. They have a disconnect in their control panel as she did in the dream.

Every time I see this disconnect in people who have benefited from my assistance or point of view and I have shared my heart with, I can't lie, I am disappointed. It is such a gift to experience such a lifetime where individuals are able to regain their individual power and to be shown a simple yet powerful way to do it. Wouldn't you want this for all those you love? Wouldn't it be worth the risk of the possibility of rebuke?

The more you share truth, the more you poke through all limitations and breathe new life into the planet. It is not done through arguing. It is done by standing in your own center. We, as a group of individuals, will be collectively manifesting greater love for all life. Let's not waste another crop of sacred potential. Let's salvage the crop in the field. Let's break down the walls of resistance in the world to divine love and kindness.

Every step you take in the advancement of your personal empowerment and truth is a leap forward in the advancement of humanity. Feel the empowerment of sharing! I certainly do by sharing truth with you. Feel my love and gratitude as well.

Healing the Emotional Wounds of Gay People

I woke up a little bit ago from a vivid dream. When my dreams are that vivid, it means that they are real in a different vibratory rate. When I remember them, it means they are pertinent to something or someone. I was doing healing work in a subtle way.

In the dream, I had just moved into a new house. I was led over to the neighbor's house. It was unfinished and had many rooms. There was a room where a few older adult men were living. They were all gay. The man who answered the door was very receptive and kind. His roommates came out to meet me out of curiosity. They were cynical and made derogatory remarks about themselves being old queens. I did not find it amusing although I was respectful of their defenses. I understand the ploy of insulting one's self first before someone else can beat you to the punch.

In the dream, I had three different books of mine that I

was sharing with them. It is nice to know that my books are manifested in the dream state. At first, they seemed indifferent, but I felt that they were really receptive under their guarded exterior. I felt their kindness under their pain. I loved them all in spite of their inability to trust.

When I awoke, I realized how difficult it must have been, and still is, for people to be gay in a hostile environment. It is better now but not better enough. I was very glad to think that I am healing the wounds of such dear souls who have been demonized for their personal preferences in regards to love. It is an ugly world that despises you because of who you love. What a private hell it must be or has been. I am hoping that speaking so blatantly about truth helps change the culture. I hope that my dream meant I am healing the wounds of these dear souls.

I may be wrong. I don't have the personal experience to back this up, but I understood from the dream that it has been more difficult for gay men than gay women. Perhaps gay men strike a fear chord in men more deeply than women. I think it is helpful to validate this pain and send healing love to all who have been accosted by society. So to all gay men and woman, on behalf of humanity, I am sorry. I love you. Please forgive me. Thank you.

You can do this too if you would. It is time to melt all barriers and heal all wounds that have gotten us to this point. It is time to celebrate all in diversity and respect and to rip away all the barriers that separate us as children of love.

Hidden in Plain Sight (Why I Woke Up Angry)

I was on the astral plane, which looks and feels a lot like the physical plane, sitting in a huge group of truth seekers. Maybe you were there? It may have registered as being a dream. You may or may not remember it, but you could have been there.

Everyone was there trying to discover truth. It was a huge crowded room with so many chairs crowded around in a circle that many were pushed out by others. It was chaotic, and the very fact that it was in a circle seemed miraculous. The point of the group was to help each other discover truth for themselves.

A very sincere person had a dream experience (funny, a dream interpretation within a dream), and she was seeking answers to what it meant. I was very excited because it was about her discovering her own spiritual truth through a blue light that had a door on it that she didn't notice.

But just as I was about to help her recognize how to access her truth, someone else leaned in front of me to speak. It was a man who runs a local nature center. He got everyone's attention and was about to speak, but he was stalling because he really didn't know what it meant. He was trying to explain it to encourage people to take classes at his nature center. Everyone was attentively listening to him.

I was mad because he was being heard because he was a man with a business. He interrupted me without even recognizing it. He had an agenda to get people to his retreat. And he was making up what he was going to say as he went along. He was duping everyone.

I was also mad at myself for not having the presence to "capture" everyone's attention. I never noticed how offensive that expression was until now. I had no accolades or credentials to back me up. All I had was the answer she was looking for to access her own truth and God center. I am wondering if it is my personality flaw or if it is merely the nature of truth to be hidden in plain sight.

How Humanity Transcends

I just woke up from a very telling experience in the inner realms. I was going to an event with one of my friends. She is someone I have done a few very kind things for in this life. The event was in the top floor of an old building that used to be a church. There were so many levels of stairs that we had to climb that it felt like an incredible task. The friend ran ahead of me with an excuse. She ended up meeting another friend somewhere in the top levels and never looked back to me. I cried like a baby as I continued to the top.

When I got to a level almost to the top, it was a waiting room of a lot of people I was familiar with. I saw a friend or two whom I had really helped with the work I do. Then I saw a lot more people. Each one of them was someone who knew the people I had helped. They knew me but indirectly. No one seemed to particularly like me.

Everyone was standing around or sitting in a hodgepodge of old furniture. No one was talking or having fun. No one seemed excited that they were in attendance of what was supposed to be a fun event. No one talked to me. They weren't interested in me at all. I came all happy, but no one engaged me, not even the friend that I knew.

I ended up sitting with a few other people on a couch that was in the middle of the concrete floor. I could move the couch around easily by pushing it with my feet and I moved it over to talk to my friend, but he was distracted with his other friends and had little to say to me. He seemed to know many people there and was more interested in engaging them. He seemed not to even like me either.

Then another room opened up and there were old outdated games to play. They were situated in a square seating design around the room and everyone could play them. They were so old that they were like antiques, but a lot of people didn't seem to mind and played them as if they didn't notice. I feigned interest and sat at one of the games but couldn't tolerate playing. I got up and could walk outside right from that level. There was more activity outside. There was some joy there and the event started to get lively. People were starting to come alive. Those who just arrived were getting used to not just milling around doing nothing.

There was a young man outside enthralled in working on

a car of some sort. He was to be some kind of kindred spirit to me. As I looked around, people were doing an array of activities outside. They were engaged in so many interesting events. They still weren't engaged with each other as much as possible, but at least they were starting to do things that they loved.

When I woke, I had no idea what this experience meant. I immediately asked my guides. Then it all made sense. The stairs were in a back area of the church. The event was something very important. The stairs represented access to higher consciousness. My friend, whom I had helped, simply used me to access higher consciousness.

She had no affection for me and felt no kinship to me. She simply used me to access higher aspects of herself for her own gain and really had no interest in higher consciousness. She was simply using me to gain access. She is not the only one. Most people I have known in this lifetime have used me this way. My friend who left me showed me that I have been assisting people to gain higher realms this whole life. My tears represented the pain it brought to my human self to love so dearly, knowing I was merely being used when I dearly craved connection.

The fact that the stairs were within an old church that continued so high that it felt like a castle turret represented how people throughout history were trying to access higher consciousness through loyalty to their kingdom and then their religion, but both were outmoded structures. The stairs symbol was used to give an understanding of how long people have been waiting for this event that was taking place in the dream.

The people that I recognized were the people I directly helped through sharing my gifts. Everyone that they knew represented to me how many people were indirectly helped through my sharing what I do. Them having no interest in me showed little understanding of my contribution to them or humanity. They had little understanding of the process of transcendence and of what was actually taking place for them. They seemed not in attendance because it was a wonderful celebration but milled around with the same indifference that they show in their lives.

The fact that they were not mingling showed that people still think they are transcending in a vacuum. Waiting for the doors opening to higher consciousness, people don't realize so many are waiting with them. They are not alone. So many of our experiences on earth have been a conditioning to keep us isolated. It was to prevent us from realizing how connected and empowered we already are.

So as people feel advancement into higher awareness, they are still affected with the brainwashing of going it alone. It is a ploy that has been used in time and space to enslave the masses. It is no longer relevant. In fact, the illusion of time and space has also been used to enslave the masses. People can energetically mingle and connect in love, joy, gratitude and friendship. They have always had that option.

The doors opening up to the next room was people entering the mental realms. As a rule, when you see geometric shapes, puzzles or equations in a dream it is a signal that you are in the mental realms. So many people waiting for higher consciousness were playing the games of the mental realms. Some knew they were outmoded, but many of the people had nostalgia with these old games. They stayed enthralled at the games instead of advancing outside, which represented higher consciousness.

The people outside were starting to relax and feel comfortable. There were no doors to go outside. You needed to merely get up from the mental games and continue to go outside. People there were entertaining themselves by doing what they loved. They were living their purpose. They no longer waited for some invisible host to entertain them or tell them what to do. They did not wait to be told to go outside. They took it upon themselves just to get up from the games and go. They proceeded to create activity and purpose for themselves. This is what higher consciousness is about. You don't need to wait for anything.

There were more and more people making it outside to higher consciousness. Until one goes outside, the party--or life--may seem dreary or tedious. Life is not just waiting around to see how it turns out. You provide the secret sauce to life. So many people made it to this party because I have been sharing love my whole life. They needed me to create this venue for them to figure it out because they were still entrenched in an outmoded system. That is what my writings and healing practices do. It gives everyone access to higher consciousness. The more people that will grasp this understanding and start inviting people to the "party," the sooner higher consciousness will prevail and old consciousness will dry up.

The game room was no more interesting to many of us even though some are still enthralled in war, manipulation and greed. These things are nostalgia for some. The more that people move out of that room and proceed outside, the more those who are playing at the war games will realize they are playing in an empty room. They are then more apt to proceed to higher consciousness as well. This is a simple understanding of how humanity transcends and your part in making that happen.

Also, be happy with the event that we are attending. We have all waited so long for such an event to take place. Can't we just please enjoy it and each other a little better now?

Empowering Yourself in Your Dream

If you ever have a dream where you are being stolen from, deceived, diminished or compromised in some way, address it right in the dream. Get your power back. It is your dream! If you are not able to address it in the dream, go immediately into contemplation upon waking and take back what was taken from you. In doing so, you will be empowering yourself.

Just Hang up on Fear

There are different types of dreams. Some are pure experiences that are happening in real time in the energetic worlds beyond the physical, some are garbled with symbols that need to be deciphered. Some dreams are teaching exercises given from a wise source. It would benefit most people to keep a dream journal to write down their dreams upon awakening. That way, they can know what certain symbols mean and create their own dream interpretation dictionary for themselves.

Dream symbols are very personal. Since each person has had different experiences, someone who is rejuvenated by the water may have a different reason for it showing up in their dream than one who has drowned. Someone who lives in a part of the world that is arid would have a different meaning to dreaming about water than someone who swims daily.

There is another form of dream that is used too often by power groups with agendas. They are dreams of infiltration meant to control the people with fear. They are a means of hitting home a point about something that someone is told they should be afraid of. It shows up in their dream as a reality. It is meant to control what they allow to happen in their Universe based on the dream. It has been used through the evolution of time to keep people fearful and contained.

When facets that are trying to control the masses send them out, they are similar to mass mailings. They are unwanted results and fearful imagery showing up in your dream experiences. Be clear! These dreams are planted by an outside source using power of suggestion. They piggyback on your own personal weaknesses. So they mix the fear with something personal to you. This customizes the affect on you. It sounds strange, but the powers that control the masses understand how this works or else advertising wouldn't be a multi-billion dollar industry. They will use your love of family, children, life and safety and the fear of losing them in a horrifying way to weaken you defenses and gain control of your common sense.

Here is how it happens. When the 2008 elections were coming around, I had recently returned from captivity. Since I was sensory deprived, it heightened my own natural abilities. My perceptions became so acute that I perceived in energy, beyond words and even thoughts. I spent all my time alone and watched and had little influence. But I watched the political conventions because I was fascinated seeing the play of power in energy. After watching one convention, I had a surreal awakened dream experience as a result.

It is hard to describe in words. A movement of one of the political sides was a stream of power that flowed right past me and passionately kissed me on the lips. It was very subtle but pervasive. It slid right in like an oozing stream and came in to seal the deal in winning me over. I was able to see through the ploy. It was a disgusting kiss. But I knew that this is what this agenda was doing, sending out psychic wooing to all those who watched the convention. It was using this tactic because I was love-starved and this would be my weakness if I had one. I was seeing the inner workings of psychic manipulation. I was shown how a person's dreams were violated similarly so a telemarketer can violate dinner time. It happens and the responsibility is upon to the homeowner or the one being violated to just hang up.

I just woke up from a similar dream that was trying to instill fear into me. I understand the agenda so I want to awaken other people who may have gotten this same "mass mailing" of fear in the dream state. The dream was simple. I was on the inside of a house and I couldn't go outside because there were groups of women in black burkas. They had overtaken the path and were mean to me when I tried to walk by. They were talking loud and cackling and this was really distressing to me.

I know by watching the news that the fear point that is being used is that the Islamic State will infiltrate our country. This dream was an energetic deliverance of that fear bomb. This dream had none of the spiritual fiber or richness of my usual dream state. It was specifically showing me what was being sent out to others who are susceptible to this worry. I have had sensitive people tell me that they feel something bad is going to happen. In many cases, they were recipients of these fear bombs.

It puts a personal signature on the fear. It does know how to hook you in, just like a car salesman knows how to look for subtle cues of how to sell you a car. I do not like loud noises. I feel sound as physical touch. So to have people making noise outside my window would be distressing to me. If I were not aware of how the psychic game of dream control worked, I would have woken up very distressed.

But instead, I saw it as an opportunity to dissipate the effectiveness of this mass attempt. The good news is that it was a very diluted attempt to induce fear. But there are people out there who may fall prey. The trick is to assist those who process these dream experiences as real threats to their life and liberty. They don't even have to remember the dream for it to have an impact on their fear level. That is the beauty of such sorcery.

These kinds of things are the exact reason that I focus so much on love. Love is the opposite of fear and love is the cure for fear. If we, as a group, choose love over indulging in fearful imaginings of the onslaught of the enemy, then the attempts of control through fear will be powerless.

People will ask me to get caught up in these streams of fear. I ruthlessly refuse. They believe that I am naive. But I am not. I treat fear the same way a mother would treat a child who was having a temper tantrum. I ignore the child until it stops demanding my attention. It is the way. Whenever one is afraid of something, unless it is an organic fear of their own death, it was instilled there by someone who has something to gain. It really is as simple as this. To make it any more complicated is to give your power away to something besides love.

To choose love in every situation is not naïve, but pure fortitude. This is what Gandhi did; this is what Mother Theresa did. Many of the souls that leave this life in greatness have mastered this ability. We all can do it now. It is time. It is not corny or naive to be kind and loving. That is just another lie of power to prevail.

Love is ruthless in its purity and effectiveness. Love is not weak. Love is pure strength. It is time for us all to forgo looking at love through the cheesecloth of fear. It's time to accept our own masterful skills of knowing love in its entirety. Doing this will abolish fear once and for all.

Love and Life Beyond the Physical Realm

There are things that show up in our life that mean something deeper than what is on the surface. They are clues to help us discover more of who we are beyond the confinement of this one lifetime. They are like dream symbols except they appear in our everyday life. If we know what these symbols mean, we can use them in a similar way as the initial clue in a cryptogram puzzle to unlock a deeper meaning to our lives.

My one friend started seeing a specific species of hawk when her cherished husband crossed over. It would comfort her to see the hawk when she was missing his physical presence. She would hear it screech across the sky at the same time daily as if to reassure her that he still loved her and that they were still a team. She indeed felt his presence whenever she thought of him, was feeling lonely or needed to make a decision about her affairs.

One day, she called me very upset. She saw her hawk

symbol joined by another hawk. There were two of them. They were flying together the whole time she witnessed them. She interpreted this to mean that he had moved on. Sometimes it takes only one wrong thought to waiver us from our center. I would not usually interfere when someone is interpreting their own symbols and tell them that I knew better, but in this case it was the compassionate thing to do.

The second hawk was a symbol for her to know that she and her husband were still together and that the process of him stepping out of the physical body did not dissolve the ties of love between them. There is an aspect of her that is as free as he is and also unencumbered by a physical form. That aspect of her and her husband are still together and still interact as a married couple.

Knowing this was an incentive for my friend to delve deeper into her own dream and astral plane experiences. When one is on the astral plane, it is as real and solid as the physical world is now to us because we are in a body of a similar vibratory rate to the plane of existence. Her husband and she have many adventures still and it all began with her paying attention to her waking symbols and disciplining herself to remember her dreams.

Making the Most of an Addictive Personality

An addiction is a fervent passion for a substance or experience of some kind. It has been deemed a negative trait. But an addictive personality is someone who is driven to find the love and meaning in something beyond themselves. It is almost as if they are aware of the veil of illusion that separates themselves from the incredible love and they are hell-bent on discovering it, even if they have to turn over every stone or look inside every bottle to find what is being withheld just outside of their grasp.

It is a tough thing to get a sense of such incredible love and completion just beyond the horizon of a linear reality. What does one do with that? There is a way to harness that enthusiasm and to get a peak behind the curtain of mediocrity. It is to throw your passion into your purpose.

By doing what you love full throttle, you will be moving beyond the linear conformity and using your passion to manifest an exponential existence. Feeling bad about who you are and what drives you is like translating an expansiveness rainbow into a gray world. We have all done this in shame, guilt, self-loathing and derision.

It is time to use the extra flaps of "us" as winds in the sails of life. Instead of denying our unique attributes so as to conform, use them to propel yourself into awesomeness. Can you imagine a world where all guilt and shame was converted into empowerment? That is what we do here.

You are amazing! You have nothing to feel guilty about. You are wasting energy worrying about insignificant things. You are looking for validation in all the wrong places. You play it meager when you care what others think. You are on the threshold of empowering the masses simply by empowering yourself in the quiet corner of your own world.

Do what you love with the passion of looking for your next fix. Throw yourself into the dynamics of living in unabashed passion. You make angels weep with your sincerity, grace and kindness. It is a noble act to honor this in yourself and convert all the inner conflict into jet fuel to propel yourself into awesome.

It is wonderful to see you burst over the sky.

My Conscious Dream

In the middle of the night, I was helping a client of mine. I was telling the client to look into a straw basket. The basket held all the different aspects of the client. Then I noticed a crazy foreign energy in there that was hiding. It was all tangled and dark, hideous and bad. It hid behind humor and amusement to go unnoticed. It was affecting the client and interfering with the client's life. It needed to go.

I just zapped it out with my intention and electrocuted it and dissipated it. I also used it as a surrogate to zap it out of a whole group of people (maybe all my Facebook friends, maybe more). The electric current from the one in the basket skipped to the one in everyone else. It looked like a web of electrical current scanning the whole group. The thing was gone from everyone. It was just wiped out!

I am sensing that many will feel something gone. Please let me know if you feel different and more at peace. I just like to get a sense of the interconnection of us all and share those insights with others. Because when we care about the betterment of all, it uplifts every single one of us.

Prophetic Dreams of a Wise One

A dear friend who has the most dynamic dreams shared two different dreams with me. They explain the dynamics that are going on between male and female energy in the world.

The first one she told me about had an alpha male acquaintance in it. He kept begging her to come back to him. This was odd because they were never in a relationship. He kept begging and begging but she stood her ground. He finally relinquished and, in doing so, took off a ring and gave it to her. It felt like she was being freed of him and getting her power back.

In the second dream, there was a businessman that has benefited from doing the taps. In the dream he was so happy and enthusiastic. He is a very nice man, but in the dream, he was trying to fit my friend for shoes. He insisted that she wear business attire black loafers. She told him that she didn't need the shoes, but he didn't hear her.

These dreams are conveying how the paradigm shift in the world is being processed by individuals. On some level, male energy knows that women are being empowered, so he is trying to win her back. He is almost insistent on it. This may be reflecting in your lives. The man grants the woman her freedom even though it isn't his to grant.

Then male energy starts getting on board with female energy being empowered, so he wants to help. He believes it is going to look like male energy. That is why the man was insisting on the woman wearing business shoes. He insists that female energy show up similar to male energy. This is not necessarily the case.

Things are changing. Lies are being uncovered, elephants are retiring, women are being empowered, people are dropping their facades and individuals are standing their ground. They are showing up original and unique and blurring the lines.

Release Cowering to Others' Truth

I just got off the phone with a long time client. She was crying because of what she had done in a dream, or more accurately, what she didn't do. She wanted me to help her feel better. But what she didn't realize was that she was tapping into a Universal issue that is relevant to everyone.

In the dream, there was a beloved priest she respected and some of her dear family members. She watched this wonderful man shoot and kill a deer. To her, the deer are sacred. They were all hunting and killing the deer she loved so much. She didn't want to offend them so she said nothing. They continued to kill her beloved friends and piled them up in her kitchen. It was appalling to her and yet she said nothing.

They then delegated people to cook up the excessive amount of her deer friends and she was beside herself. But instead of doing anything about it, she distracted herself and used the excuse that she was too busy. Then she tried to find someone else who she felt was more powerful to talk to the people and stop them from their horrific activities. She did nothing and nothing got done.

She called me as I was writing and tuning into my Spirit Guides. I already knew that there is an annoyance with people who don't share what truth I put out there. There are so many people who benefit from my assistance and yet they don't share what is possible with others. Why don't they share? They are afraid of what others will think. If they are still afraid of something then they are still more fear based than love based. They are using all that I share as ego gratification and not perpetuating truth. So all that I share is not nearly benefiting others as much as it possibly could be.

This longtime client was tapping into a systemic problem in the uplifting of consciousness. People are waiting for other people to share truth or they are waiting for truth to burst out there so they can jump on the bandwagon. They are all waiting and yet doing little to assist. In doing little or nothing, they are adding to the resistance of others to find truth. It is awful that some people can't even recognize the spiritual gift that is being freely given to my client. But what is worse is people who recognize the gift and still hoard it for themselves out of fear or apathy. Shame on them. It is not a shame from any outer source but their own hypocrisy and spiritual paralysis.

There are still so many souls suffering in the world. Innocence is being destroyed every day. People sit back and wring their hands and argue about right action and yet do nothing in sharing the techniques that I so generously and graciously give out to assist in the uplifting of humanity. What self-loathing must go on so people who perceive the truth still refuse to share. And that is what my client was experiencing when she called this morning.

I was so happy that she was being shown what her refusal to perpetuate truth was actually perpetuating the opposite. She was not capable of being a helpless bystander. She was affected by the fate of others. Her acknowledging her missed opportunity was actually a good thing. It was nothing new that she was doing, but now she was aware of the effects of her inability to own her spiritual convictions. Hopefully this message will reach more than just her.

I just put out a huge set of taps to release one's connection with the personification of negative energy. Only one person bothered to share those with others. The Spirit Guides who work diligently to pull people out of suffering were disappointed by this. They were disappointed that such astute people would wield their free will this way. They compel me to write such a post now. If there is one offense to the Spirit Guides, it is an enlightened soul who sits on their laurels.

You can only encourage a soul for so long. At some point they have to unfurl their own wings and fly into the wind to experience the current themselves. Sharing what resonates is a good way to test the currents before one is ready to fly.

(Say each statement three times out loud while continuously tapping on the top of your head at the crown chakra and say it a fourth time while tapping on your chest at the heart chakra.)

"I declare myself a surrogate for society in doing these taps; in all moments."

"I release cowering to others' truth; in all moments."

"I release the belief that others' truth is more important than mine; in all moments."

"I release dismissing my truth as weak, wrong, or misguided; in all moments."

"I release avoiding accountability by cowering to others' truth; in all moments."

"I release the lack of understanding by cowering to others' truth; in all moments."

"I release all the fear that has been instilled in me that causes me to cower to others' truth; in all moments."

"I release blindly accepting the fate that cowering to

others' truth defaulted to me; in all moments."

"I release blindly adhering to others' truth; in all moments."

"I release being enslaved to others' truth; in all moments."

"I release the belief that I need to cower to others' truth; in all moments."

"I release giving my power to cowering to others' truth; in all moments."

"I release giving my carte blanche proxy by cowering to others' truth; in all moments."

"I extract all the fear that others' truth has put on me; in all moments."

"I release my individuality being thwarted by cowering to others' truth; in all moments."

"I release being deduced to a statistic by cowering to others' truth; in all moments."

"I release blindly adhering to cowering to others' truth as my truth; in all moments"

"I release ignoring my gut reaction in regards to cowering to others' truth; in all moments."

"I release dissipating my own effectiveness by cowering to others' truth; in all moments."

"I remove all vivaxes between myself and cowering to others' truth; in all moments."

"I remove all tentacles between myself and cowering to others' truth; in all moments."

"I remove the long ugly claws of cowering to others' truth from my beingness; in all moments."

"I remove all engrams that cowering to others' truth has put on me; in all moments."

"I remove all programming and conditioning that cowering to others' truth has put on me; in all moments."

"I send all energy matrices into the light that cause me to cower to others' truth; in all moments."

"I command all complex energy matrices that cause me to cower to others' truth to be escorted into the light by my guides; in all moments."

"I recant all vows and agreements between myself and cowering to others' truth; in all moments."

"I remove all blessings between myself and cowering to others' truth; in all moments."

"I remove all curses between myself and cowering to others' truth; in all moments."

"I sever all strings, cords and wires between myself and cowering to others' truth; in all moments."

"I dissolve all karmic ties between myself and cowering to others' truth; in all moments."

"I remove all the pain, burden, fear, limitations,

disconnectedness, futility, unworthiness and illusion of separateness that cowering to others' truth has put on me; in all moments."

"I take back all the joy, love, abundance, freedom, health, life, wholeness and ability to discern that cowering to others' truth has taken from me; in all moments."

"I shift my paradigm from cowering to others' truth to the joy, love, abundance, freedom, life, the ability to discern and wholeness of my own divinity; in all moments."

"I transcend cowering to others' truth; in all moments."

"I am centered and empowered in the joy, love, abundance, freedom, life, ability to discern and wholeness of my own divinity; in all moments."

Simha, the Dream Hero

I was very tired today but was compelled to go to a grocery store that is pretty far away. For some reason, I had to go to this particular store. I finally got the motivation to get into the car and drive much farther than usual. It wasn't very busy when Simha and I arrived.

As we went into the main door, a woman coming out of the store started talking to Simha. She seemed very excited. She told Simha that she knew her. Then she looked at me and told me that Simha came to her in a dream and helped her. We had never seen this woman before, but I am used to people telling me that I have helped them in the dream state so it wasn't that strange to me.

The woman told me the whole experience. She said she was very scared in her dream. It was pitch dark and there was a fork in the road. She did not know what to do. Suddenly, Simha came out of nowhere and put the woman on her back. Simha then carried the woman away to safety.

She said that she knew it was Simha because she had the same white around her mouth. We hugged and she left so grateful to meet her dream hero. That was the reason I had to go to this grocery store exactly when I did. This woman needed to meet her dream hero.

Taking Classes in the Dream State

There are some dreams that are universal and occur again and again during the course of our lives. One of them is the dream of being in school.

Many people think that heaven is a stagnant state of consciousness, that nothing happens after you cross. But this is the furthest thing from the truth. In fact, your spiritual education is more relevant after you cross than it is in your waking life.

It is because this lifetime may seem like you are taking a vacation from the spiritual journey. You may be here to rest which is equivalent to taking a light load of credits in college. In fact, this lifetime could be dedicated to learning one pesky lesson that has been elusive such as compassion, gratitude or self-love.

Many people will have a dream of being in a classroom or of taking a test that they are failing. It is their higher self reminding them that they are here to learn and grow. They are not here to forget their studies. They are not here to be indifferent and unaware.

Everyone's lesson is personal. What one person has learned, another person may struggle with. This is true on earth as well. When we remember we are here to learn, it changes our perspective. It gives us the overview to understanding. We may be able to exude more compassion when we don't take the homework so seriously.

When one has a dream of being in school, they should pay attention to the details. Pay attention to the other students, the teacher, the classroom and the lesson. This is your higher self giving you a clue whether you are progressing in your particular lesson or not. For example, if the other students are people you knew in your past, it could be telling you that you are lagging behind on your lesson. Perhaps you are stuck in the past.

Everything is relevant to you. There is no need to be concerned when you land in a classroom in the dream state. It could merely be a reminder that you are a student of life and whatever you may think is important in your life may not even be a question on the test.

The Capacity of Women to Love

I was shown in the dream state one night the incredible capacity of women to love, the amazing things she will overlook and how she can forge a whole amazing life out of remnants and promises of potential. Also, how her shifting this dynamic is vital to the upgrade of humanity.

In the dream state, I was shown all the ways I invested incredible energy into the possibility of a relationship with never really receiving much back. I used all my resources, ingenuity and creativity to prop up a man who seemed totally indifferent to me. With my creative imagination and hope chest of possibilities, I forged a subpar partner with this man of my dreams. His only real gift, from what I could see in the dream, is that he tolerated me.

In the dream, this short, balding, unattractive man was the object of my desire. (In true female form, competition is distasteful to me so I chose someone that I didn't have to compete with any woman for.) He was renovating a bar as a business. (I don't drink or enjoy being in settings where people drink.) He was spending his days there as if the bar were already open and he was a great success. (Lack of awareness on his part of the disconnect between trying to be successful and really being successful.)

In the dream, he was too lazy and disinterested to really be a success. But I was his cheerleader and this fed that need in him to seem successful. This man never talked to me directly (disinterested in me). Yet I was enamored with every aspect of him. I exuded love and filled myself just with the thought of him. (I was feeding my own need for love and gave him the credit when he was doing nothing to deserve it.)

I would wait on him in all the ways that made me happy to do so. He was indifferent to me and took my efforts for granted. In the dream, I poured him fresh cream for his coffee. (Since I have recently gone off dairy and opposed using dairy in my personal life, it was showing me how I compromise my values to please him.)

He had a friend who needed a job. There was someone paying for a part-time painter. I negotiated with the person hiring to work out all the details so I could bring the job to his friend. I was at first going to give it to someone I have put all my creative energy into supporting in the past in hopes that this would make him want a relationship with me. (They were showing me all the time and energy I wasted in this life pouring myself into a man to make him a success simply for the promise of having a relationship.)

In the dream, I was so happy. I was full of love, promise, hope for the future, desire to have a baby and love for this man who was safe and indifferent to me. In the dream, he did not waste an ounce of energy thinking or caring about me. He simply tolerated me. The dream was showing me, so painfully and clearly how unbalanced my dynamics are with men. The unworthiness I exuded in myself was polar opposite to the great lengths and ingenuity I could exude and how empowered I could feel in imagining this lump of coal as a diamond.

It is not easy to admit this. When I was a child, my father and grown brothers never talked to me. They ignored me completely as I used the stockade of energy of my new life force to try and please them. This was the role I was imprinted with. Being ignored and waiting on a man was synonymous to me with the innate love I felt as a child, the love that just permeated my essence. It was my own energy field that was buffering me in love and contentment and keeping me exuded in the joy of giving. The man was just really a prop to induce my perpetual state of dynamo.

This is how my life was until too many humiliations, defilements and abuses threw my energy system out of whack. It wasn't that men had changed towards me. They were consistent. It was my own energy system that got broken. It was my energy system that was feeding me so much love, contentment, ingenuity and possibilities. Too bad I had to waste all that energy by directing it to a lost cause.

The dream gave me hope. Not for myself, but for all women and men out there. If I was having this experience in the dream state, then it was being pumped into the awareness of the collective. Humanity was receiving a dose of awareness and an upgrade in how they debase themselves, even desecrate themselves for others.

I sensed that the dynamics that I was becoming aware of in the dream experience were infusing awareness into all the relationships in the world where one person takes on the role of martyring the reverence of their beautiful life force in deference to an indifferent participant.

It also showed me how female energy could use the tsunami of hope and potential that they pump into the succubus of male based intentions to actually heal the world of all its transgressions. If they would only remove men from their targets and shower their love on the world. In a way, by empowering the indifference of male slanted intentions, it is actually female energy that is feeding the imbalance of the world simply by pouring all of her love and intentions into the shortsightedness of male energy.

This dream showed me how it is a relatively simple shift. A little awareness goes a long way.

The Inner Exchange

When I have dream experiences, sometimes they seem as real as being awake in the physical. Because they are. It's just that there are so many other experiences happening in the dream state because we aren't beholden to linear time on the other side. It is an exponential experience and the physical brain has to filter it down to a linear timeline and perception. So much is lost in the remembering or translation.

On the other side, I was sitting in a mall terminal with lots of empty seats around me. Simha and I were waiting for our journey back to the physical world. Two young women came over and sat next to me. Right next to me.

There were hundreds of seats around and they wanted to sit next to me. I was so angry.

I got up and started ranting at how inconsiderate they were. They didn't care. They felt entitled. They thought nothing of violating my privacy. So I let the older of the two women have it. I told her that her feelings of entitlement were the reason she was so unhappy. In fact, her selfish disregard of others is what caused her to have such severe depression. This took her aback.

She wondered how I knew about the depression. She thought I must have seen her pick up depression medicine at one point. I just told her no. "I am a dynamic healer and it is obvious that your selfishness is related to the depression." This she took in. It ruminated within her. It was a seed for a change in consciousness.

Maybe I will meet her in this physical world at some point. Our connection was already formulated in the more subtle realms. When I woke up, it was like having a great epiphany for all those who suffer from depression. Perhaps they need to focus less on themselves and more on others. This doesn't quite sound earth shattering now, but it does seem to be a seed for all those who are looking for away out of it.

The worst thing you can do when receiving a diagnosis is to curl up into it and let it define you. The diagnosis is something to push off from and swim into healthier waters instead of wearing it like a martyr or a victim. Those who are vested in a business of disease would want you to do that. But that is more to define their importance rather that your own empowerment.

The Righteous Complaint

Recently, I had a bad experience with a local professional. I wanted to write an online review of my interaction under the ruse of helping other people. But it really was a desire to vent or to punish him for not treating me the way I wished him to treat me. The motive was ego driven.

That night, in a dream, I was in the man's home. It was very hectic. I was hired to be a nanny, but the children were all over the place. The house was really unorganized and it had several scattered rooms that seemed not to be related to the rest of the house. The father was trying to give me a tour and instructions of how to take care of the kids. But he couldn't even find them in the house. It was so chaotic that he didn't know where the baby was and the other kids were left unsupervised.

When I woke up, I immediately received the spiritual message of the dream. If I chose to interfere in this man's life through writing a bad review, I would be involving myself in his personal affairs. By doing this, I would, on some subtle level, be responsible for the care of his personal life. It was not worth the satisfaction of writing an unkind post.

Visiting Loved Ones Who Have Passed

The thing is that we visit our loved ones that are passed in the dream state. It is so much like being here when we are unencumbered by the physical body that it is very healing. It is like everyday life. The only problem is that most people don't remember it when they awake. This causes a bit of a frustration for our loved ones on the other side who have just visited with us and then have to see us be sad in the morning when we drop back into our physical body.

Worlds Within

There are incredible worlds of beauty and wonder within ourselves. We have to sort through the silt of our physical life to get to it. That is what many dreams do. In a way, our physical issues rise to the top, close to our conscious psyche, to be dealt with and released. They are sometimes intense enough to be thought of as nightmares.

Those Who Trap Souls

A client had an inner experience. Her dreams have become so real and interactive that they deserve a distinction from the passive experiences of dreams. She has developed this skill simply by regularly writing down her dreams as she woke, also by willing herself to participate in the experiences she witnesses.

In the experience, she was driving into a discount store. The driveway was partially hidden by bushes so she drove in blindly. When she got in the driveway, she realized it was really a dead end with no way to turn around. She locked up the car and went into the store. The manager confronted her. He said he had to confiscate her car because it was parked where it did not belong. From her training to be proactive, my client fought to get the car back.

Her car represented her ability to travel in the inner dimensions. The discount store represented groups that offer a shortcut to heaven without the individual learning spiritual law where love is exemplified. The driveway being a dead end represents the doctrine of religious beliefs that don't allow you an "out" if you see that they lead nowhere. The store manager is a power monger who uses deceit to trap souls and rob them of their ability to explore the inner realms. The truth is that love is the true coin to expand one's consciousness and ensure spiritual freedom.

It was this woman's ability and capacity to love that empowered her to stand up to the manager of the store and maintain her freedom. Of course, she is confident that I will assist her if she ever gets in a jam. The beauty of doing this particular set of taps is that you don't need to know who is trying to trap soul. You just need to do them and be reassured that you are insuring the freedom of the multitudes. You will be helping souls who will never ever recognize your assistance.

(Say each statement three times while tapping on your head and say it a fourth time while tapping on your chest.)

"We declare ourselves surrogates for humanity in doing these taps; in all moments."

"We release being manipulated by all those who trap soul; in all moments."

"We release being deceived by all those who trap soul; in all moments."

"We release the genetic propensity to accept those who trap soul; in all moments."

"We release being suckered by those who trap soul; in all moments."

"We release being blind, deaf, and mute to our subtle senses; in all moments."

"We awaken all our subtle senses; in all moments."

"We release needing those who trap soul to feel safe; in all moments."

"We release being stuck in the primal mode of fear; in all moments."

"We release being shackled to those who trap soul; in all moments."

"We release owing all those who trap soul to be our common denominator; in all moments."

"We release being subjugated by those who trap soul; in all moments."

"We release being poisoned with those who trap soul; in all moments."

"We release being enslaved to those who trap soul; in all moments."

"We release being enslaved by those who trap soul; in all moments."

"We nullify all contracts between ourselves and all those who trap soul; in all moments."

"We release all systemic allegiance to those who trap soul; in all moments."

"We remove all vivaxes between ourselves and all those who trap soul; in all moments."

"We remove all tentacles between ourselves and all those who trap soul; in all moments."

"We remove the claws of all those who trap soul from our beingness; in all moments."

"We release being ruled by those who trap soul; in all moments."

"We remove all programming and conditioning that all those who trap soul have put on us; in all moments."

"We remove all engrams of all those who trap soul; in all moments."

"We send all energy matrices of all those who trap soul into the Light and Sound; in all moments."

"We command all complex energy matrices of all those who trap soul to be escorted into the Light and Sound; in all moments."

"We send all energy matrices into the Light and Sound that perpetuate all those who trap soul; in all moments."

"We command all complex energy matrices that perpetuate all those who trap soul to be escorted into the Light and Sound; in all moments."

"We recant all vows and agreements between ourselves and all those who trap soul; in all moments."

"We strip all illusion off of all those who trap soul; in all moments."

"We remove all masks, walls, and armor from all those who trap soul; in all moments."

"We shatter all glass ceilings that all those who trap soul have put on us; in all moments."

"We eliminate the first cause in regards to all those who trap soul; in all moments."

"We remove all curses between ourselves and all those who trap soul; in all moments."

"We remove all blessings between ourselves and all those who trap soul; in all moments."

"We strip all entitlement off of all those who trap soul; in all moments."

"We remove all the pain, burden, and limitations that all those who trap soul have put on us; in all moments."

"We remove all the fear, futility and unworthiness that all those who trap soul have put on us; in all moments."

"We remove all the apathy, indifference, and devastation that all those who trap soul have put on us; in all moments."

"We remove all the rejection, abandonment, and illusion of separateness that all those who trap soul have put on us; in all moments."

"We remove all that we have put on all others due to all those who trap soul; in all moments."

"We take back all that all those who trap soul have taken from us; in all moments."

"We give back all that we have taken from others due to all those who trap soul; in all moments."

"We collapse and dissolve all those who trap soul; in all moments."

"We release resonating or emanating with all those who trap soul; in all moments."

"We extract all those who trap soul from our sound frequency; in all moments."

"We extract all those who trap soul from our light emanation; in all moments."

"We extract all those who trap soul from all 32 layers of our auric field; in all moments."

"We extract all those who trap soul from our whole beingness; in all moments."

"We abolish all those who trap soul as a construct; in all moments."

"We shift our paradigm from all those who trap soul to Love and Acceptance; in all moments."

"We transcend all those who trap soul; in all moments."

"We are centered and empowered in Universal Love and Spiritual Freedom; in all moments."

"We resonate, emanate, and are interconnected with all life in Universal Love and Spiritual Freedom; in all moments."

*Soul is like the word fish here in that it is the same word for plural and singular.

Utilizing the Dream State for Self-Growth

Many people think that dreams are random. This is not my truth. Dreams are our higher wisdom's attempts to awaken us. But there is a curtain between this life and our wholeness to prevent us from being overwhelmed here by the vastness of our experiences. The curtain that divides the states of awakening and our physical existence are as dividing as they need to be. The more we are committed to delving into ourselves, the more we will be shown. For some, it is a thin veil that divides the two states.

I never share my dreams. But I was guided to do so with a dream that I woke up from to show others how to carry the information of the dreams into their contemplative state to empower themselves.

In my dream, the town was in a frenzy. It was terrified about running out of food. As I was walking over the bridge into town, I noticed there were feces next to the river. The porta potties were filled so people were defecating next to them. The river was contaminated as well.

In town, the supermarket was in a frenzy. The shelves were being emptied and everyone was in chaos. I walked around calm. The deli clerk offered me some items and I politely refused. I was calm and nonreactive.

When I awoke, I immediately knew what this dream was about for me. It was a message for me, not some generic person but for me. It was utilizing all my experiences to show me an aspect of myself a little better.

Here is what my dream means to me: Since I was starved nearly to death a few years ago, it has been difficult for me to suppress the urge to eat. If I get hungry, it creates a panic attack in me. The same has been true with exercise. Doing either creates the trauma in me that I existed in during that year of captivity. The frenzied people in the dream are my cells. They are panicking because I have been successfully dieting for the last five months. They are terrified of being starved to death. Also, the feces are all the toxins that my body is dumping more quickly than the river can carry away. But my higher awareness walked around the store knowing that everything will be fine. It was calm and nonreactive.

Using this information, I can improve my state of affairs in contemplation. In a quiet time, I merely go to the town and reassure all the town's people (which are the cells of my body) that they will not go hungry. I replace all the bakery items on the shelf with vitamins and water that are very filling and plentiful. I visualize everyone calming down and being happy with the lighter improvements to the local diet. I see everyone working and productive and happy. I see the feces (which represents the byproducts and toxins of losing weight) being cleaned up and the river washing away and clear. I visualize the sun shining, everyone happy and productive, many children playing and laughing and everyone satisfied.

Any dream that one has is the ability to recreate themselves in their desired state. This is not random. It is a tool for all to use. Some will say that they don't remember their dreams, but it is because the indifference made them stop looking at them. Tell yourself before you go to sleep at night to remember your dreams. And when you wake up, figure out how to use the information that you have been given to improve your quality of life.

Why You Are Dreaming More

Because we are so much more than the physical us, you are now becoming privy to your true activities. They should almost feel like real experiences now instead of broken up symbols. We are all working very hard to assist the raise in consciousness of humanity. I wake up sometimes just to rest.

Your Christmas Gift to the World

I just woke up from a disturbing dream. It was about a Christmas party. Everyone was going to see the new baby. But the focus was all on the older sibling. There were no snacks, no gifts, no warmth and no joy in going to this event. Everyone was in their new clothes, but it didn't matter because nobody appreciated anyone else. Being all decked out in a setting where no one cared made everyone feel uncomfortable in their own skin. It is like they were always so unhappy but without any warmth around them, they felt it more.

The five year old was worshiped. Everything was about her. There was no place to really sit but the child had the couch to stand on. They were singing songs out of a megaphone. They were cute, but it was mandated to adore them so people were over it. The child was singing really loud and was to be on television to sell their very expensive clothes. The proceeds would go to buying them more clothes.

At one point, I was going to play along and sing a song with them. But I had to stand on a lopsided stacking of toys to emulate the child's height of standing on the back of the couch. I could not make a usable stool to stand on. A few of us went to the counter where the drinks were supposed to be served. It was laughable. There was just an empty counter next to an overflowing trash container of empty cups.

Everyone knew it was a joyless party and planned to leave to find somewhere they could go dancing. We made our excuses and everyone was leaving early together. As we were leaving, one of the guests started mentioning the death of Lincoln and how it would be interesting to write a script around that. There was a bit of support for that as we left.

This dream had very deep meaning. The obnoxious toddler is what we have allowed the holiday to morph into. It was supposed to be honoring the birth of something sacred, but it has morphed into indulging the worst traits of our character that are taught to and developed in our children. That is what we do when we indulge them to the degree that is happening. When we shamelessly spoil children in the name of all that is sacred, we do a disservice to all of humanity. This loveless party was what society has become. The baby never even made an appearance. It was all about the spoiled rotten child accumulating more.

The lack of snacks and warmth was symbolic of there not being anything offered in a spiritual sense to anyone who attended the party. It was only an exercise in wearing new clothes with no joy or goodness imbued in the process. The void feeling in the guests is the byproduct of all the focus being on the child. There was none left for anyone else. Everyone was conditioned to go along with the joyless party and only secretly mocked the derided feeling of being obligated to attend. This depicts the lack of reverence in general.

Society has morphed into a demonstrative display of greed by using the baby (the birth of Christ) merely as an excuse to indulge. My trying to perform next to the child on a stool made of toys to bring some meaning back to the party was very important. It meant that no one is able to bring meaning back into society because of the limitations set up by outmoded belief systems. The toys represent limitations in beliefs, laws and doctrines that prevented anyone from gaining empowerment, awakening or transcending in totally following societal dictates.

The empty cups meant that all the sweetness and benefits that could possibly be accessed through the holiday have long been drunk by guests who had come and gone. That the holiday has nothing to offer in sustenance except what one can possibly bring to it themselves. It has been overtaken long ago by materialism. Our society is totally depleted and devoid of being able to offer anything to its members except what the members bring to the table to share with others. All outlets of groups giving to the individuals have been bankrupt due to excessive materialism.

People leaving early is indicative of people showing up in society out of obligation but going somewhere else to express their spirituality. The woman wanting to write a script was showing how female energy is now being used in the attempt to freshen the old state of consciousness of society to prevent it from bleeding attendees. This is something to be aware of and we are already seeing it transpire in the media by propping women up in male energy roles to seem like they are embracing female energy. Anything based on physical attributes and competitiveness is male energy. The child in the dream was a pretty little girl. It depicted the short shelf life on physical attributes. Everyone else at the party was treated as irrelevant.

Here is your gift to the world. You can assist people everywhere in bowing out of worshipping materialism in the guise of paying homage to what is sacred.

(Say each statement a total of four times. The first three times, say it while tapping continuously on the top of your head. Say it the fourth time while tapping on your chest.)

"We declare ourselves surrogates for humanity in doing these taps; in all moments."

"We release being manipulated by materialism; in all moments."

"We release being deceived by materialism; in all moments."

"We release the genetic propensity to be materialistic; in all moments."

"We release being stuck in the primal mode of materialism; in all moments."

"We release being shackled to materialism; in all moments."

"We release allowing materialism to be our common denominator; in all moments."

"We release being subjugated by materialism; in all moments."

"We release being surrounded by materialism; in all moments."

"We release being indebted to materialism; in all moments."

"We nullify all contracts between ourselves and all materialism; in all moments."

"We convert all materialism back into Joy, Love, Abundance, Freedom, Health, Success, Truth and Wholeness; in all moments."

"We release all loyalty to materialism; in all moments."

"We remove all vivaxes between ourselves and all materialism; in all moments."

"We remove all tentacles between ourselves all materialism; in all moments."

"We remove the claws of all materialism from our beingness; in all moments."

"We release being ruled by materialism; in all moments."

"We extract all materialism from our understanding of spirituality; in all moments."

"We remove all programming and conditioning that materialism has put on us; in all moments."

"We remove all engrams of materialism from our beingness; in all moments."

"We send all energy matrices of materialism into the Light and Sound; in all moments."

"We command all complex energy matrices of materialism to be escorted into the Light and Sound; in all moments."

"We send all energy matrices into the Light and Sound that intrude upon our spiritualty; in all moments."

"We command all complex energy matrices that intrude upon our spirituality to be escorted into the Light and Sound; in all moments."

"We recant all vows and agreements between ourselves and materialism; in all moments."

"We strip all illusion off of materialism in all forms; in all moments."

"We remove all masks, walls, and armor from mass

materialism; in all moments."

"We shatter all glass ceilings that materialism has put on us; in all moments."

"We eliminate the first cause in regards to materialism; in all moments."

"We remove all curses between ourselves and materialism; in all moments."

"We remove all blessings between ourselves and materialism; in all moments."

"We strip all entitlement off of all those immersed in materialism; in all moments."

"We remove all the pain, burden, and limitations that materialism has put on us; in all moments."

"We remove all the fear, futility and unworthiness that materialism has put on us; in all moments."

"We remove all the apathy, indifference, and devastation that materialism has put on us; in all moments."

"We remove all the rejection, abandonment, and illusion of separateness that materialism has put on us; in all moments."

"We remove all that we have put on all others due to materialism; in all moments."

"We take back all that materialism has taken from us; in all moments."

"We give back all that we have taken from others due to materialism; in all moments."

"We collapse and dissolve all materialism; in all moments."

"We release resonating or emanating with materialism; in all moments."

"We extract all materialism from our Sound Frequency; in all moments."

"We extract all materialism from our Light Emanation; in all moments."

"We extract all materialism from all 32 layers of our auric field; in all moments."

"We extract all materialism from our whole beingness; in all moments."

"We abolish all materialism as a construct; in all moments."

"We shift our paradigm from materialism to Joy, Love, Abundance, Freedom, Health, Success, Truth and Wholeness; in all moments."

"We transcend materialism; in all moments."

"We are centered and empowered in Universal Joy, Love, Abundance, Freedom, Health, Success, Truth and Wholeness; in all moments."

"We resonate, emanate, and are interconnected with all

life in Universal Joy, Love, Abundance, Freedom, Health, Success, Truth and Wholeness; in all moments."

Dampen Psychic Energy

Last night in the dream state, I spent time with the displaced children. I was with a couple of boys who were brothers. One was a teen about twelve and one was about six. They are numb and dazed. We were having lunch in a cramped space with a lot of others in cramped space. I was merely being present with them so they did not feel alone.

I was able to mock up the nurturing love of their parents. If their parents weren't so traumatized, they may be able to be present for themselves even from afar. But they are trapped in an experience of terror. That terror creates psychic energy that those who created the situation harvest to use for mass control. It is not unlike the monsters in *Monsters, Inc.* scaring the children to fuel their energy grids. There is a grain of truth in fiction.

I was acting as a presence to love and nurture the children so that they can stay whole during this insanity that is using them as scapegoats. I would implore everyone who reads this to put their attention on spending time with the children during the time they sleep.

Just simply set the intention before you fall to sleep. Simply say to yourself; "I go to the children who are being imprisoned."

Or, "I go to those who are most in need of love."

Pay attention to your dreams. The experience may seem so normal (because it is beyond the conscious mind), that you may overlook its importance. But it is very important. Go to the people in the world that are being traumatized the most. You may show up to them as a Guardian Angel, a friend or merely a kind stranger. Love and support them as much as possible.

Dampen the psychic energy that is being used to perpetuate fear and control. When people are afraid, they revert to primal mode. In primal mode, people's higher abilities to reason are deactivated and they are easier to control. LOVE DAMPENS THE PSYCHIC ENERGIES OF CONTROL. In being loving, you will be preventing those in power from perpetuating further egregious acts.

SECTION THREE: INSPIRATION

All People Are Takers

All people are takers if you choose to see them that way. You may well bring that out in them if that is what you choose to see. I prefer to look past all the clouds and see the sunshine of love within everyone because everyone is kind and wishes to give from the heart. This is how I see everyone. I may get my heart broken once in a while, but I much prefer that than living with a heart that is mangled and distorted to see only bad things in others.

The world is a horrible, ugly place for so many. This is what they choose to see. They nod and agree with each other's evidence of how awful things are. They lament over politics and global issues and, in doing so, they pour their beautiful essence into feeding such beasts.

Or, the world is a magical, wonderful place where the human heart shows evidence of resilience, patience, fortitude and kindness a billion times a minute all over the world. Individuals are loving, dreaming, and creating amazing wonders to bring joy, comfort and relief to the multitudes. The world is changing, shifting and morphing to manifest wonders beyond the concepts that are presently fathomable.

You matter. Where you focus matters. Which reality you invest your energy into matters. The milk of human kindness is a real essence. You have access to an exponential bounty of it. Yes, you are empowered. May you be empowered in beauty, wonder, luster and light. May you feel my love in the invisible ether and awaken you to a new dawn of enlightenment.

We do this together in our agreement and approval to do so. Let's choose the wonder.

An Exercise to Transform Every Moment into Feeling Like a Holiday

(Say each statement three times while tapping on your head and then say it a fourth time while tapping on your chest. Complete each statement the four times and then move onto the next one.)

"I declare myself a surrogate for all life in doing these taps; in all moments."

"I release being enslaved to the past; in all moments."

"I release dipping into the past; in all moments."

"I release pulling the past into the moment; in all moments."

"I release weaving the past into the moment; in all moments."

"I remove all vivaxes between myself and the past; in all moments."

"I remove all vivaxes between the past and the moment; in all moments."

"I remove the claws of the past from the moment; in all moments."

"I remove all tentacles between the past and the moment; in all moments."

"I remove all programming and conditioning that the past has put on the moment; in all moments."

"I remove all engrams of the past from the moment; in all moments."

"I remove the physical onslaught of the past from the moment; in all moments."

"I remove the emotional onslaught of the past from the moment; in all moments."

"I remove the hiccup of past experiences from the moment; in all moments."

"I remove the echo of past experiences from the moment; in all moments."

"I remove the mental onslaught of the past from the moment; in all moments."

"I release allowing the past to disturb the calm of the moment; in all moments."

"I release allowing the past to disturb the joy, love, and abundance of the moment; in all moments."

"I release allowing the past to disturb the freedom, health, or success of the moment; in all moments."

"I release allowing the past to disturb the peace, life, or wholeness of the moment; in all moments."

"I release allowing the past to disturb the beauty, enthusiasm, or contentment of the moment; in all moments."

"I release allowing the past to disturb the spirituality, enlightenment, or confidence of the moment; in all moments."

"I release allowing the past to disturb the interconnectedness, empowerment or ability to discern in the moment; in all moments."

"I strip all illusion off of the past; in all moments."

"I remove all masks, walls, and armor of the past from the moment; in all moments."

"I dissolve in the light and sound all energy matrices of the past; in all moments."

"I command all complex energy matrices of the past that inflict themselves on the moment to be dissolved in the light and sound ;in all moments."

"I release being pulled out of the moment by the past; in all moments."

"I release being led around by the past; in all moments."

"I nullify all contracts between the moment and the past; in all moments."

"I recant all vows and agreements between the moment and the past; in all moments."

"I remove all curses between the moment and the past; in all moments."

"I remove all blessings between the moment and the past; in all moments."

"I sever all strings, cords, and wires between the moment and the past; in all moments."

"I dissolve all karmic ties between the moment and the past; in all moments."

"I withdraw all the energy of the moment from the past; in all moments."

"I remove all the pain, burden, and limitations that the past has inflicted on the moment; in all moments."

"I remove all the fear, futility, and unworthiness that the past has inflicted on the moment; in all moments."

"I remove all the primal urges and archaic structures that the past has inflicted on the moment; in all moments."

"I remove all the beliefs, rituals and illusion of separateness that the past has inflicted on the moment; in all moments."

"I shatter all glass ceilings of the past from the moment; in all moments."

"I collapse and dissolve the past; in all moments."

"I release the moment resonating with the past; in all moments."

"I release the moment emanating with the past; in all moments."

"I extract all of the past from the moment; in all moments."

"I extract all of the past from the moment's sound frequency; in all moments."

"I extract all of the past from the moment's light emanation; in all moments."

"I shift the paradigm of the moment to totally in the moment; in all moments."

"The moment transcends the past; in all moments."

"I am centered, empowered and imbued totally in the moment; in all moments."

"I resonate, emanate and am interconnected with all life exponentially and perpetually in the moment; in all moments."

At No One's Expense

Ever since I was a little girl, I used to be kind and do the right thing to gain the approval of my team of Spirit Guides. It has proved a good technique for me. I have gained insights and incredible strengths that others don't yet recognize in themselves. I tirelessly work on being the kindest, most noble person I can be despite the horrific outer experiences and heartbreak that I have endured. I did it to emulate my Spirit Guides and resonate with the same caliber as them.

Why would I mimic people? They are the ones that offend, scorn, humiliate and ignore. I would prefer to see others not as the wounded souls they appear to be but as the Spirit Guides they are in training to be. In doing so, perhaps I may hasten their tutelage. Perhaps soon we will all walk this earth as Ascended Masters. Then we will have a good belly laugh at no one's expense.

Awakening

Within crusted walls of embedded emotion

Bombarded by waves of perpetual commotion

Is a permanent "me" determined to stand

Slough off adversity like layers of sand.

Draw in the Light from a far away source

To stand firm in the Love seems par for the course

Reverberating in music, a most precious choir

Break through the dross, confusion and mire

Emanate, vibrate, reverberate, resound

Be inundated with such beauty I unfurl and rebound

Show others imprisoned what awakening can be

Humbly resonating loving and free.

Be a Visionary

We limit each other all the time. This statement is limiting in itself. Language started out in the caveman days to convey vital information. But any time one puts a cap on the actions of another or holds the other person's experiences as truth, we are all held to the lowest common denominator. Only the lowest bar is achieved.

How many times have we all heard, "You are going to get sick if you...," "If you don't do this, you will...," "You will fall and break your neck if you..."? We aren't even putting our own experiences on others; we are burdening the human spirit with fears we have grandfathered in from wherever.

The four-minute mile, breaking the sound barrier, every stride in civil rights were all thought impossible to achieve. It took someone to see beyond the immediate horizon to raise the bar for all and for others to agree that it is a worthy reality. All it takes is someone, anyone, to hold true to a higher vision and for others to open up their consciousness to allow it to manifest. It may start as only a door cracked open, but there will be a tipping point to a Universal belief system. And when resistance is met, and the opposing view screams louder, it is evidence that the consciousness is being stretched into realization.

Here are some of the visions I hold. Please feel free to hold them with me:

Spontaneous healing

Disease wiped out of the analogues of human experience

Joy, Love, Abundance and Freedom for every individual

Communicating through nonverbal cues

All beings supporting each other

Accessing energy sources that don't deplete the planet

People thinking and creating for themselves

Everyone contributing their gifts

All life, including plant, animal and mineral being valued

Interplanetary travel and community

Mass forms of control and manipulation being wiped out

Nature being valued and protected

Universal kindness resurfacing on a mass scale

Music, dance and self-expression being the norm.

Please don't mistake a visionary with someone in denial and feel the need to point out all the ills in the world. I am not naive. I have consciously witnessed atrocities that would keep many adults up nights, but I have also seen and loved past them. So can everyone if they choose. Light can only be snuffed out for a while, but it is the eternal. Light and love always prevail.

Becoming Free

Peace is your birthright. If you do not have peace, you may have to forgo some of the trappings of illusion to reestablish it as a mainstay. Do this by challenging the things that do not nurture you and see if they are worth the discord that they provide.

For example, if you are living your life for the love and respect of others, do an inventory of whether their love and respect has the street value that you once believed that it did. See if those that they do respect are actually living such a glamorous life. Better yet, take note of whether that person, persons or group really do love and respect themselves.

Perhaps they are looking towards others to fill an innate emptiness in their own makeup. If that is the case, you are better off not in their safe catch.

If you are looking at someone who has great wealth and thinking that entails great peace, take a glimpse behind that illusion as well. There is a lot of legwork to maintaining great wealth that is not depicted on the screen of envy. Perhaps you are given the exact amount of wealth and clout that you can handle while maintaining wellbeing.

Regardless, the best form of peace is to relax your atoms in a conscious surrender. This is done through gratitude. If one can relax their atoms during an undesirable situation, it is only to serve them in their quest for self-empowerment. Self-empowerment is a state in which Joy, Love, Abundance, Freedom, Health, Success and Wholeness dwell.

In a place of empowerment, these attributes are defined by you and are not dangling carrots to lock you into a world of illusion. You become the defining faction and are no longer defined or judged by others, at least not in a way that matters to you. You become free.

Being Free of the Cage of Human Consciousness

Have you ever seen an animal that was so used to living in a cage that it was afraid to come out. The cage seemed to provide all that it needed for so long that it couldn't even fathom being without it. This is how we are as people. Our cage is the human consciousness.

The human consciousness is such a contradiction. It

emphasizes trust in things that illicit fear and are not congruent with us at our core. We, in our true form, are dynamic souls bursting with love and light. Anything that is not blissful joy is part of the cage or the process of removing ourselves from the cage.

The Joy and boundless Love are waiting for us beyond the bars that we look through. It is our highest celebrating to unbar ourselves and realize ourselves as a pure expression of love.

Here are some taps to assist:

(Say each statement three times while tapping on your head and say it a fourth time while tapping on your chest.)

"I release the fear of leaving the cage; in all moments."

"I release the fear of existing beyond the cage; in all moments."

"I release confusing the cage for home; in all moments."

"I release the belief that the cage is nirvana; in all moments."

"I release my dependency on the cage; in all moments."

"I release encouraging others to stay in their cage; in all moments."

"I release the belief I will be alone and abandoned for leaving the cage; in all moments."

"I release my loyalty to the cage; in all moments."

"I release the belief that others are stuck in a cage; in all moments."

"I release keeping others caged; in all moments."

"I release fortifying the bars of the cage; in all moments."

"I release sabotaging my own liberation from the cage; in all moments."

"I release sabotaging the liberation of others; in all moments."

I recant all vows and agreements between myself and the cage; in all moments."

"I remove all curses between myself and the cage; in all moments."

"I dissolve all karmic ties between myself and the cage; in all moments."

"I remove all the pain, burden and limitations that the cage has put on me; in all moments."

"I release all that I have vested in the cage; in all moments."

"I take back all the Joy, Love, Abundance, Freedom and Wholeness that the cage has taken from me; in all moments."

"I release resonating with the cage; in all moments."

"I shift my paradigm from the cage to Joy, Love, Abundance, Freedom, Life and Wholeness; in all moments."

"I shift my paradigm from the cage to enlightenment; in all moments."

Being in Agreement

There is nothing that a pure intention fueled by positive energy can't overcome. When two or more come into agreement with such a thing, it is exponential. That is what I do for others; I agree with them at their highest potential, however they express this.

I am still taken aback by people who argue for the opposite. If I tell someone that they are abundant beyond compare, they will argue with me on the side of poverty. The same is true if I see happiness, health or love for someone. They will argue on the side of sadness, pain, and loneliness. It makes me tend not to put such a high intention out there for others so they don't have to protest so much. It is like they think that I am invalidating them.

When someone gives you a compliment, accept it. When someone shares their aspirations, support them. Who is anybody to give them a reality check when all the variables are different for each person? Think of what you are literally doing when you are being the devil's advocate. When someone tries something new, don't be there on the sidelines waiting for it to fail. When someone is finding their legs, don't clip their wings. You can show your greatness simply in supporting others in delving into theirs.

Every story of achievement has a foundation of adversary. At this point, we have all forged our way through the trenches of hard knocks. It is time to give each other a hand up over the wall instead of a cold shoulder. How about this statement: "I support you in whatever you do to further your happiness and the wellbeing of others." Can you support this intention?

Here is a Universal agreement that is worthy to support: That everyone live in Joy, Love, Abundance, Freedom, Health, Success, Security, Companionship, Peace and Wholeness, however they manifest them without harming others.

Being Present in the Moment

Each moment, no matter what is outwardly transpiring, is laden with such contentment. At any moment, at any time, conjure up any or all of these experiences and enliven them in the present:

- Wearing warm cozy pajamas nestled with a good book

- Cuddling with the love of your life

- Your favorite team winning the championship

- A warm cup of cocoa/cider/tea

- Watching your child sleep

- Waiting out the storm while having all the necessities

- Accomplishing a great task

- Sharing your gifts in an appreciative arena

- Hearing a genuine compliment

- Receiving a very special gift

- Saying "I Love You" for the first time

- Awaking from an incredible dream

- Feeling beautiful/handsome

- Hugging your furry family member

- The first day of vacation

- Quenching a big thirst/hunger

- Seeing someone you have assisted thrive

- The kindness of a friend

- Heartfelt laughter

- Your connection to nature

You have all these moments and more in your own repertoire. And if you are the one going through the list thinking you don't identify with all the items, you are missing the point. Catch that tendency and tweak it. Make your own list. Have all the great moments ready to conjure up at will.

Make a list of the good moments in your life. Write them out in little papers and keep them in a jar if it helps. Every time you feel the need to shift back into joy, take one out and read it at random. Give this assignment to your children. They can collect a lifetime of little papers. Train them and yourself to get in the habit of writing them down.

To shift from worrying or complaining and into contentment is a form of Mastership. The Universe gives us more of what we focus on. This is a simple tool to acknowledge and manifest more Joy, Love, and Abundance into our life.

Beyond a Broken Heart

If people realized what wonders were beyond the broken heart, they would give in more easily. The truth is the heart is resilient beyond all measure. It is tapped into the infinite source that knows no matter what outer appearances seem, love will prevail. Even if it is after the illusion has halted through the decay of the physical body. Love will prevail.

This is the mainstay of life. If we did not all believe this on some level, we would not continue to exist. We would not try. We would not prevail. We would not succeed.

Love is inevitable and will have its way in the end. This is not a question. The question is not if; the question is when. It can happen in an instant or it can seemingly take forever.

So what prevents love from prevailing? It is the stubbornness of the mind. The mind is like the big brother that thinks he knows everything. The heart is the little sister who realizes the truth but goes along with everything the mind says because she has no need to upstage him.

This is the heart. The heart concedes, reveals, prevails, endures, revels, embraces, expands, empowers and imbues. The one thing the heart doesn't do is break. When someone thinks their heart is breaking, it is the mind that is in peril. The mind is shattering from its wants, opinions, desires, righteousness, superiority, indignation, drama and stance. It is actually the mind breaking and not the heart. Let it.

Let the mind shatter into a trillion shards of preconceived notions. It is inevitable. When you sweep them all away, you will be left with a glorious loving nature. This is the true self standing at the helm of a loving heart. When that twinge of pain comes, know that it is a crack in the surface that shellacs the facade. Instead of wincing from it, delve into it and thrust yourself into the pain. The more that you crack it open, the more you can surrender to your true nature. It is a realm of love that is so profound that the

284

only expressions are gratitude, humility and awe.

Blurring the Lines

If you can feed the birds, why can't you feed the squirrels?

If you cry at a sad movie, why can't you cry for the multitudes in plight?

If you can love an innocent baby, why can't you love every baby?

If you can find an easy solution, why can't you see the world finding resolve?

If you can tell the truth once, why can't you tell the truth always?

If you make one promise, why can't you keep all promises?

If you lie to others, you also lie to yourself.

If you dilute your integrity, you dilute your whole essence.

If you give up on others, you give up on yourself.

If you shut off from seeing the plight of the masses, you close off whole wings of your inner chambers.

If you make excuses, you are arguing for your own limitations.

If you attack others, you are waging war.

If you defend yourself, you are accusing others of waging war.

If you see with the eyes of love, you will see love everywhere.

If you get excited about life, life will be exiting.

If you do something different, the world will be new again.

If you raise the bar on what you will accept, everyone will stop hunching over.

If you receive this message, you are able to hear truth.

If you do something with your awareness, there is hope.

If there is hope, there is compassion.

If there is compassion, there is a connection.

If there is a connection, there is a willing heart.

If there is willingness, fear will fall away.

When fear falls away, understanding will emerge.

Hearts will open.

Lives will heal.

Awakening happens.

Love is accepted.

Love is shared.

Love is realized.

All then awaken.

All are empowered.

All are free.

Breaching the Realms to Awakening

What people are starting to realize is that you can't give your energy through devotion or dedication to another group or person and also have it to empower yourself. At one point, you are going to have to decide if you want to take a back seat in your own spiritual endeavors or if you want to be fully realized of your own potential. Everything we are is a spiritual endeavor. Just because we deny it is so or lost our way, does not make it any less real.

Make no mistake. Your whole reason for existing is to realize yourself as the God-Being that you are. You have a unique vantage point to life. You have been brutalized and walked beside and behind the down trodden. This has built up a great empathy in you and an understanding into the subtle mechanisms of compassion.

Who is more qualified to don the humble greatness of omnipotence than one who has been violated and abused at every turn and still has the capacity to love? This world has been your training ground. But you are breaching the realms of awakening. How do I know that? You are reading this message.

"Come on in, the Water Is Fine"

We all exist in an ocean of Joy, Love, Abundance and Freedom. We are all in perfect harmony and peace with all the other atoms in the ocean. Imagine your happiest most fulfilling experience and magnify it a million times over. This is the actuality of existence.

In our first lifetime, we are given a little boat to maneuver around in. This is our ego. It is meant to assist us in gaining perspective on the vastness of our life. But it creates a sense of separation within us. We believe we are not part of the ocean but alone, invisible and unloved.

We outgrow the need for the boat. It becomes a hindrance. But the fear of being submerged without it is terrifying. So we keep riding around. The sense of separation and loneliness becomes unbearable. We bump into the other boats as a way to ease the isolation. We are desperate to feel connected.

It comes to a point when one realizes that there is no joy in damaging the other boats. There is more pleasure in helping others. We help them fix their boat. We have compassion for them being so dependent on their boat which distracts us from realizing how dependent we are on ours. One gets caught up in patching up the other boats and ends up splashing around in the ocean. Some happily swim away from their boat to assist others. They are so enthralled in helping others that they hardly notice.

Before one realizes it, they are free styling in the infinite ocean of Joy, Love, Abundance and Freedom. It is then we are equipped to reflect infinite joy, love, abundance and freedom back to others. We may still have a boat, but it is obvious that we swim freely at will. Our confidence and love shine through. When we are consumed with kindness, it is the same as saying, "come on in, the water is fine."

Creating Balance Through Giving

When I give a gift, I don't hover around and wait for a thank you. I allow the reverence of giving and the capacity to give to be the reward. I don't stop the process of giving by waiting for a response. That interrupts the flow of giving. Only those who are out of the habit of giving do this. The rest of us understand the sanctity of our position.

The sun doesn't micromanage who receives its light and warmth. It trusts that the gift will reach the receptive. The clouds don't lament emptying themselves of all they are in service. Giving is the cycle of life. The clouds will reinvent themselves over and over again and give all that they are to the process. The Universe runs on giving.

At some point, man interrupted the natural process of giving in himself. Probably because of his "great mind," he thought he knew better. It was probably around the same time he subjugated woman. Woman understands giving and nature. She is so giving that she has been overcompensating for man's taking. For so long, she has been trying to maintain a balance through giving. It is not working. As much as female energy has given, male energy has taken more.

Male energy has taken so much that he has left the planet crippled. It does not quench his thirst for taking. He just uses his talents to figure out new ways to take. He loves to rape. He invents new ways to rape even the land. Those that protest get shouted down, subjugated or demonized. It is time for male energy to rest so it can gain reason.

The way that male energy can be restored to the natural balance of nature is to be met by female energy. She needs to teach male energy the benefits of giving. Everyone that gives happily all that they are without trepidation or resentment restores the natural balance of the world. Let all give according to their capabilities. May we all be stretched in our capacity and willingness to give. In doing so, we, as a species, return to nature and are made whole.

The Crossroads

We are at a fork in the road of evolution. The way we think, react, believe and interact has all been conditioned into us and has led us down a dark path. We have forgotten our personal strength and ability to forge our own way.

We have relinquished the mighty adventure of a rustic life filled with scraped knees, bruised dreams and hopeful intentions. We have relinquished that satisfying feeling of falling into bed completely exhausted and content for the uneasy ability to slip into soft complacency.

We have chosen the mushy unfulfilling fate of conformity for far too long. It has led us to the brink of disaster in a morally corrupt world where we blatantly allow elected officials to desecrate humanity. Every time we use our energy to judge, attack or diminish someone else, we are reinforcing the debauchery of the standards set for us in an archaic time.

We have evolved beyond the limitation of allowing insecure, unbalanced men from forging our future. We have indulged in our own petty whims of indifference and grudge matches that are like dull little droplets that converge into creating the path forward in a dismal future. We have chosen "fear" for far too long.

It is time for all of us to reassess the reactionary state in which we live. When is the last time we made a selfish choice? Was it really selfish or was it just unpopular to the status quo? How did we find ourselves sitting in a soft chair throwing disparaging intentions to others with no more ill intentions than our own? We are so angry at ourselves for being complacent but are so complacent that we don't realize we are angry at all, let alone with ourselves.

So we throw nasty comments into the computer screen

hoping they will stick somewhere. We hope to get a rise out of someone. Hope to get a reaction somewhere. Only for the hope to know that we still have the ability to make a difference by hurting someone who is at arm's length whom we may never meet. It is so easy that way, isn't it?

Yet we play right into the hands of those who wish to control us. We have chosen to play it small. We are mad at ourselves for our limited role and so we attack others we can not see in a home we can't know and use this to feel empowered. Instead, we need to merely use our discipline and strength to forgo assaulting others from afar. This merely sets the precedent of what we do as a collective.

Every time you exercise a gracious act, withdraw from a justified attack, refrain from arguing or one-upping another, you are steering all of humanity clear of a disaster. You are at the helm. You, in your seemingly small insignificant life, are the blueprint for how humanity ventures forward. The more you choose honorably on all sides, the more you will see honor reflected in our collective world. That is the secret of life.

The secret of life has always been that it is not what happens to benefit you that matters. It is what you do and how you proceed to benefit others. The quality of life for all of humanity improves when the quality of your own thoughts and intentions improve. How often do you give thought to the wellbeing of people on the other side of the planet?

We can build all the walls we want to, but that doesn't

preclude us from breathing the same air as others, having our hearts beat in rhythm with them, and having the same hopes and dreams for our loved ones as they do. Could you love a dog that was rejected, abused or neglected on the other side of the world? Then why can we not love a person the same way? Why are we conditioned to feel so robbed when another person thrives? Why does it have to be "us versus them"? Is there not room for all to thrive?

It is time to uncover the little pockets of indifference and the conditioned responses that glaze us over. It is time for us to live, love, react and forge on with a one heart intention because, like it or not, we are all in this together. The whole process of war brings us to a realization of commonality. We can come to that conclusion without the devastation. We don't need the harsh lessons to awaken ourselves. All we need to do is to take better heed of our own intentions and send them out in the spirit of inclusiveness instead of division.

Contribute to World Peace: Crumble Down the Resistance to World Peace

People frequently complain about the length of the tap exercises I post. Or, they tell me how hard it is to sit there and do them. I am not sure if it has occurred to anyone that it is difficult for me to write them and that I have resistance in forging them from nothing with no payoff to myself in doing so. In fact, I know people will criticize and complain. Yet I work through the resistance to bring them to you on the off-chance they will assist someone in feeling more empowered in their life.

Hearing people tell me how difficult it is to do the taps, or diminish them and me by comparing them to any old taps, used to take wind out of my sails. But knowing that it is helping others who do forge through the resistance is the motivation. Think about it: If you do nothing, you get more of the same. So why not try something abstract in an exercise in doing something?

I have a lot of resistance to writing this series of taps. Yet I know it's necessary for the advancement of peace in the world. Let's all work through our resistance together and send out a proactive intention to crumble down the resistance to world peace.

You will be surprised at how much energy doing all these taps will free in you.

(Say each statement three times while tapping on your head and say it a fourth time while tapping on your chest.)

"I declare myself a surrogate for all Christians and Jews in doing these taps; in all moments."

"I release hating Muslims; in all moments."

"I release demonizing Muslims; in all moments."

"I release being the enemy of Muslims; in all moments."

"I release the belief that I am superior to Muslims; in all moments."

"I nullify all contracts with Muslims; in all moments."

"I withdraw all my energy from hating Muslims; in all moments."

"I extract all the hate that I have projected onto Muslims; in all moments."

"I dry up all psychic streams that mandate the diminishing of Muslims; in all moments."

"I send all energy matrices into the Light and Sound that compel me to hate Muslims; in all moments."

"I command all complex energy matrices that compel me to hate Muslims to be escorted into the Light and Sound; in all moments."

"I remove all engrams of hating Muslims; in all moments."

"I remove all programming and conditioning to hate Muslims; in all moments."

"I strip all illusion off of hating Muslims; in all moments."

"I remove all masks, walls and armor that hating Muslims has put on me; in all moments."

"I eliminate the first cause in regards to hating Muslims; in all moments."

"I release being immersed in hating Muslims; in all moments."

"I untangle all my energy from hating Muslims; in all

moments."

"I release the genetic propensity to hate Muslims; in all moments."

"I dissolve all of the hating of Muslims with the purity of Divine Love; in all moments."

"I view all Muslims from the vantage point of Love; in all moments."

"I remove all vortexes between myself and hating Muslims; in all moments."

"I dry up all instincts to hate Muslims; in all moments."

"I recant all vows and agreements to hate Muslims; in all moments."

"I remove all curses that I put on hating Muslims; in all moments."

"I remove all blessings that I put on hating Muslims: in a moments."

"I sever all strings and cords between myself and hating Muslims; in all moments."

"I dissolve all karmic ties between myself and hating Muslims; in all moments."

"I remove all the pain, burden, and limitations that I have put on all Muslims; in all moments."

"I remove all the fear, futility and unworthiness I have put on all Muslims; in all moments."

"I release ostracizing Muslims; in all moments."

"I give back all that I have taken from Muslims; in all moments."

"I extract all hate of Muslims from my Sound Frequency and the Universal Sound Frequency; in all moments."

"I extract all hate of Muslims from my Light Emanation and the Universal Light Emanation; in all moments."

"I release individually or universally resonating or emanating with hating Muslims; in all moments."

"I transcend hating Muslims; in all moments."

"I shift my paradigm from hating Muslims to seeing all souls as pure love; in all moments."

"I am centered and empowered in seeing all souls as pure love; in all moments."

"I resonate, emanate and am interconnected with all life in seeing all souls as pure love; in all moments."

∎∎

"I declare myself a surrogate for all Christians and Muslims in doing these taps; in all moments."

"I release hating Jews; in all moments."

"I release demonizing Jews; in all moments."

"I release being the enemy of Jews; in all moments."

"I release the belief that I am superior to Jews; in all moments."

"I nullify all contracts with Jews; in all moments."

"I withdraw all my energy from hating Jews; in all moments."

"I extract all the hate that I have projected onto Jews; in all moments."

"I dry up all psychic streams that mandate the diminishing of Jews; in all moments."

"I send all energy matrices into the Light and Sound that compel me to hate Jews; in all moments."

"I command all complex energy matrices that compel me to hate Jews to be escorted into the Light and Sound; in all moments."

"I remove all engrams of hating Jews; in all moments."

"I remove all programming and conditioning to hating Jews; in all moments."

"I strip all illusion off of hating Jews; in all moments."

"I remove all masks, walls and armor that hating Jews has put on me; in all moments."

"I eliminate the first cause in regards to hating Jews; in all moments."

"I release being immersed in hating Jews; in all moments."

"I untangle all my energy from hating Jews; in all moments."

"I release the genetic propensity to hate Jews; in all moments."

"I dissolve all of the hating of Jews with the purity of Divine Love; in all moments."

"I view all Jews from the vantage point of Love; in all moments."

"I remove all vortexes between myself and hating Jews; in all moments."

"I dry up all instincts to hate Jews; in all moments."

"I recant all vows and agreements to hate Jews; in all moments."

"I remove all curses that I put on Jews; in all moments."

"I remove all blessings I put on hating Jews; in all moments."

"I severe all strings and cords between myself and hating Jews; in all moments."

"I dissolve all karmic ties between myself and hating Jews; in all moments."

"I remove all the pain, burden, and limitations that I have put on all Jews; in all moments."

"I remove all the fear, futility, unworthiness I have put on all Jews; in all moments."

"I release ostracizing Jews; in all moments."

"I give back all that I have taken from Jews; in all moments."

"I extract all hate of Jews from my Sound Frequency and the Universal Sound Frequency; in all moments."

"I extract all hate of Jews from my Light Emanation and the Universal Light Emanation; in all moments."

"I release individually or universally resonating or emanating with hating Jews; in all moments."

"I transcend hating Jews; in all moments."

"I shift my paradigm from hating Jews to seeing all souls as pure love; in all moments."

"I am centered and empowered in seeing all souls as pure love; in all moments."

"I resonate, emanate and am interconnected with all life in seeing all souls as pure love; in all moments."

• •

"I declare myself a surrogate for all Jews and Muslims in doing these taps; in all moments."

"I release hating Christians; in all moments."

"I release demonizing Christians; in all moments."

"I release being the enemy of Christians; in all moments."

"I release the belief that I am superior to Christians; in all moments."

"I nullify all contracts with Christians; in all moments."

"I withdraw all my energy from hating Christians; in all moments."

"I extract all the hate that I have projected onto Christians; in all moments."

"I dry up all psychic streams that mandate the diminishing of Christians; in all moments."

"I send all energy matrices into the Light and Sound that compel me to hate Christians; in all moments."

"I command all complex energy matrices that compel me to hate Christians to be escorted into the Light and Sound; in all moments."

"I remove all engrams of hating Christians; in all moments."

"I remove all programming and conditioning to hate Christians; in all moments."

"I strip all illusion off of hating Christians; in all moments."

"I remove all masks, walls and armor that hating Christians has put on me; in all moments."

"I eliminate the first cause in regards to hating Christians; in all moments."

"I release being immersed in hating Christians; in all moments."

"I untangle all my energy from hating Christians; in all moments."

"I release the genetic propensity to hate Christians; in all moments."

"I dissolve all of the hating of Christians with the purity of Divine Love; in all moments."

"I view all Christians from the vantage point of Love; in all moments."

"I remove all vortexes between myself and hating Christians; in all moments."

"I dry up all instincts to hate Christians; in all moments."

"I recant all vows and agreements to hate Christians; in all moments."

"I remove all curses that I put on Christians; in all moments."

"I remove all blessings I put on hating Christians; in a moments."

"I severe all strings and cords between myself and hating Christians; in all moments."

"I dissolve all karmic ties between myself and hating

Christians; in all moments."

"I remove all the pain, burden, and limitations that I have put on all Christians; in all moments."

"I remove all the fear, futility and unworthiness I have put on all Christians; in all moments."

"I release ostracizing Christians; in all moments."

"I give back all that I have taken from Christians; in all moments."

"I extract all hate of Christians from my Sound frequency and the Universal Sound Frequency; in all moments."

"I extract all hate of Christians from my Light Emanation and the Universal Light Emanation; in all moments."

"I release individually or universally resonating or emanating with hating Christians; in all moments."

"I transcend hating Christians; in all moments."

"I shift my paradigm from hating Christians to seeing all souls as pure love; in all moments."

"I am centered and empowered in seeing all souls as pure love; in all moments."

"I resonate, emanate and am interconnected with all life in seeing all souls as pure love; in all moments."

"I declare myself a surrogate for all religious denominations in doing these taps; in all moments."

"I release hating Pagans; in all moments."

"I release demonizing Pagans; in all moments."

"I release being the enemy of Pagans; in all moments."

"I release the belief that I am superior to Pagans; in all moments."

"I nullify all contracts with Pagans; in all moments."

"I withdraw all my energy from hating Pagans; in all moments."

"I extract all the hate that I have projected onto Pagans; in all moments."

"I dry up all psychic streams that mandate the diminishing of Pagans; in all moments."

"I send all energy matrices into the Light and Sound that compel me to hate Pagans; in all moments."

"I command all complex energy matrices that compel me to hate Pagans to be escorted into the Light and Sound; in all moments."

"I remove all engrams of hating Pagans; in all moments."

"I remove all programming and conditioning to hate Pagans; in all moments."

"I strip all illusion off of hating Pagans; in all moments."

"I remove all masks, walls and armor that hating Pagans has put on me; in all moments."

"I eliminate the first cause in regards to hating Pagans; in all moments."

"I release being immersed in hating Pagans; in all moments."

"I untangle all my energy from hating Pagans; in all moments."

"I release the genetic propensity to hate Pagans; in all moments."

"I dissolve all of the hating of Pagans with the purity of Divine Love; in all moments."

"I view all Pagans from the vantage point of Love; in all moments."

"I remove all vortexes between myself and hating Pagans; in all moments."

"I dry up all instincts to hate Pagans; in all moments."

"I recant all vows and agreements to hate Pagans; in all moments."

"I remove all curses that I put on Pagans; in all moments."

"I remove all blessings I put on hating Pagans; in a moments."

"I severe all strings and cords between myself and hating Pagans; in all moments."

"I dissolve all karmic ties between myself and hating Pagans; in all moments."

"I remove all the pain, burden and limitations that I have put on all Pagans; in all moments."

"I remove all the fear, futility and unworthiness I have put on all Pagans; in all moments."

"I release ostracizing Pagans; in all moments."

"I give back all that I have taken from Pagans; in all moments."

"I extract all hate of Pagans from my Sound Frequency and the Universal Sound Frequency; in all moments."

"I extract all hate of Pagans from my Light Emanation and the Universal Light Emanation; in all moments."

"I release individually or universally resonating or emanating with hating Pagans; in all moments."

"I transcend hating Pagans; in all moments."

"I shift my paradigm from hating Pagans to seeing all souls as pure love; in all moments."

"I am centered and empowered in seeing all souls as pure love; in all moments."

"I resonate, emanate and am interconnected with all life in seeing all souls as pure love; in all moments."

"I declare myself a surrogate for all religious denominations in doing these taps; in all moments."

"I release hating Atheists; in all moments."

"I release demonizing Atheists; in all moments."

"I release being the enemy of Atheists; in all moments."

"I release the belief that I am superior to Atheists; in all moments."

"I nullify all contracts with Atheists; in all moments."

"I withdraw all my energy from hating Atheists; in all moments."

"I extract all the hate that I have projected onto Atheists; in all moments."

"I dry up all psychic streams that mandate the diminishing of Atheists; in all moments."

"I send all energy matrices into the Light and Sound that compel me to hate Atheists; in all moments."

"I command all complex energy matrices that compel me to hate Atheists to be escorted into the Light and Sound; in all moments."

"I remove all engrams of hating Atheists; in all moments."

"I remove all programming and conditioning to hate Atheists; in all moments."

"I strip all illusion off of hating Atheists; in all moments."

"I remove all masks, walls and armor that hating Atheists has put on me; in all moments."

"I eliminate the first cause in regards to hating Atheists; in all moments."

"I release being immersed in hating Atheists; in all moments."

"I untangle all my energy from hating Atheists; in all moments."

"I release the genetic propensity to hate Atheists; in all moments."

"I dissolve all of the hating of Atheists with the purity of Divine Love; in all moments."

"I view all Atheists from the vantage point of Love; in all moments."

"I remove all vortexes between myself and hating Atheists; in all moments."

"I dry up all instincts to hate Atheists; in all moments."

"I recant all vows and agreements to hate Atheists; in all moments."

"I remove all curses that I put on Atheists; in all moments."

"I remove all blessings I put on hating Atheists; in a moments."

"I sever all strings and cords between myself and hating Atheists; in all moments."

"I dissolve all karmic ties between myself and hating Atheists; in all moments."

"I remove all the pain, burden and limitations that I have put on all Atheists; in all moments."

"I remove all the fear, futility and unworthiness I have put on all Atheists; in all moments."

"I release ostracizing Atheists; in all moments."

"I give back all that I have taken from Atheists; in all moments."

"I extract all hate of Atheists from my Sound Frequency and the Universal Sound Frequency; in all moments."

"I extract all hate of Atheists from my Light Emanation and the Universal Light Emanation; in all moments."

"I release individually or universally resonating or emanating with hating Atheists; in all moments."

"I transcend hating Atheists; in all moments."

"I shift my paradigm from hating Atheists to seeing all souls as pure love; in all moments."

"I am centered and empowered in seeing all souls as pure love; in all moments."

"I resonate, emanate and am interconnected with all life in seeing all souls as pure love; in all moments."

Feel free to continue doing these taps for other denominations. Notice how spacious it feels in the atmosphere from doing these taps. This exercise is you being a dynamic advocate for world peace.

Divine Providence

The world thrives on the kindness that we all are able to exude. When we speak about what a horrible place this is, we make it a self-fulfilling prophecy. It just became a little less nice to that person that you just mentioned that to. Since man has killed off so many inhabitants that exude goodness, it is up to us who are aware to take up the slack and consciously pour love, gratitude and positive vibes back into the ground.

People think I am unrealistic. I am very realistic. People who disconnect from their responsibility to give back to earth are like middle management. Meaning, they see half of the picture and believe they are privy to the whole scope. Half of the picture is seeing what can be taken. The higher visionaries understand that what needs to be taken, needs to be replenished and more, to sustain balance.

Believe it or not, there are some people who are happy to run this world to the ground. They believe that by the time it is depleted we will have discovered another planet to conquer or discovered a way to sustain ourselves in a toxic world. This is the belief system that we interrupt with our kind intentions in the world. It doesn't matter how warm and fuzzy they make their fracking commercials and how they sidestep the word fracking. This is the intention that they have. Pay attention to what you are watching. The more heartfelt the commercial, the more poison or destruction they are trying to feed you. Love is endless, but it isn't perpetuated by eating food that is laden with toxins and carcinogens.

It is our responsibility to put kindness back into the world. It is a sort of enzyme or a vitamin to life to do so. It may not be taught anymore, so some may have to dig deep to do this. For some, it may mean simply turning off the negative streams of the news and commercials in their life, or to stop using gossip, complaints and health issues as a topic of conversation. Another thing someone can do is to keep asking themselves as they go about their day, "Am I taking right now or am I giving?"

We have been trained to be takers and depend on establishments to give to us. This has made us weak and dependent as a society. The way to counter this is to change the energetic flow of this dynamic. We do so by giving in every possible situation. It can range from just being kind, saying something uplifting, allowing someone else to go first, checking in on a neighbor or doing something totally out of your comfort zone.

The more you give, the more giving will feel empowering, not only for you, but for others. I never realized I was a healer. I just started out listening to people on the phone because they had no one else to talk to. I went to massage therapy school and realized that I could move energy with my loving intention. I combined the two and now I help people release devastating issues that they have not been able to relieve anywhere else. I went from having no self-esteem to helping others sharing whatever experience I possibly can share. It was done simply with Divine Providence and my desperate desire to contribute.

Most people don't realize how dynamic and empowered they are. Most people are just starting to wake up and look around as if awakening from a deep fitful slumber, perhaps a nightmare. But now is the time to wipe the sand from our eyes, shake off the sleep and awaken to the dynamic potential that we are. We are the best of the best of us. We have examples of what one determined person can do. We have evidence of what one determined group can do. It's time to roll up our sleeves, unlatch our hearts, retrain our minds, shatter all glass ceilings and shake each other into action.

Plant a tree, grow a garden, feed the starving, take in a stray, invent a better way of doing things, become self-sustaining, take others into consideration, show up positive, let a stranger go first, interrupt the gossip, take the higher ground, question authority, ask "why", ask "why not", dream big, let things go, see the other point of view, forgo grandstanding, forgo taking sides, see the good in all, draw it out, take up a hobby, live your dream, live your purpose and encourage others to live theirs.

Be the leader, teacher, helper, healer, and lover of life that you are slated to be. We are the co-facilitators and saviors to our own fate. Use this moment as a turning point to shift into the new paradigm. See each other the way that I see you: Joyful, Loving, Abundant, Healthy, Whole and Free! Most of all, see us all Empowered.

Emptying out Hell

This is what I was doing right before I awoke in my physical body. I was anointing older people on a beach as they reached a shore. At first, it was a couple, but then it was a lot. They were crossing over and waiting to be assigned to heaven or hell. I held their heads like one would in a cranial sacral massage but from above because they were bowing to me thinking I was an official agent of God.

I wasn't anointing them because they needed anointing. It was because that is what they believed they needed and I was there to assist them. So I infused a greater understanding into them of the inner worlds so they could enjoy the freedoms of them without being encumbered with their earthly belief systems.

It seemed like hell was on one side and heaven was the rest of the world. Hell is a place of regrets. It was empty. Apparently, my job was to upgrade people's understanding so that they didn't lock themselves in hell. So my job was to empty out hell.

I am not telling you this because I am the only one who is capable of doing this work. I am telling you so you can do the work too. By understanding what happens when someone crosses over, you are capable of instilling an upgrade in understanding to them before they cross and perhaps those who are already on the other side. Hell is no longer an option. It was always built on instilling that belief in others.

The upgrade in humanity is in not thinking I am wonderful for what I say I do and what resonates as truth. The upgrade is in knowing you can do it too. You know it. Stand on the beach with me and release those crossing or have crossed from their misunderstandings. We do this work honestly, respectfully and with the deepest gratitude for being capable of serving in joyful awareness.

Encouragement!

Whatever you are experiencing, no matter how impossible, or discouraging, please know that it is temporary. Even the most limiting confinement can only hold our physical body. Our minds and hearts are free to roam the Universe, to discover new planets and connect with enlightened beings and species that we may never be able to physically meet.

Any form of limitation is an opportunity to have experiences beyond the preconceived limitations. The dam does not confine the river; it merely changes the flow. You are a river! You cannot be stopped from thriving. You are too magnificent for that. Depression is merely a temporary eddy in the stream. It is not the whole river.

Take in the whole view of you. Step back from what you think you are. Pull out of the eddy. Anything that anyone else can do, any great feat, you are also capable of and more!

You Are Blessed

You don't need prayers as much as understanding. You need to lift a lantern into that dark abyss and look into every crevice. What you thought was your ambrosia was laced with cyanide. The Universe just knocked the goblet out of your hands as you were raising it to your lips. You are not stricken down. You are blessed by the invisible hands of protection. You are loved.

Certainly it is inviting at the mouth of a cul-de-sac. But once one has entrenched themselves in a dead end, it sometimes takes pain to knock one back into the awareness to find themselves.

Sending you love. I am excited for your growth. You can gauge it by the depth of the pain that you are feeling. It is incredible. It leaves the old you in the dust.

Evidence of Love's Existence

I was starving and exhausted beyond compare. In my mind, even though I wasn't allowed to think (my captor would know), I ran a thought loop through my head that defied my captor's attempts to break me. His programming was that I was disgusting, reviled, and hated by all that was pure and sacred and that all the angels thought that I deserved to suffer in a miserable eternal existence of pain.

He laughed and scoffed at my humiliation and the more that I suffered, the happier he was. He would invent ways to draw out my anguish. He would eat in front of me and mock me as he forced me to work in over one hundred degree heat until I was exhausted and emaciated. He told me that God hated me, that I had defiled all that was good to such a degree that God wanted to see me suffer and was pleased at my misery. Not because God was unkind, but because I was such a disgusting waste of existence.

There was really nothing from my history that obviously contradicted his statements. I had a large family that didn't seem to embrace me. I had made no great strides in the community to show evidence of the contrary. I had no family of my own. He took my dog from me and convinced me that my dog, whom I had rescued, really hated me. He made me serve the dog as a king because it was an extension of him.

My brain nearly gave up the ability to think rationally. It had exhausted the possibilities to counter his programming. But there was one statement from my spiritual teachings that kept me alive: Soul exists because God loves it. I existed so God must love me. It was the one irrefutable argument I had in my mental and physical fog. It defied all his efforts to break me. I existed. God must love me. I was lovable. Others exist so God must love others. So now I am connected to all through this realization. I am connected to all through the Love. That is all that remained of who I was. I AM the evidence of Love's existence.

Expound Your Joy

I facilitated a private remote session. It was for someone who was familiar with my work but had never had a private session. It took her two years to get to the point of scheduling one. As soon as I heard her voice, I could tell so much about her. She was very kind and agreeable, but she held layers of pain underneath the kindness and used being nice to buffer her from any pain.

She had been tortured in many lifetimes. Her causal body (the aspect of her that holds the records of past lives) was so scarred and mutilated that I could not do a regular session with her. On the surface, she was very capable and willing. But if I led her through the taps that I would another client, it would have registered as torture to her on a certain level. This would be cruel.

So I sang many songs that were uplifting to her. I sang songs from some artists that she liked but only knew their cover songs. Some were from the seventies. The artists from past eras tapped into a freedom and expansion of consciousness that is lost in the present era. Creativity in the subtle realms is less accessible to musicians now because of lack of receptivity to it in society.

As more people share openly about subtle realms and greater expansion of consciousness, a creative renaissance will emerge. This creative renaissance will be the precipice of world peace because more and more people will be enthralled in sharing their gifts. Less interest will be put on acquiring a nest egg and more emphasis will be put on milking every moment of the most love and kindness for all, which is what I try to do with my writings and healing work.

The singing was like a healing balm to a weary soul. She could feel a lightness and relief come into her that had been missing. She admitted that she loved music and had allowed it to shut down in her life. I explained that we are sound frequencies and light emanations woven together to give the illusion of form. When we listen to music, we are hearing God, in a way, in our native tongue. She liked this.

We did do a few taps. It seems like she had pleated her life and folded it into a very narrow band of experiences to conform to the specifications of life in such a linear society. All these folds of expanded awareness and consciousness were neatly pleating her expansive self. We let out the pleats.

(Say each statement three times while tapping on your head and say it a fourth time while tapping on your chest.)

"I release pleating up Joy; in all moments."

"I release pleating up Love; in all moments."

"I release pleating up Abundance; in all moments."

"I release pleating up Freedom; in all moments."

"I release pleating up my Health; in all moments."

"I release pleating up Success; in all moments."

"I release pleating up Creativity; in all moments."

"I release pleating up Peace; in all moments."

"I release pleating up Beauty; in all moments."

"I release pleating up my Enthusiasm; in all moments."

"I release pleating up Contentment; in all moments."

"I release pleating up Spirituality; in all moments."

"I release pleating up Truth; in all moments."

"I release pleating up Purity; in all moments."

"I release pleating up Innocence; in all moments."

"I unfold exponential Joy; in all moments."

"I unfold exponential Love; in all moments."

"I unfold exponential Abundance; in all moments."

"I unfold exponential Freedom; in all moments."

"I unfold exponential Health; in all moments."

"I unfold exponential Success; in all moments."

"I unfold exponential Creativity; in all moments."

"I unfold exponential Peace; in all moments."

"I unfold exponential Beauty; in all moments."

"I unfold exponential Enthusiasm; in all moments."

"I unfold exponential Contentment; in all moments."

"I unfold exponential Spirituality; in all moments."

"I unfold exponential Truth; in all moments."

"I unfold exponential Purity; in all moments."

"I unfold exponential Innocence; in all moments."

"I release pinching my Sound Frequency; in all moments."

"I expound my Sound Frequency; in all moments."

"I release pinching my Light Emanation; in all moments."

"I expound my Light Emanation; in all moments."

Global Peace

G - Godly

L - Love

O - Overflowing

B - Beyond

A - All

L - Lines

P - Pure

E - Energy

A - Always

C - Caring about

E - Everyone

We can do this with our thoughts and our intentions. Those "in control" may shove fossil fuel consumption down our throats to keep the world enslaved to coarse energy. That is their stronghold. But we do not need to allow our thoughts and intentions to be crude as well. That is on us.

Be:

- A ruthless advocate for kindness

- A hopeful optimist

- A champion for truth

- The holdout in selling out

Gain victory over your perspective.

Believe:

- In fairies

- The goodness of trees

- The reincarnation of our dear ones

- That kindness prevails

- In the innate goodness of others.

Know:

- That all lives, in all forms, matter

- Fear is mostly induced to gain control

- Hate is merely stagnant fear that can be dissipated with love

- It can happen in an instant; it doesn't need to take time

- You are an empowered, love generator that has never been taken on the open road.

Celebrate:

- Effortlessly showing kindness

- Being a holdout for truth

- Champions of daily gratitude

- Life-Love-Awakening

- Truth gaining a foothold.

Shake hands with yourself, God and love in everyone you encounter.

Spill over the brim with enthusiasm and compassion.

Awaken everyone you meet with your optimism and kindness.

Interrupt those who are complaining with reasons to be grateful.

Offer a smile more easily than an opinion.

Forgo the need to challenge others' talents or convictions.

Allow others the space to breathe in the love and kindness patience exudes.

Use gratitude to open up all your energy systems.

Spill love into the world. Saturate it.

Convert all that seems hopeless or limiting into positive intention by churning the gratitude around in you and melting all into love. Be a tumbler of love.

Feel your own omniscience.

Be a "know it all" for awakening.

Have a God complex! By all means have a God complex!

Every being was robbed of their potential when they were born into the lie that there is only one son of God. This lie is choking the planet and making slaves of us all.

We:

- Are all the sons and daughters of God

- Are indeed awakening

- Must be accountable

- Must hold all beings and ourselves sacred

- Need to speak our truth and it will create a pathway for the love.

Grace

G - Give kindness to all

R - Respect the sanctity of all souls

A - Attune to what is the highest good in every situation

C - Consider the vantage point of all others

E - Empathize with everyone

Grace is artistry and a skill like all others.

It can be cultivated, nurtured and taught.

What we do in each act of grace is empower the integrity of humanity.

From each act of Grace:

- Illumination of spirit is revealed

- Heaviness lifts

- Hearts unburden

- Silent pleas are answered

- "Resolve" unfurls its wings

- Insights take their first breath

- Paths are cleared

- Innocence is nurtured

- Kindness is empowered

- Hope is restored

- Resolve is instilled

- Quietude is respected

- Peace expands

- A way is secured.

What you do in Grace is:

- Eliminate the primal urge to initiate hostile acts

- Forgo the path of petty indifference

- Repair all divide

- Create resiliency in the intricate woven fabric of life

- Reclaim wonder for all those in your wake

- Teach lost souls a way to be found

- Demonstrate a dying art to fervent generations

- Enlighten the murky hallways of tradition.

Your acts of Grace:

- Bring relief to those who are desperate in their own plight

- Satiate those starving to know kindness

- Address the deprived in whatever way they have been depreciated

- Illuminate dark corners of the world

- Wipe the brow of faces you may never see

- Hush the muted cries of indifference

- Ripple out into a sea of kindred spirits

- Sing to the sweetest aspect of every point of light

- Attune the heart of goodness with the voice of reason

- Uplift all souls to their own quickening to enlightenment

- Anchor your stance as a mighty force for mass enlightenment

This is what you choose to do or not do, every moment.

You have this much power.

You always have.

Harness the Gratitude of the Moment

(Say each statement three times out loud while tapping on the top of your head at the crown chakra and say it a fourth time while tapping on your chest at the heart chakra.)

"I tap into the reverence of the moment through gratitude for my great capacity to love; in all moments."

"I tap into the reverence of the moment through gratitude for the sanctity of my breath; in all moments."

"I tap into the presence of the moment through gratitude for being unshackled; in all moments."

"I tap into the reverence of the moment through gratitude for my ability to reason; in all moments."

"I tap into the reverence of the moment through gratitude for my heart beating in synchronicity with life; in all moments."

"I tap into the reverence of the moment through gratitude for nature; in all moments."

"I tap into the reverence of the moment through gratitude for my present condition of being unfettered; in all moments."

"I tap into the reverence of the moment through gratitude

for my ability to quiet the mind; in all moments."

"I tap into the reverence of the moment through gratitude for my ability to shift gears into the sacred space of gratitude; in all moments."

You Are Awesome

Has anyone told you lately how awesome you are?

You have survived incredible feats just to be here. You have conquered demons, slayed dragons, beaten the odds, rolled with the punches, sidestepped landmines, grabbed the glass ring, given it your all and risen to the cream of the crop just to be here.

The fact that you have blocked all but this lifetime out so you can concentrate on the task at hand does not diminish your journey.

Please don't let anyone tell you that you are not amazing or that you are unworthy. Your sheer presence in this world contradicts that very statement. You are evidence of amazing.

If life feels mundane, accept it as a respite and embrace it. There is so much wonder that reveals itself when the mundane is scrutinized for the opportunity it is. May you transcend the illusion of mundane and turn each moment inside out to reveal the wonder and splendor of an adventure. Play through dear friend. Play through!

- "Life" by Jen Ward

How to Undo a Logjam

Barter is the original currency. When necessity gauged the actual rate of exchange, the hard work, sacrifice and importance to the family's survival could be felt and traced in a product or service offered. It had substance.

The monetary system is one big game of chicken. It is an agreement to pretend. An arbitrary number is assigned to a person's time. They somehow fall into a slot that needs to be filled by a person with the ability to conform. They need show only a hint of individuality so they stand out slightly above the other drones but not enough to rock the boat of establishment.

Passion, creativity and exuberance are squelched out at every turn. Complacency and peer approval are the prison of conformity, especially in the work place. There needs to be so much talent, drive and vision for one soul to try to make it over the wall into personal expression and freedom.

Society pays people to not perform. They bow out with an excuse of disability because they don't fit into the spectrum of what is valued as performance. They weave their complacency into a full blown victim consciousness and hide behind those who are really in need. The real deficiency is the lack of value this society puts on individual subjective talents. Society chains the human spirit by housing the able and monetarily rewarding so many that deem themselves disabled. This is the true energy crisis, the lack of heart.

One side is blaming the other. Both sides together are like a black and white cookie. One side wants to cut everyone off, and one side wants to validate everyone who bows out as needy. Both sides are the extreme. The government itself, through its structure, has locked all its constituents into a "them versus us" mode. It is paralyzed in inaction as one side cancels the other side out. We don't have to go on a rampage as society to solve this issue.

The sweeping change that so many are desperately seeking does not happen at the top. There needs to be a ground swelling of appreciation for a person's worth. How many people do you know who want to start a business, but they are afraid to put a worth on themselves? Help them. Build them up. Put a high value on them. Pay someone for their service. Buy local. Local is usually someone who is using their skills and talents to be productive in society. Let's reward them. Practice today by just saying something of value to those who work and serve. Flip a switch within that forgoes the criticism and makes a conscious choice to give gratitude. We can do this! I support us in this.

As a group, we are feeling powerless. How do you undo a logjam? You move one component at a time. The more we empower those who still have the heart and drive to attempt success, the more we pave the way for the next person. We can do this as Americans. We can agree to do this. This is the one issue that we may be able to reunite with. No more trashing the other side. No more wasting energy on feeling powerless. Let's move all our support and passion to anyone still willing to succeed. Let's give our heart to them in the form of monetary reward.

I Am Alone Today

There is no one in my life who wishes to spend time with me today. No one really cares about me. I don't matter. I must be so annoying to be around that no one wants to even extend human kindness to me. It is irrelevant to everyone here whether I exist or not. I must be hard to love. I don't even attract life partners because there is nothing attractive about me.

These are the thoughts that the human consciousness of the mind bombard me with. These are the thoughts that induce pain and dredge up old instances of injury and indignation. But I choose to turn down the channel on such silly notions. I listen to my heart.

This is what the heart tells me:

Being with people is a distraction. The Universe is strengthening your capacity to be imbued with love by not having you believe that it originates from other people.

You give so much of yourself. You need to pour that love into the world and not waste it on those who feel entitled to it.

You are being blessed to have all the humans pushed out of your life so that you can develop your ability to love other species of life and have an intimate relationship with life itself.

You are too aware to be trapped in the conventions of social culture. If the Universe left it to you, you would be distracted all the days of your life trying to please and placate others.

Everything that you are given daily in life lessons and spiritual awareness becomes a part of you even when you cross over. You are rich and abundant beyond compare in the spiritual realms. Others are starving for your spiritual gifts. Don't waste energy or momentum by focusing on those around you who don't see your greatness.

Isn't life a thorough teacher to provide you with a buffer from people adoring you? All those around you who don't see your greatness assist you so well in staying focused on the sanctity of the moment and not being distracted by the illusions.

No one can see you because so few people see truth, beauty and love in the world. You resonate so closely to truth, beauty and love that you have indeed become invisible to the average human.

Your spiritual light is very bright. For some humans, it blinds them. In this world of illusion, the way they respond to that is by being put off by you. But that is only more reason to have compassion for them.

All the security and material comfort that humans strive to accrue is only their limited attempt to own the intangible gifts that come so readily to you.

The Universe is gifting you with isolation so that it can help you drop out of the illusion of the moment and become alive, aware and expansive in the true interconnection of all.

God is not punishing you. You are being gifted with great insight and lasting spiritual capabilities every moment. By ignoring the mind's taunting, you are awakening to the sanctity of all life.

You and your gifts are so important to the world that you are not allowed to waste this existence being caught up in the illusion of the day and the pettiness of man.

Thanksgiving is a day to teach others as a group how to be grateful and how to interconnect with others. You have already learned these lessons so you do not need to go through the tedious lesson plans that other humans need.

Wanting what other humans have is like wishing to go back to kindergarten because you like coloring. You create masterpieces my friend. Use your abilities to do so.

These are some of the things that my heart tells me. It also tells me that I am being used as an example to show people how the shift from human consciousness to spiritual consciousness is done. It also tells me that there are those out there who need to hear this. That this is what their hearts have been telling them as well. Those who need to hear this will find this message and realize that they are loved and important in the scheme of life. They matter and are dearer than all the homespun celebrations can convey.

Please get a sense of how important you are to life and the transcendence process from the mundane to the dynamic. Use any pain that you may endure as a benchmark of the greatness of your true self. May you realize your true worth in the expansion of consciousness. You matter. You really do. You are loved beyond compare. You really are.

Some will argue with this that they can't matter because they don't outshine others in this life. You are not paying attention. It is a lie of the human consciousness that you must be great on the backs of others. That is how male energy has programmed the world.

But female energy embraces greatness as a sisterhood where all are happiest when everyone is at their best. That is the reality of where human awareness is headed. By dropping out of the lies of the illusion, you can plug into the expansiveness of the ultimate truth. As one succeeds in the true sense, we all succeed.

Here is to the success of the human species to transcend. I love you all. Every single one of you. Because I can. And that is a gift that human loneliness has afforded me. I would not trade that for anything.

I Have No Sympathy for You!

I have no sympathy for you

Sympathy is such a low vibration

It is the cousin of pain

Or unworthiness

Sympathy is given from a vantage point of above

It is looking down

It is saying, "Poor you, I am better and you are not"

It is the same color as a festering wound

To give you sympathy, is to paint you with a debilitating brushstroke.

You do not really want sympathy

You want validation

I validate you

You want reassurance

I reassure you

You want to know that you are special

You are special

You want to know that everything will be okay

Everything will be okay

Wanting sympathy is you asking for a hand up

But giving sympathy is holding you down as you are trying to get up

Both are ineffective

You can have compassion

Compassion is acknowledging your journey without

asking you to stay there

Compassion is saying, "I have been there and have survived it. You will too."

You can have empathy

Empathy is saying, "I understand what you are experiencing. You are not alone."

Sympathy is keeping one paralyzed in the position of need

You are too dynamic for that

Sympathy is an agreement of lack

You are too important to believe that this is you

Receiving sympathy comes at too high a price

Rip off the bandages and kick out the crutch of sympathy out from under you

Pick off the scabs of the old you

Celebrate the new skin of empowerment

You are honored

You are respected

You are experienced

You are whole

You are awakened

You are strong

You are accomplished

You are empowered

You are healed

You are loved

There is no sympathy for you

Only friendship and respect

Because that is what you deserve.

If

If I had physical wings, I would use them to shelter those who were stuck on the ground from the elements. For where would I go that would free me from knowing that others were being pummeled where they stand?

If I had a voice that could be heard around the world I would use it to sing in any key to those who have forgotten that they can sing as well. The scorn and judgment of those who belittle my gift would pale compared to the exhilaration of even one soul feeling empowered.

If I had might, I would use it as a means of reminding all others what their empowerment looks and feels like.

If I had legs and arms to span the world, I would walk up to every heart that aches and hug them with my whole being so that they could remember what the warmth of kindness felt like.

Then maybe they could fly, sing, walk and hug others as well and awaken all souls from their unrest.

Love Is Air Born

It is hard to keep knocking on a closed door. But you have to allow the realization that there are other open doors out there experiencing the same thing. It is not fruitless. The love we exude is air born and permeating through the vents. Those who keep out the love with closed doors and clenched fists must at some point breath it in to survive.

It Really Is That Simple

Blind loyalty builds up resentment. Male energy has dominated all the possible engrams in distorting the importance of those who serve humanity. As much as those in true service reject such adulation, it is still an engram etched in this world. It is a glass ceiling on humanity. It is an unhealthy dynamic for individual growth.

For as soon as you elevate someone, you have just lowered your own stance. Those in true service to humanity do not wish to see individuals debase themselves. Any practice that expects this does not honor the true nature of God.

Service is all about elevating the one assisted. People try to elevate me, but I am just fine where I am. I am grateful for the respect because it is the same respect that I give. I wish everyone else to merely elevate themselves. That is all that needs to happen for truth and love to prevail. Everyone must simply elevate themselves in service to life in some way. It is really that simple.

Kind People

Kind people are like walking, breathing wading pools of love. Others are going to want to be around them to drink of their kindness. They may merely want to be around them in hopes that the kindness will permeate their pool. It is a great accomplishment to be kind when the world has shown you its ruthless side. It is amazing when all you do is reflect love back to it.

If you are kind, the world will most likely want to be around you. Others will unconsciously be drawn to you in hopes to feel your kindness through osmosis. So if you are delayed in traffic, if supermarkets fill up around you, when the person in front of you painfully delays the flow of your transaction, please remember your base nature.

Kindness is using you to raise the benchmark on kindness in the world. When you are pushed almost beyond your limit of patience, please remember who you are at your core. Remember wherever you are, no matter how tired, hungry or overtaxed you are, you are first and foremost kind. Also, that you can maintain your kindness because you realize to your core that you are incredibly loved.

Kindness As the Benchmark

What if it were inevitable for another nation to become the leading superpower in the world? What if they chose to emulate America in doing that? Wouldn't you then want America to depict the highest kindness, compassion, benevolence and goodwill affordable?

The benchmark that we set in excellence is the water level for the whole world. Isn't it important then to transcend all pettiness? Don't we need to allow for human error in judgment if we are to keep raising all humanity to the cream? What is our responsibility in accountability?

Let's Choose to Be

If I say the statement, "Everyone should feel comfortable in sharing love freely," it most likely elicits a subtle negative reaction of a deviant act being committed. Think about it. This is no accident.

We have been programmed and conditioned to respond negatively to good things and be comfortable with negative imagery and scenarios. This is no accident. Why does the term tree hugger conjure up such a negative response? What are the connotations that accompany it? Is it a sweet harmless person sensitive to the importance of all forms of life? Or is it some flaky, unbalanced person who is out of touch? Why? Why is it such a bad quality to respect trees?

It is because society has been programmed and

conditioned to feel more comfortable with negative expressions than positive ones. Someone may wince at outward expressions of love and kindness in their most innocent state. Are they too syrupy? But that same person will think nothing of swearing and talking of debauchery in everyday interactions. Violence is becoming the norm. Why? Because we are being conditioned to accept it.

The fix for this is for those who are able, to be more mindful of the negative imagery that is conjured up during their daily interactions. Challenge subliminal responses and imagery that they induce. This in itself dissipates their effect. To create a greater change, people can introduce kindness back into everyday interactions. Trust shouldn't be regarded as naive. Kindness shouldn't be regarded as being flaky. And love shouldn't be viewed as a vulnerability or weakness.

Society has been on autopilot for way too long. It is now time for people to initiate some self-responsibility and take ownership of the world we live in. We are not passive bystanders. We are leaders, teachers, innovators, creators, healers and empowered if we choose to be. Let's choose to be.

Life Is a Buffet

Life is like an "all you can eat" buffet. You get to choose from the experiences that you have. We are more empowered than we give ourselves credit for. We manifest everything that we focus on. That is the reason to focus on Joy, Love, Abundance, Freedom and Wholeness. When people tell me about their problems, I want to say, "Stop choosing them from the buffet."

Instead of telling me about your problems, tell me about your dreams. Tell me how much you love your family. Tell me a funny story about your pets. Share with me your artwork, music, ideas, projects, what you are proud of, what makes you happy, what you are excited about, what your favorite team is, where you are going on vacation and all the miracles that happened during the day.

When someone is living like a victim, it is like waiting for the waiter to come and serve up a daily special of disappointment. When someone is having problems, I wonder why they are choosing them from the menu. What we focus on is what we manifest. That is the simple cause and effect of life.

There are so many experiences that are waiting to manifest. I invite and encourage everyone to at least choose from the a la carte menu!

Light Workers - Spiritual Farmers

There is an innate belief system that prevents people from gaining their potential. It is the fear of failing or reaching a dead end. It is not possible. Life always forges ahead. You are an eternal being. You have existed beyond all time. You are an expression of Light, Love and Sound that took form and will always exist. Any failure that you ever met has been temporary. Your existence in this moment is evidence of that.

When you were pressed into form, you took on some of the qualities of form. They have permeated your belief system and cause you to create less freedom for yourself. The more you identify with form and less with Light, Love and Sound, the more limitations you create for yourself.

Life is a big experiment. We have all learned to play it small and identify so much with form that we believe we are this compilation of chemicals from the earth. But what inspires our passion? What fuels our soul? What awakens our memory of ourselves as infinite omnipotent beings? It is feeding ourselves with what is our source.

Physical food is necessary as fuel for the physical body. Nurturing is important to the emotional or astral body. Mental acuity is important for the mental body. So Light, Love and Sound are important for the spiritual body or soul. That is why being a Light worker is the soul's equivalent of being a farmer.

Our human spirit needs sustenance to feed the soul. Love, Light and celestial music are the breath of the ethereal self. Those who strive, heal, teach and inspire others are creating fodder for the spiritual self. When one is immersed in fear, regrets, problems, unworthiness and doubt, they are starving their own soul.

That should be reassurance to those who dream, strive, break through resistance, love beyond any confines and give without any fear of being diminished for doing so. The process of distributing kindness is a tangible form of feeding the intangible soul. So many people are starving because they don't realize that they need to give to "eat" as a spiritual being.

When people brag about being a light worker, as subtle as it is, I wonder why are they so proud of feeding themselves. Doesn't everyone have to feed their soul? Giving is a form of eating in the spiritual worlds. There are so many souls starving of nutrients. Teaching them to partake in love and kindness is a means of teaching them to nourish their soul. It nourishes ourselves as well.

So really, the only form of failure is believing in failure. The only real death is forgoing to strive out of fear of failing, which is a form of death. Death is a stagnant energy. Many people who are breathing on earth are dead because they are afraid to do anything out of fear of a physical death. This puts them in an energetic catatonic state. They are already dead.

Those of us who love others, ignore their shortcomings, inspire the greatness in them, encourage dreams, forge a path for them to be empowered, heal their hearts and teach them to discern with their minds are bringing the spiritual dead back to life. It is not enough to show up once a week and declare your loyalty to a pie in the sky deity. One has to show up every moment confident and kind, courageous and vulnerable, empowered and flawed, to the task of pouring kindness and virtue back into this world.

Judging others creates a paralysis. This stuns the spirit and clips one's wings. It doesn't do much for the one being judged either. The more we lead with kindness, open our hearts, and refute the inevitable illusion of gloom that is literally in our drinking water, then we can revive a legion of angels and awaken the masses.

Love As the Initial Cause

Ignorance is ignorance

Abusing power is abusing power

Complacency is complacency

People are people

Judging is judging

Hate is hate

Love is Universal

The same invisible hate that goads ISIL to murder

Has its foothold in America in proselytizing hate against gays

What is the difference?

Hate is hate

God is not a hater

People who think God hates are making God in THEIR OWN IMAGE

The lesson in power is getting old; those of us who Love choose a different experience

It is time for the shroud of ignorance to be cast from the eyes of the complacent

Let each soul of love speak up just a little more in defense of love

There is nothing noble in being meek

The meek shall inherit the earth

Those who are empowered in love will inherit all of heaven

When you speak truth in your small world, the ripple of truth ebbs out and bends the sword of power

When you are loving and kind in your day, power dries up a little bit more on the other side of the world

You are no bit player

You are just not afforded the ability to see the effect of your cause

Make love and kindness your cause and watch how quickly it takes hold in the world

Don't wait for someone else, you be the initial cause

You know you want to

You know you are able

You know how dynamic and empowered you are

Make love your impassioned pleas to all humanity

Make love be your benchmark of this life

Make love be your golden footprint

Save the world from the ruthless acts that you hold secret
memories of

Take a stand

And when you fly away...

You will be carried away with you own wings of love.

Love's Final Decree

Wait out the pain

It does have an end

Like looking up at the clouds

For the rain to descend

Let it drip through your hair

And fall to the ground

As the force of the break

Reverberate and resound

Crack open the nut

Where the anguish was held

Pull out the shriveled meat

That caused you such dread

Recover your composure

From that punch in the gut

No, you aren't shattered

You're still the whole nut

Recover your dignity

Walk away clean

You are guided in all endeavors

By forces unseen

Refute the notion

That you go it alone

You are honored as sacred

There's no sin to atone

Let the silence and loneliness

Cut through the facade

Rip through layers of bullshit

As the angels applaud

What you hold dear

As your own private hell

Drives you to hear truth

As clear as a bell

As truth now personified

To this we agree

To hold space in this world

For Love's final decree.

Merry Christmas Right Now

What if Christmas was truly a state of heart that we could access at any time? What if Christmas is more about simply emulating the kindness of an enlightened soul and the total opposite of drawing lines in the sand? What if it doesn't happen once a year but every moment? What would be the point of gifts, decorations and music except to convey that feeling to others?

What if Christmas could be experienced in a much simpler way? What if each kindness was sharing the Christmas Spirit? What if each smile did the same? Why can't it? Why not? Here's me saying Merry Christmas right now.

Miracles

Miracles aren't meant to be witnessed. That is why there seems to be so few of them. Miracles are meant to be experienced from the vantage point of rolling up one's sleeves and creating them out of our own wonder. From this unique point of view, they may not seem so dramatic, but they are all indeed miracles. In fact, so much of our existence is a miracle that it is more efficient to ask, "What is not a miracle?"

Overcoming Complacency

Before I woke up, I was explaining to a group of people what they are doing when they go along with something that they don't believe in. It doesn't have to be a big moral issue but something that doesn't resonate with them as useful or truth. It could be as small as not speaking up when someone else is being teased and it doesn't feel right, even when that person is yourself.

We think it is okay to suck it up and take whatever

someone dishes out because we don't want to hurt their feelings. But what about the feelings of all the others they are stepping on? We don't want to take a stand because they may push us down. Well they have been pushing us down all along in little increments.

We are afraid to address them, but they are afraid of us. All they have as a defense is their loud obnoxious demeanor. They don't have truth or being right on their side. They only have their bluff. Once you penetrate their boisterous facade, they will rescind. It may be uncomfortable for a bit, but it is still better than giving up your empowerment to a bully.

In the dream, I was using the example of a younger girl who lost her virginity to some creep but then felt it didn't matter, that she didn't matter, so she allowed anyone to sleep with her after that. That is what we do when we don't stand up for ourselves in the little ways. If we can't do it ourselves, how can we expect the collective to do it in a big way? How can we expect humanity to take back empowerment for all from the bullies and blowhards in power if we don't do it for ourselves? It is in our own life that we learn to distinguish the difference.

It is in our own lives that we empower goodness and kindness to be the law of the land. We are the droplets of love that converge to form the river of consciousness. What we do, who we are and what we stand for matters, for we are the hearts and hands of the river of humanity.

Paint a Palette of Kindness

You are a miracle of the infinite dipped in physical form.
There is no need to choke on physical thoughts, drown in
physical emotions or be paralyzed in physical existence.
No. You are so capable of being, loving and expressing
yourself in the physical world while never missing a step
of a beautiful dance with the infinite.

You are like a paintbrush that never gets confused into
believing it is the paint. You are the instrument of such
artistry of kindness using a palette of the coarsest
vibrations that the Universe supplies as a palette. You do
this all with maintaining your flexibility and resilience.
You are not one to dry up and get stiff in a jar. That is not
your fate my friend.

You have learned the trick of dipping yourself often into
the infinite well of kindness and love. You spread yourself
more fluidly and effortlessly and leave a trail of your
wonder wherever you go. Your colors are exquisitely
expressed through all that you choose to partake of. Your
life is a gallery of masterpieces signed with your own
artistry. Be bold and confident and take ownership of all
that you do.

The secret is in dipping into the well. It has always been
that simple.

People are saturated in hearing how bad and inadequate
they are. They are tired of feeling inferior. They know they
have an aspect of themselves that is dynamic and unique
and they keep that tucked away out of fear of being

rejected. The truth is, we have all been rejected. What is the risk in speaking our truth at this point? We have all been brought to the lowest common denominator.

It is time to start pulling each other up just by seeing that incredible spark of genius in each and every individual. It is there. I see it in you. You know I see it in you. So if I can see it, everyone can see it because we are all made of the same stuff. We are all made of dreams and bones and blood and desire. So why not nurture that spark of divinity in each being and start a blazing fire of passion and exuberance in the very breath of humanity?

People are starving to connect to their own soul in the face of another. A smile, a kindness, an honest exchange and a heartfelt communication are all opening the doors to doing that. When more and more people start looking past the persona and engaging the loving heart within, the sooner we are all happily, lovingly exchanging with each other all that is good and kind. As of yet, perhaps many have theirs still locked away on a shelf somewhere within. It is time to raid the heart…in a good way.

Perpetual Prayer

There is a sense of separateness in the way that we think, feel and act. We may believe that all the things we think, say, feel and do are in increments and that is not really accurate. We wake up, perform our morning routine, perform our work, interact with people one at a time, get some exercise, do some meditation/prayer and go to sleep. We are doing everything in little boxes like they are separate from everything else. What if we looked at them as if they were not?

If we went through our life like everything we are doing is happening all at once (which is a valid metaphysical perspective), then our integrity would be based on the consistency of our actions, thoughts and feelings being in agreement. This is what being centered is all about.

I see all these inconsistencies in people because to me they are happening in real time. I am not engaging in a linear way. When I interact with someone, everything that they have ever said and done is right there in front of everything I have ever said and done. They don't recognize this because most people filter out all that is happening except what is striking their senses in that moment. Also, it can be very humbling.

Imagine that everyone perceived in this way. People could no longer gossip about another and then talk directly to them as if they had not. Both of those aspects of them would be present all the time. One could not lament about how awful their life was and then brag about how successful they are. Their story would have to remain consistent because it is. One could not operate from the vantage point that they are imbued with kindness if all their unkind acts were seen at the same time.

People have become savvy. They may not realize it quite yet, but they are seeing all these things combined in people. We see the inconsistencies. We may not articulate it, but we know what is going on. Have you ever watched *The Daily Show* with Jon Stewart where someone takes a stance for or against something with righteous indignation and then he shows video clips of how they are contradicting an earlier stance? This is a depiction of how people contradict themselves. It is happening with almost everyone in real time.

This concept can be overwhelming. A simple technique to help ourselves live less compartmentalized and more centered is to take whatever we do presently as worship and overlay that with what is going on in our daily life. If we can align those two things, a lot of inconsistencies would evaporate. Because mindlessly going through our day and consciously showing incredible reverence and gratitude are polar opposites.

Think of when you are in that heightened state of gratitude. Now, in your mind, go through your day as if you are also doing whatever brought you to that state of reverence as well. It may be going to church, prayer/meditation, giving of yourself in some way, being present with a loved one, etc. Everything you do, imbue it with a state of incredible reverence. This has so many obvious and unconscious benefits and it may seem really easy, but it can be very difficult to maintain.

This may be why yoga is so beneficial and simplistic but meets with such resistance. Because it is blending the inconsistencies between action and reflection until the self merges into oneness.

If you want to work with this way of being, it might help to use the technique above and adopt the affirmation: "My life is a perpetual prayer." It may also be even beneficial to do this tap:

(Say this statement three times while tapping on your head, and say it a fourth time while tapping on your chest.)

"My life is a perpetual prayer; in all moments."

"The world is perpetuated into the Heart of Love through me; in all moments."

"All individuals and interactions are blessed through my Grace and Kindness; in all moments."

Precursor to Living One's Purpose

When you wake up each morning, get in the habit of not jumping into your day. Lay in bed for as long as you feel you can afford to. Use that time to remember your dreams and to think of positive things that you are happy about in your life.

It feels like doing this is indulgent, but what it is doing is allowing you to transfer easily from the dream state to the waking state. It aligns all your different components (or bodies). It allows your thoughts, feelings, and the experiences that you were accessing in the dream state to align with the physical body, so they are all working in accordance with what is the best expression of you.

Think of the times you weren't able to do this. When you jumped out of bed and started running the physical body without the insight or fortitude to regulate whatever comes at you emotionally or mentally, you may overreact or overthink the whole day. It is best to honor all aspects of yourself as vital components of your balance and grace, which they are. Your mind and emotions are wise council to keep you in tune with your innate wisdom. They are not very good leaders for they have a tendency to work against each other when they are in charge.

If you are to embrace this into a routine, try to start the day with something that you love to do because this is a way to balance all your components as well. Think of when you are creating something. You are leading with the highest intention (goal to create). You are then using your emotions as an adviser to gauge what is working and what is not. You use the mind as an adviser to council you on what is the next course of action. You use your experience as the means to bring yourself to the goal that the intention (which is an agreement between the mind and emotions) sets as course.

This is why creative ventures are so important. They train all the components of one's self to work in harmony with the others. Manifesting in any type of hobby, no matter what that hobby is, is a precursor and a steppingstone to living one's purpose.

Purpose

You did not come here to feel good. You came here to be an advocate of truth and to lead the unenlightened to a state of realization. It is not about being warm and fuzzy with complacency but to get lost in the adventure of life. It's about digging in, getting messy, being tested, feeling vulnerable.

It's about that first realization that breaks through the sleeping sickness of society. It is not about feeling or thinking; it is about BEING! Being Alive! Being Love! Being Truth! And if it takes a few days or lifetimes of discomfort to have all humanity realign to truth, then so be it.

Raising the Bar on Normal

I woke up this morning and had an inner prompting (a nudge) to jump out of bed and run and do errands like I used to when I was younger. So, of course, I lay back down to sleep again and waited for it to subside. But then my inner teachers or spirit guides or innate wisdom downloaded the understanding of why into my conscious mind.

It reminded me of the freedom I used to feel in just jumping in the car and going. It said that people in the world are getting back to that natural state of wonder that they used to have. So a way to assist is to tap into it for myself and write a post to share some other ideas with how to do that and why it is important.

I got clear direction about how to assist the shift in consciousness. It is to do things that are spontaneous, that we love, and take up those things that we used to love to do when we were young but let fall along the way. I was told that the world is moving back to order and so to pick things up and straighten as we go will become as natural and ingrained as what it used to feel like to be messy.

I was giving a list of ways people can assist in a shift in consciousness or at least to go along with the flow of it. These are really exciting times and people are feeling it. So here is list of ways to approach life in a new state of consciousness.

Break old patterns by doing things out of your routine:

- Go for rides, hikes, walks, or runs

- Sing out loud

- Do things that you used to do for fun

- Take up old hobbies

- Brush off old talents

- Treat strangers like friends

- Figure out a way to do things that you have always wanted to do

- Be spontaneous

- Strike up meaningful conversations with strangers

- Change your appearance

- See things from other vantage points

- Proclaim your strengths and talents without a hint of recoiling at doing so

- Say exactly what you mean when you mean it

- Straighten up your environment as you go

- See the good in everything

- Live life as Benjamin Button, as if you are getting younger

- Stop living in expectation of getting old, sick or dying

- Be as creative and bold as a bipolar hippy

- Forgo worrying.

The consciousness of the world is moving towards a loving and spontaneous place where everyone is so busy enjoying life that they have no energy or inclination to control or judge others. The more we all get there in our own life, the more that we help manifest it in the world. Who knew that all the overactive, attention deficit, hippies, dreamers, creators and innovators were merely tapping into the future before their time. Here is to raising the bar on normal and thinking so outside the box that the box disappears in hindsight.

Recognizing Ourselves as Pure Love

Because of vibrational resonance, it takes less effort to focus on the negative issues in the world than the positive ones. The mind seems to go there by default. And where the mind goes, the vibration of the whole person seems to go. And where one person goes, many more go as well.

It is like being easier to hold a heavy object to your side rather than to hold it up at eye level. But if you raise it way over your head, develop your muscles and do it often, it can be really easy to raise a heavy item over your head, lock your arms and carry it there.

That is kind of what needs to be done with our vantage point in the world. The world has been so heavy. Every horrible thing that happens in the world is paraded on the airwaves to get attention and elicit more negativity. Then it makes us all think and talk about these horrible things. This is everyone holding the heavy object very low to the ground.

We all have to exercise our muscles, not to focus on the negative things, but to focus on the positive things that happen in the world. We will have to lock our arms and hold our attention high. This is done by not indulging in the negative issues. It is done by focusing our attention on all the good things that happen everyday. What are they? Here is the start of a running list of things that are happening right now in the world that are positive and wonderful.

Please make your own list or add to this one. Please keep

it close as a reminder of all the wonderful things that are happening in the world that we never hear about. Tune into them energetically and support them. This is the way to elevate the vibrations of all.

Right at this very moment:

Couples are falling in love

Sunshine is bursting through the horizon and warming the day

Someone is risking their life

Children are playing in innocence

Someone is creating a masterpiece

A genius is being born

Innovations are being created to uplift humanity

Power is dwindling its grip

Students are learning

Animals are being cherished

Pets are being spoiled

The hungry are being fed

The discouraged are given hope

Strangers are sacrificing their lives for others

Kindness is being given, demonstrated and

perpetuated

Mothers are nursing their newborns

Babies are being swaddled

Dads are bragging about their kids

Siblings are looking out for each other

Dreams are manifesting

Glass ceilings are being shattered

Stars are being born

Realizations are awakening

Old ideology is dying

Souls are crossing over peacefully

Revelations are being made

New ideas are being accepted

Lovers are embracing

Gratitude is pouring out

Communities are rebuilding

Nature is being appreciated

Adversaries are conceding

Hearts are being encouraged

Humanity is awakening

Our connection to all others is being recognized

Trees are exchanging our stagnant energy with clean energy

Creativity is flowing

Limitations are being lifted

Spiritual law is being understood

Humanity is awakening

We are embracing ourselves in the reflection of others

Love is perpetuating

Laughter is resonating

Vibrations are rising

We are healing

We are empowering

We are empowered

We are recognizing ourselves as pure love.

(Say each statement three times while tapping on your head and say it a fourth time while tapping on your chest.)

"I define myself as Love itself; in all moments"

"I define myself as Integrity itself; in all moments."

"I define myself as Success itself; in all moments."

"I define myself as Fitness itself; in all moments."

"I define myself as Health itself; in all moments."

"I define myself as Joy itself; in all moments."

"I define myself as Abundance itself; in all moments."

The art of living is a craft just like any other. Life doesn't happen to you, just like the field doesn't happen to the farmer, the canvas doesn't happen to the painter or the clay doesn't happen to the sculptor. Life is the raw material that we forge and mold our greatness from. Living a life serenely and yet profoundly is what becoming a master of life is all about. Any master craftsman doesn't wait to be told how to breathe life into their artistry. Their internal sense of knowing guides their hands, heart, choices, words, and even their very thoughts. This is the key to mastering life.

The Best of All Worlds

There is a pain barrier that is similar to the sound barrier. Once it is passed through, the Joy, Love, Abundance, Freedom and Wholeness are exponential and limitless. We are now breaking through that barrier to have more and more people realize the depth of what is possible beyond linear experiences.

I am proud to have broken through this pain barrier to report to all others the incredible contentedness and satisfaction that are on the other side. If you are in pain and it feels hopeless and never ending, please keep going. You are piercing the wall of the facade that human conditioning has constructed. Keep going. Keep going. You are moving into a more expansive state of being that makes the pricks and pains of life seem irrelevant in comparison to such incredible bliss.

You no longer have to wait until you cross over to experience this. You can now do this while still clothed in your physical self. It is literally having the best of all worlds. See what awareness can afford you just by reading this? Imagine what else is waiting to be revealed and experienced to and by you. Doesn't it make everything that has been experienced to this point, oh so worth it?

The Community Pool of Humanity

What we do here with our sweet love is to crumble the corners of hate, fear and derision in the world until all are immersed in the ambiance and splendor of their own divinity. Love is not shared or practiced as a hostile takeover, austere practices or a gaudy show of power. This is not possible because it would deviate from love and veer into power or manipulation.

Love is perfected in the recesses of our own reverent journey. We have been gleaning the dew that is collected from the mist of our anguish. We distill it into the succor of sincere compassion and offer it to those who have been separated from their own empowerment.

In doing so, we enhance our own fortitude and resilience and pour the wisdom of our experience into the community pool of humanity.

The Kindest Thing to Do

The Dark Ages never really ended. Humans have just become more savvy in their ignorance. Having a stomach for war, diminishing those who are different, believing they are the superior species, and being selfish and gluttonous with the abundance of resources are all evidence that humans are still in the Dark Ages.

The good news is that there are glimmers of enlightenment reaching the planet. There are those who see through the facade, share kindness between species, value more than the concepts of wealth, discern for themselves and are breaking free from the shackles of centuries of conditioning.

The hope of humanity rests in the arms of those who love willingly, live gratefully in their purpose and empower the individuality and discernment in all. They do so willingly without meeting others for contempt of their uniqueness or trying to outdo them.

The way out of the Dark Ages is to meet all in the sisterhood of kindness. We have tried doing it in the brotherhood of man, but that has just evolved into brother killing brother and desecrating his sisters. Embracing the sisterhood of kindness is still left untried and untested.

This is the time to realize the difference between kindness and weakness. Kindness is not a weakness. Kindness can take care of business when it is necessary. It is time to take care of business. It is time to take back one's empowerment. It is the kindest thing to do for the planet and all its inhabitants.

The Precipice of a New Era

My life is kind of an experiment. I know that I can release the emotional issues of an individual. Their energy system can then regenerate the whole body. This is called healing. It has even been proved effective in a group.

We have all seen great minds get overtaxed and close. We have all seen loving hearts be opened so wide that they get overwhelmed and rescind. Yet we have seen so very few open hearts working in perfect synchronicity with an open mind in one body. A few names come to heart: Gandhi, Nelson Mandela, Wayne Dyer.

What if it were possible to empower each individual to become as effective as your average worldly inspirational teacher? What if it were possible to teach how to connect the mind and heart to be in perfect symmetry of effectiveness with each other? What if it could be taught to the masses? What if the healing that I do on individuals could be done to the world at large?

This is my goal. My purpose is to uplift, inspire, show, teach, heal, validate, love and empower as many individuals in the world as possible. There is such a divide right now between those of the heart and those of the mind. It has been an unspoken, perhaps unrecognized, schism in humanity.

My intention is to heal that rift. To awaken the great minds of those who have been dismissed and open the loving hearts that the indifference of stark intelligence may have closed. The mind and heart work in unison. The great minds of the world need to sit at the feet of the tree huggers and discover the nuances of what they are missing. The loving hearts of the world must melt the apathy and indifference of great intelligence. They must be reminded that they are still an aspect of nature. In doing so, they may remember their true nature.

The ramifications of what is possible have not been tested of what an intelligent heart and a loving mind can accomplish together. It is my goal to nurture this partnership in all souls so that it can reflect in the Universal humanity of man. I have stumbled upon these insights and have gained the fortitude and courage to share them. Once they are uttered and shared, they sprout wings of their own. I encourage you to empower truth within yourselves. You, in doing this, are teetering the precipice of a new era.

The True Social Divide

When I was really at a low point, I got a voucher to go to an "upscale" donation site to get furniture and clothes for myself. I felt very blessed. I was so grateful that people who didn't even know me had come together to help me.

There was a woman who was at the site at the same time. She started to complain. "There is nothing here," she said. "It has really been disappointing lately." She went on to complain about every service she was receiving with a resounding disdain. Seeing the situation from her vantage point left me a little wilted.

It occurs to me that no one likes to be without. No one likes knowing others are in need. It is the spirit of a person to give when there is need. So why is there such a problem with helping others in need? This woman crystallized the issue for me.

The social divide isn't about economics. The true social divide is between the grateful and the ungrateful. No one minds giving to someone who appreciates it. Gratitude is a form of payment when that is all a person can give. But when someone is not grateful, then anything they are given is a form of stealing.

That is the problem with all the social safety nets that are put into place. Once they are implemented for all, they become expected, and once they are expected, they are no longer appreciated. That lack of appreciation is what bankrupts a community. The lack of gratitude is the great form of depletion that is playing out in America.

There are rich people that are ungrateful as well, and they are part of the problem. No one is exempt from being plugged into the Universal Love Lattice that we are all a part of. All must contribute their energy in the form of talents, time, attention or intent. If one does not, they are dead weight to the rest. This is an inner form of exchange that some see so clearly that they try to mandate outwardly, which is the issue. Service looks and feels different to all. Some may be able to give with only a smile, but a sincere smile is priceless to one who is need of it.

The only way to mandate this is to hold all to a higher standard. The bar is so low in some circles that it needs to be raised just to crawl under. We need to return to a society that doesn't celebrate disease but rallies around the genius, the innovator, the survivors and the heroes so that they can help everyone see those qualities in all.

We have got to stop using hate tactics and return to kindness and civility as a factoring system. We can start by seeing the nugget of good in everything instead of waiting for someone to make a mistake so that we can use it against them. We can give a hand up and lead by example. Ignore all the evidence of what is wrong in the world and focus on what is right. Use our attention to focus on the good to help more good manifest.

It may seem like an overwhelming prospect, but it is doable. We have evidence of great individuals uplifting humanity. What if that is the bar we chose for all to measure up to? What if we looked for the genius in all and did so consistently, so all could start to see the genius in themselves? This is how I choose to live. This is me creating the world that I envision. This is me ignoring all but the greatest in everyone. I invite you all to join me in my world.

The Universal Experience

The more I facilitate private sessions, the more I am shown that our deepest angst and the things that we cling to and hide so desperately are exactly what others are clinging to as well. The conditions may be different, but the struggle with the experiences is universal.

There seems to be a formula to life. Love, angst, abandonment, denial, recovery, acceptance and transcendence are all conditions that individuals need to conquer in their life's tutelage. We are all working on different lessons and from different vantage points so it creates the illusion of separation.

To overcome the condition of life, know that whatever you are experiencing, another is touching upon in their own life in some degree and in some way. Knowing that the pain you share is experienced in some degree by everyone else may take the sting out of it. Once you can see the same issues in others, you may be able to see how they struggle with it, how they endure and how they love beyond it.

These incredible desires to love and belong and to be seen in a gracious light are the universal commonality of existing. Once one sees this, they can get a sense of the incredible journey each has been on to love and be loved at all costs. This is where we connect. This is the point where we forgo all differences and are united as one.

There is no need to look back at the dark. Focus only on the brilliant light and not any shadow that may be cast by your form. Your purpose is to perpetuate the light, not to dwell on the shadows that are cast in contrast to its brilliance.

Thriving with Abuse

All the abuse that you have ever endured was never meant to break, isolate or devastate you. You were never meant to recoil into a ball of victim consciousness. All your experiences were meant to dry up the dross and burn off the edges that have collected upon the pristine of your essence and allowed you to be complacent in shallow waters.

You are being cleansed and rejuvenated so that you realize the depth and the range of your own capacities to love. You are being immersed in every experience so that you can register such compassion. Your depth allows you to merge with any soul in lack and ease their angst with the golden caliber of your caring.

You do this not by immersing in their dross and feeling around for their heart. It is done by seeing them in purity, goodness, and wholeness and ignoring all that doesn't shine with the same caliber as your own essence. It is spiritual law that you enhance what you put your attention on. So see the goodness in others that is desperate to be acknowledged and realized.

Focus on kindness to others with your own understanding of what it means to you to be valued with kindness. Value others to the same depth that you value your own breath. This is how you manifest goodness in the world. This is how you make all your experiences of poor treatment count for something. This is the alchemy of transforming lead into gold.

Show every soul how important they are in the dance of life. Thank your socks for warming your feet. Thank your car for the collection of atoms it has become to bring convenience to your day. When you do this, it is easier to exchange gratitude with your co-workers, your furry family and the trees that give you breath and lay down their lives for you every day for your indulgent pleasures and comforts.

The more you embrace your own experiences with gratitude and reverence, the more you will embrace the gratitude and display a reverence for all of life. Victims are just those who haven't realized the interconnection between their plight and those who suffer all over the world. Once the switch is turned on and one forgoes the personal tribulations to embrace the wondrous simple connection between themselves and all of humanity, they are forever changed.

Their light is more vibrant. Their childlike wonder is reinstated. Their capacity to love is stretched beyond all measure. They are connected forever to absolute truth directly through innate knowing. They even are capable of sharing their incredible gifts because they have been tempted and deterred in all ways and yet they still rise out of the ashes like the Phoenix.

You may be that Phoenix. If you are, you must know that you are adored by all the heavens. It is only the crude dross of this world that disdains you. How could it not? You shrivel it up with a mere glance. You threaten its very existence. Of course, the dross is going to use every means to diminish you. Be of no concern; the heavens shine through such things soon enough. You are whole and are ever important in the greater mechanisms of life. The part you play is important. All is well.

Please share this message with someone who has endured much. They have waited a long time for such outer confirmation. Please tell them that they matter and that you see their greatness. For some, it is what they need to hear to shine once again. This post is a small homage and acknowledgment of their great contribution to humanity. Please recognize their greatness. Please recognize your own. You are all loved beyond measure. It is time to start being immersed in the validation of love.

Unconditional Appreciation

People don't mean to let you down. They are just limited, shortsighted and have selective memory. The key is in not being dependent upon them. Be grateful if they follow through but always have a plan "B" handy. That is the way to not be thrown. It is a way to stay empowered. Also remember that it is the Universe that provides all your providence. It is accessing willing parties at the time to do this. But the gifts always are beyond the giver.

That does not mean not to be grateful to the giver. It means the opposite. Be very thankful when they are present for you, for they may not always be called to do so. Know that you are gifted with their assistance, so when they are not able to help you, still have gratitude enough to send to them regardless. This is giving unconditional love. This is what whomever has ever showed you a kindness deserves.

Your love and appreciation of others should not be dangled in front of loved ones like a peanut thrown to a performing monkey only as they serve you. This treatment is unworthy of them and you.

Validation of My Own Journey

Some people are still stuck in linear thinking. We are transcending linear thinking. The state of the world is proof that people are not learning from their mistakes. Energetically, they have built up what I call engrams, which are like eddies in a stream. They are caught in continuous thoughts, feelings and behaviors.

Defending the ego is being caught in an eddy or mind loop. Nobody is wrong. It is just that so few have an example that is not tainted with selfish motives or laden with their own eddies. Society itself condones the eddies and sanctifies them with approval. Anything that tries to interrupt the engrams gets met with derision or worse.

I put out truths as a way to interrupt the eddies that exist in society and in a person. I don't get fame, riches or glory for this. I regularly get met with contempt. But this is my purpose. I have survived the most horrendous treatment to be at this point to share truth. I did not expect to be in this position. But here I am.

The reason I am here is because the old way is not working. In the old paradigm, people believed that they were separate units devoid of responsibility to anyone. In the new paradigm, we know ourselves to be all connected. So the time we spent on pettiness and stroking the ego cannot be indulged as easily because what the individual harbors, they bring to the collective. The collective needs to be nurtured with love.

Souls in all forms are still suffering at the hands of those still learning their lessons. It is time for individuals to hold themselves a little more accountable. Tough love is a way to interrupt the eddies of the individuals and stark truth interrupts it for group engrams as well. The more people hold themselves accountable and shift in their personal dynamics, the more that the collective shifts into a place of humanity for all.

Humanity isn't just people. It is all the animals, trees, waters and rocks and earth itself that are affected by the insidious selfishness of the human ego.

I have been like a jellyfish in this lifetime. I have been born under the harshest circumstances with no defenses. I have had some powerful protection from guides who wanted me to survive. It is just recently that I started sharing truth and I have been attacked by some pretty savvy male energy that wanted to put me in my place. They want to put female energy in its place. They want to squelch truth in any form. My Spirit Guides have knocked them on their ass and some have come back to apologize.

I never know what I am going to write until I am told in inspiration what to write. My life has been one big field study in human nature. I have not enjoyed the same milestones in this life that others have enjoyed. I was cursed at birth by a drunken mother who had tried to get rid of me all through my gestation period. No simple milestone that other people have had, have I had to indulge in. Birthdays, friends, family, joining groups, and celebrations, being nurtured or even loved were all things I have not been privy to in this lifetime. This life is me doing field study on these topics. It was a short synopsis on all the ways people diminish, scorn, deride and try to kill goodness.

So now that I have a voice and an ability to help others, I absolutely know I am led here by a higher purpose. As it contrasts the experiences of this lifetime, I know that I am here to assist. So people can argue and dismiss what I share, but it is a missed opportunity for them. I am here. That is my proof of my purpose. I have survived with no agenda except to teach individuals the skills they need to empower themselves and to redirect their intention back into love.

It is only in taking back our individuality from all the groups and empowering our own empowerment that we thrive in the new paradigm. It is not by diminishing, negating, or assaulting those who have a sincere intention to help others. Every single unit of life contributes so much to the quality of life for the whole. Humans just need to realize the damage they have done with their pettiness of purpose and taking mentality. It is time for them to rediscover their loving nature as a group. My motivation is to help that transformation to love as much as possible and to drive it if need be. To do any less would be an invalidation of my own journey.

We Matter!

Your talents and gifts aren't meant to exist in a vacuum. They are meant to be spilled into the world to make it beautifully complicated. The world is not meant to be a black and white world of good and bad. It is supposed to be a multidimensional colorful array of wonderful attempts at being awesome. There is no perfect flower or one song to sing. There is music, color, fragrances and dynamic expression for all types of preferences.

To hold back your skills until everyone will love them will be sealing yourself in a sarcophagus of complacency. The world doesn't realize it loves you yet. You haven't introduced yourself to it. The most aware people are aware of those around them. They take their subtle cues from subtle realms. Quit trying to outsmart the world by rejecting yourself before they get a chance to do so.

You are not that self-aware yet to realize that even if you were perfect, someone would reject you because they are really rejecting themselves. It has never been about the other person loving or rejecting you. It has always been about what will you do to gift yourself? What will you do to empower yourself? What will you do to amuse yourself?

The multitudes are waiting to build their gifts on the back of your accomplishments. This is the tag team of humanity. Why are you stopping up the gears when we are all experiencing the stagnant existence that happens when the multitudes do that? We are still unclogging the gears of past generations who have done this religiously. They are the ones that still choose war over creation and still choose power over love and still chose fear over acceptance. We are not they. Let's wash their stain from the face of humanity and continue with our arts.

We love! We accept. We share. We discern. We plant. We grow. We feed. We heal. We empower. We ensue. We believe. We nurture. We know. It is just time to do all these things together. We are not one little person. We are everyone and we matter!

We, as a species, are meant to finally realize our potential in greatness. It is not through wielding power. It is through unclenching our fists, rolling up our sleeves and opening our hearts.

What Awakening Entails

Lamenting over an unrequited love is just letting go of the third dimensional bullshit. In the higher worlds, there is no strong attraction because that is only movement through the emotional body. Your love has evolved quicker than your understanding. You can love everybody at once, and you can love them at such a pure state that there is no need, want or even desire to possess.

As the world is awakening, so is our comprehension of love. All the want, need and desire is what causes so much pain and unrest in the world. It will be good when people outgrow it. You are capable of having a deep, satisfying love with any being in the world.

The person who triggers you to that passion is merely a flint to ignite such love. That is what the true purpose of a love interest is and really always as been--to stoke the flame of your omniscience and exponential ability to love. Stoke that love, not for ownership in a small way, but to ignite the world in the exponential Joy of Divine Love.

That is what awakening entails. Being in love makes it easier.

This is an important time in the manifestation of higher consciousness. Now is not the time to feel defeated by futility or want, but to be empowered by your own capacity and depth to give of yourself to another being. Not just one being but the whole. As more awaken to this prospect, we will dry up the hunger to take and hoard in the world. All will pour their wealth of abilities and aptitudes back into the collective. You are onto something.

What Came First:

The limited funds or telling the Universe one is broke?

The first sign of aging or telling the Universe one is old?

The first achy bone or telling the Universe one is sick?

The first hint of sadness or telling the Universe one is depressed?

The onslaught of problems or telling the Universe one can't?

When we tell others our problems, we are proclaiming them to the Universe. This is how the Universe then defines us.

When one deals with lack in any way, it is a temporary lesson. The more one identifies with the lesson, the longer it will linger as a part of them.

When anyone asks any question of you, don't trade your power for a quick fix of sympathy. Tap into the sacred aspect of yourself and answer:

I Am Happy!

I Am in Love!

I Am Rich!

I Am Healthy!

I AM Free!

What we do here is of no small matter. People are intentionally being starved, women are being raped and enslaved, species are being eliminated and humanity is being eradicated all over the world. None of that is eliminated with adding more hotheaded power-seeking egomaniacs to the mix. The only thing that halts the desecration of humanity is the exponential perpetual pumping in of higher awareness and divinity through kindness to all corners of the world. We do that individually and allow it to reflect in our leader of choice.

The fear and hate must be dampened and squelched by an onslaught of higher standards. It is up to us to put that in place. It needs to be done. There is no more catch up time for a learning curve. You as an individual matter and you must embrace that stance to save the fate of the world. We are all superman in that way.

Who Am I? Who Are You?

Labels are thrown around as weapons. If you put a label on something, it conveniently prevents the need to delve further. In the world that we live in, these labels are an outmoded means of compartmentalizing everyone. We

If one stops using labels to demonize others then we are back to engaging people on their merit and not a sound bite. People are so wonderful and complicated. We need to stop demonizing others for a political gain. This is done in the name of God. Does not everyone see the hypocrisy in that? In what good book does it say hate and judge, demonize and reject, label and diminish? Why do people not challenge that hypocrisy more?

I am a liberal - I look for the good in all others so there is understanding.

I am a conservative - I reserve judgment of others. I am very stingy in that way.

I am a Christian - I strive to live with the same integrity as Jesus Christ. I get as upset about the hypocrites as he did. Except these days they are politicians and not tax collectors.

I am pro life - I believe in quality of life for all living beings.

I am pro choice - I believe everyone has the right to bring an unwanted baby into the world if they have the means to take care of it, much to the chagrin of that child.

I am a tree hugger - When all humans have turned away from me, trees were there to give comfort. I am still trying to wrap my head around why someone who is grateful for the contributions of such magnificent living beings is demonized.

I am a patriot - I am very grateful for my place in the world. It affords me the comforts and safeties that I get to appreciate.

I am a constitutionalist - I appreciate the great efforts that the forefathers put into creating the Constitution so that the rights of all could be honored. They thought through every scenario they could imagine so that the United States could maintain its integrity. It sickens me that their very process is used to strong arm the American people into being held at literal gunpoint again and again in our streets and our communities.

I am a socialist - I believe that everyone matters in society.

I am an immigrant - My DNA is German and Irish. Thank God that trek to this land is over.

I am God fearing - I fear those who use God to achieve an agenda.

I am a hippie - I believe in love, music, healing, and expressing one's self beyond the confines of a nine to five existence.

I am repressed - I don't sleep around. In fact, I live like a monk.

I am the moral majority - I morally police myself and am harder on me than others would be.

I am a silent majority - I don't always speak my mind out of fear of being demonized for my view. I like to blend.

I am transgender - I love and appreciate the beauty and

strengths of both sexes. I don't need to merely choose one of two polar opposites to framework my identity.

I am an animal lover - Animals bring so much of the love and contentment to the humans who have been rejected by other humans. They deserve to be idolized simply for doing that.

I hope this blurs the lines for a few people. We don't need to be so diametrically opposed. The truth is, what many people say they are on the surface, is not what they feel they are in their heart. The heart is not so shallow and we as dynamic beings are not that simplistic. Let's stop agreeing to be depicted that way.

You Are Love, Loved and Loving

Whatever you are feeling and experiencing is valid.

However you are feeling isolated, know that so many others are experiencing the same.

You are bonded to all others by that feeling of being disconnected.

You dip from an infinite well when you pierce through the pain to scoop out the joy.

You show your fortitude and resolve by always being present with optimism and enthusiasm.

You show your compassion by allowing others to be frivolous and silly while you master the hard questions of existence.

You show your wisdom when you let go of the mental anguish, shrug your shoulders and join in the play.

You show your kindness when you allow others the space to be messy and clueless never letting on that there is an alternative way.

You show your strength of character when you go though the motions year after year and never scream out for the sheer madness of the repetition of not transcending.

You personify peace when you show others how to stretch their atoms to include more light in their personal realm simply by the act of surrender and trust.

You show your charm when you show up for others time and again realizing that they don't have the steady capacity to always show up for you.

You show your dedication to love simply by allowing others to figure out love in their own way with their own terms and their own representation of Source.

You show your abilities to manifest when you have enough food, shelter, comforts and happiness to get by without hoarding more than you need in the moment.

You show your benevolence when you are happy for others and forgo the need to compete with them in life, which is not a game after all.

You show your commitment to all life when you pour love and kindness to all other souls simply because love and kindness are your base nature.

You strive to be better, kinder, more understanding to yourself as well as others.

You give so much without realizing that you are giving at all.

These are a few of the reasons that you are so lovable, capable, worthy and aware. You are a reflection of the Divine in the illusion of physical form. You are Love, Loved and Loving. You are AMAZING!

These are some of the reasons on the shortlist of why I love you.

You Are Who You Are

Either you know yourself to be a divine spark of God with freedom of choice or a breathing piece of matter that's a victim of circumstance. Decide who you are. If you are a victim of circumstance then everyone else is a victim of circumstance as well. We are all made of the same stuff. But if you see the greatness in others, you must recognize greatness in yourself. If you then recognize greatness in yourself by default, you must take ownership of it.

You must then acquaint yourself with all the amenities that being a divine spark of God affords to you. Because being a victim in an empowered state of awareness is just too much of a transgression to reasonably tolerate. This is what so many of us are grappling with right now. We are learning the blueprints and instruction manuals of this empowered self.

To shrivel up and cower on a wind glider or soar into the setting sun sniveling on one's knees is too ridiculous for any soul to wrestle with. Stand up and operate the equipment that you were equipped with. Don't you dare allow anyone to pull you around on a string or tow you to serve their agenda. Operate under your own accord. Anything else is unworthy of the greatness of your capabilities.

Your State of Grace

Most people are not afraid to die but to be separated from their consciousness. In a manner, they are afraid to cease to continue to be them. So they pad who they are with a lot of extraneous issues to ensure their own existence. It is not necessary.

The petty things we use to pad our existence actually prevent us from experiencing the Joy, Love, Abundance and Freedom that are our innate selves. The more we identify with external issues, feelings and thoughts, the more we move away from our true dynamic awesomeness. Trust the surrender to move into your true essence.

> The more we diminish others, the more we take away from our own value.

> The more we judge others, the more we pile self-

judgment on ourselves.

The more we fear, the more we move away from our center.

The more we attack, the more we fracture our own wholeness.

The good news is:

The more we encourage, nurture, uplift, heal, teach, support, love, show kindness, and see the greatness in all others, the more we uncover our own nature.

To give to others is to gift ourselves.

To love others is to love ourselves.

To empower others is to empower ourselves.

To be vulnerable and raw to the world is to teach all others to defend less and love more.

You are the awakening that the world is waiting for.

It is in your presence.

It is in your empowerment.

And it is in your state of Grace.

Your Story Is Your Triumph

Someone just asked me if I thought God would save us. This was my response:

Yes, but not from afar. God will save us when we all take

responsibility to save each other through kindness, consideration, caring, and sometimes conceding. God is within. So when more and more people accept the responsibility of Godlike demeanor, we will be saved from within.

Don't expect the angels to swoop down from the heavens and smite the blade of the enemy. Expect the concept of enemy to dry up as you recognize the God love in each being.

Don't expect a legion of righteousness to swoop down that delivers everyone into hell. Realize that we make our own hell through our ignoble thoughts, choices and judgments. Dry up your own private portal to hell through the constant endeavor of kind actions and intentions. Motivate others to goodness through seeing the best in them. Be grateful for the good you see in others instead of picking them apart for what you perceive as a moral infraction.

Don't expect anyone to hand you a ribbon and tell you that you are one of the chosen. Innately know your worth and then no one can taint the caliber of your worth.

Don't be deceived in quantifying the value of another because as soon as you misdirect your view from their absolute inner light, you also take your gaze off your own perpetual sheen. You emanate at the level of splendor that you hold others in regard.

Don't allow others to use you as a pawn in their vindictive battle with self-worth. People can only love others to the degree they love themselves. Hitler was part Jewish. All the hate he commanded onto others was a testimony to his self-loathing. Let us not lose this vital lesson. Those who hate, judge, belittle or are adamant of the course others should take are displaying their own lack of self-approval or acceptance. Let's not assist in visiting their pathology onto the world.

Don't allow your sacred views to be harvested into a political agenda. Society has become one perpetual advertisement for violence and lacking the ability to discern. Listen to your gut or heart when you are being told something is true. If someone leads you by eliciting fear in you, they are playing you. Please don't fall for it. Counter any fearful reaction with love and watch it dissipate. In this way, you come in command of all of heaven. When you learn this, you are mimicking the lessons of all avatars. It truly is that simple.

The strength, resilience, fortitude, awareness, depth, love, kindness and discernment are in you. It has been collecting in your DNA before the understanding of DNA existed. You are literally born to overcome all the negativity that is thrown at you.

That is why your story is your triumph. Every rejection, humiliation, defilement and desecration has been etching a pathway of compassion deep within your soul memory. Those who have suffered have forged such an incredible capacity to love. It is no different than a beautiful chalice being forged from the fiercest, hottest fire. The alchemy of legend is this. This is the secret that all avatars know. You are the lost chalice that legend sought. Your alchemy is from the defilement of coarse matter to the pristine sheen of unconditional golden love.

The closer you get to the perpetual state of grace, the more that life will singe at your edges and smooth your round contour. Know that you are not being rejected by God. You are being initiated into your own awakening. You are blessed beyond measure to survive through everything that you have endured and still maintain the capacity to love.

Those with their sharp edges will implore others to focus their gaze on the purification of others. They will feign righteousness as an act of denial. But don't be fooled. Look at the ragged edges of an agenda on anyone who tries to implore you in the name of God or speaks for God as if they know something you do not. They know nothing if they don't speak with love. They understand little without kindness. They are still asleep and groggy in their dreams of power and control. Leave them to slumber or awaken them with your love, but do not join their nightmare.

Know yourself to be better than the illusion so many people are conjuring in this world and selling as truth. See the bounty they sit on as a mound of lies and pain they have doled out for others. When one benefits from the suffering of another being, they are lost in their own hell. Do not envy them their state. You in your simple state are richer in grace and awareness. That is something all the money and esteem in the world can't buy.

See the goodness in others and the world as your own private mirror. Focus on the love and kindness you see beyond the mist and summon it forth with your purity of intention. The presence unadorned with an agenda is the mostly comely beauty realized. Be as beautiful as you are. Be as beautiful as others see you.

Don't feign humility or unworthiness. That is a ploy of those who still pit others against their kindred spirits. Humility is seeing the same greatness in others that you see in yourself. There is no need to lower the bar on everyone's worth in the exercise of such things.

See the intention behind the limitations of others. Instead of attacking them for their lack of perfection, appreciate their tenacity to assist others in some way. There is no need to reject anyone because of their limitations. Perhaps your loving support will assist them more than your contempt for their lack.

Perfection is a lie. Wanting others to be perfect is sabotage to us all. Mutilating your body, starving yourself or lying about your stance just so others will deem you perfect or beautiful is a desecration to your spirit. Instead of seeking perfection in all, seek acceptance and all will be as good as perfect. Self-acceptance is something that is achievable.

I accept you all.

- Jen

ABOUT THE AUTHOR

Jen Ward is an Ascended Master. This entails being a Reiki Master, gifted healer, inspirational speaker, author of many books and an innovator of a healing modality for self empowerment. She offers a simple but dynamic protocol to assist individuals in clearing up all their energy imbalances (karma) with every person, experience, belief system and the Universe. She enables all those struggling, to cross the bridge of self-discovery, with her encouragement and instruction. Her passion is to empower the world by encouraging all individuals in their own miraculous healing adventure.

Jen is considered a Sangoma, a traditional African shaman who channels ancestors, and clears energy by emoting sounds and vocalizations. An interesting prerequisite to being a Sangoma is to have survived being on the brink of death. When it was first revealed that Jen was a Sangoma, she had not yet fulfilled the rigorous prerequisites necessary. However, in April 2008, through a series of traumas, she returned to civilization meeting all the requirements. She passed through the transforming process of enlightenment. She returned to the world of humanity a devout soul inspired to serve.

Jen currently works diligently in the physical world and in the worlds of energy to assist all souls to reach greater heights of awareness and empowerment. Those who believe they have "arrived", may be the most entrenched in the mental realms. They can painlessly free themselves without relinquishing the comfort of their current belief system. All that needs to be released will fall away naturally. "Fear, in all its subtle forms of denial and judgment, will naturally fall away."

Many people report receiving healing assistance from Jen or protection in the dream state and even more subtle realms. Jen is passionate to shatter the mentality of sitting at the feet of another. She shares truth and wisdom graciously and abundantly. Jen makes the practice of doling out truth in increments to set up the dynamic of personality worship obsolete. Her passion is to assist the world over the brink of all perceived limitations, beyond the mind's scope, into the realms of enlightenment.

Jenuinehealing.com

OTHER BOOKS BY JEN WARD

Enlightenment Unveiled: *Expound into Empowerment.* This book contains case studies to help you peel away the layers to your own empowerment using the tapping technique.

Grow Where You Are Planted: *Quotes for an Enlightened "Jeneration."* Inspirational quotes that are seeds to shift your consciousness into greater awareness.

Perpetual Calendar: *Daily Exercises to Maintain Balance and Harmony in Your Health, Relationships and the Entire World.* 369 days of powerful taps to use as a daily grounding practice for those who find meditation difficult.

Children of the Universe. Passionate prose to lead the reader lovingly into expanded consciousness.

Letters of Accord: *Assigning Words to Unspoken Truth.* Truths that the ancient ones want you to know to redirect your life and humanity back into empowerment.

The Do What You Love Diet: *Finally, Finally, Finally, Feel Good in Your Own Skin.* Revolutionary approach to regaining fitness by tackling primal imbalances in relationship to food.

Emerging from the Mist: *Awakening the Balance of Female Empowerment in the World.* Release all the issues that prevent someone from embracing their female empowerment.

Affinity for All Life: *Valuing Your Relationship with all Species.* This book is a means to strengthen and affirm your relationship with the animal kingdom.

The Wisdom of the Trees. If one is struggling for purpose, they can find love, and truth by tuning into the *Wisdom of the Trees*.

Chronicles of Truth. Truth has been buried away for way too long. Here is a means to discover the truth that lies dormant within yourself.

Healing Your Relationships. This book is a means to open up communications and responsiveness to others so that clarity and respect can flourish again in society.

How to Awaken Your Inner Dragon: *Visualizations to Empower Yourself and the World.* Tap into the best possible version of you and the world.

Collecting Everyday Miracles: *Commit to Being Empowered.* This book is a thought provoking means to recreate the moment of conception with everyday miracles. It is through gratitude and awareness. This is what this book fosters.

The SFT Lexicon: *Spiritual Freedom Technique.* Tap into the powerful ability of the mind to self-heal.

www.ingramcontent.com/pod-product-compliance
Lightning Source LLC
Chambersburg PA
CBHW062357090426
42740CB00010B/1315